CATHOLICS IN AMERICA

1776-1976

NATIONAL CONFERENCE OF CATHOLIC BISHOPS

COMMITTEE FOR THE BICENTENNIAL

BISHOPS' COMMITTEE

John Cardinal Dearden, *Chairman*
Humberto Cardinal Medeiros
Archbishop Peter L. Gerety
Archbishop Edward A. McCarthy
Bishop Joseph F. Donnelly
Bishop Raymond J. Gallagher
Bishop William R. Johnson
Bishop James S. Rausch

Consultors

Lawrence Cardinal Shehan
Archbishop Coleman Carroll
Bishop Joseph A. McNicholas

Board of Consultants

Msgr. Peter Armstrong
Hon. Genevieve Blatt
Sr. Margaret Brennan, IHM
Ms. Helen Casey
Rev. John Civille
Sr. M. Shawn Copeland, OP
Mr. Vincent W. DeCoursey
Rev. Virgil P. Elizondo
Mr. James Finn
Mr. John J. Henning
Rev. Raymond Hill, MM

Bicentennial Conference Subcommittee

Archbishop Peter L. Gerety, *Chairman*
Bishop William R. Johnson
Bishop James S. Rausch
Ms. Juanita Acevedo
Dr. Clinton Bamberger
Sr. Margaret Brennan, IHM
Mr. Joseph Collins
Msgr. Lawrence Corcoran
Dr. Jorge Dominguez
Mr. James Finn
Dr. Irving Friedman
Rev. Jesus Garcia

Rev. Michael Groden
Hon. Charles Hammock
Rev. Peter Henriot, SJ
Dr. Alfred Hero
Rev. Theodore Hesburgh, CSC
Mrs. Jane Wolford Hughes
Ms. Ann Leibig
Rev. A. J. McKnight, CSSP
Rev. Emerson Moore
Rev. Richard Neuhaus
Mr. Michael Novak
Dr. David O'Brien
Mr. Robert Pranger
Dr. Stephen Tonsor
Rev. David Tracy

History Subcommittee

Archbishop Edward A. McCarthy, *Chairman*
Bishop Raymond J. Gallagher
Bishop Robert E. Tracy
Rev. Colman Barry, OSB
Msgr. John Tracy Ellis
Dr. Philip Gleason
Sr. M. Adele Francis Gorman, OSF
Dr. Annabelle Melville
Rev. Robert Trisco

Religious Observance Subcommittee

Humberto Cardinal Medeiros, *Chairman*
Rev. Joseph Champlin
Rev. Thomas Krosnicki, SVD
Rev. James O'Donohue
Rev. Virgil P. Elizondo
Rev. Clarence Rivers
Very Rev. Walter J. Schmitz, SS

Committee Staff

Mr. Francis J. Butler, *Executive Director*
Ms. Marguerite D. Madigan *Administrative Assistant*

CATHOLICS
IN
AMERICA

1776-1976

EDITED BY ROBERT TRISCO

With a Foreword by
THE MOST REVEREND EDWARD A. MCCARTHY
Coadjutor Archbishop of Miami

NATIONAL CONFERENCE OF
CATHOLIC BISHOPS
COMMITTEE FOR THE BICENTENNIAL
Washington, D.C.

1976

Table of Contents

Foreword

by

THE MOST REVEREND EDWARD A. McCARTHY

Coadjutor Archbishop of Miami
Chairman of the Subcommittee on History
of the
National Conference of Catholic Bishops'
Committee for the Bicentennial

After George Washington was elected to the presidency of the United States and inaugurated in office, the Catholic clergy and laity of the country through a committee sent him formal felicitations. They discreetly reminded him that they deserved the religious liberty that had been assured by the federal Constitution and by the constitutions of many states, because they had taken an active part in the Revolution:

> . . . whilst our country preserves her freedom and independence,
> we shall have a well founded title to claim from her justice equal
> rights of citizenship, as the price of our blood spilt under your eyes,
> and of our common exertions for her defense, under your auspicious
> conduct, rights rendered more dear to us by the remembrance of
> former hardships.

Replying to this message, the first President expressed the "hope ever to see America among the foremost nations in examples of justice and liberality." Citizens who possess such virtues would be disposed, he thought, "to allow, that all those who conduct themselves as worthy members of the community are equally entitled to the protection of civil government." In reference to the Catholics' share in the struggle for independence and to the wartime alliance with France he wrote:

> And I presume that your fellow-citizens will not forget the patriotic
> part which you took in the accomplishment of their Revolution,
> and the establishment of their government; or the important assistance
> which they received from a nation in which the Roman Catholic
> religion is professed.

The Catholics were prompt to exercise the rights that they had won through the Revolution. In structure they soon acquired a diocese and a bishop. In numbers they gradually expanded their proportion of the population, through natural increase, immigration, and conversions, from approximately one per cent in 1776 to nearly twenty-three per cent in the Bicentennial year. In activity and property they grew correspondingly through the erection of churches and educational and charitable institutions.

The Catholics' fellow citizens of the late eighteenth and early nineteenth century may have long remembered their contribution to the achievement of American independence although not all the states immediately abolished all legal discrimination based on religion. With the passing of time and the arrival of immigrants, however, a majority of the Catholics no longer could claim to be descendants of those who had fought and died for the liberty of their country. Many of their fellow citizens began to deny their right to equal protection of the civil government as if their loyalty to the Pope in spiritual matters disqualified them or their difference of blood, their poverty, and their cultural inferiority rendered them undesirable. Paradoxically, as Catholics became more numerous, they became a more beleaguered minority. Yet in subsequent wars they served no less valorously than their religious forebears had served on the battlefields and ships of the Revolution.

Even as they were closed in upon themselves in the more populous centers, they reached out through missionary enterprises first to the Indians on the frontiers and later to the pagans of other continents. On this continent the missioners were extending the trails into the wilderness first blazed by priests from the sixteenth century on. Those heralds of the Gospel who even through the nineteenth century had in large part come from Europe were followed in the twentieth by native Americans.

In 1789 the Catholics praised Washington for the improvement of agriculture and extension of commerce that the new nation had already begun to enjoy under his administration. They did not foresee that "this prospect of national prosperity" would entail the dangers as well as the benefits of industrialization or that their spiritual descendants would in large numbers become victims of economic exploitation. Yet these later Catholics also produced champions of social justice not only for themselves but also for their unfortunate compatriots. Similarly, Washington's contemporary admirers rejoiced in the zeal with which America was animated, as they quaintly phrased it, "for the attainment and encouragement of useful literature." They were probably thinking of the freedom, previously denied them, with which they could at last open schools; they never suspected that a public system of education would later be created that would threaten the faith of Catholic children and would demand extraordinary generosity of their parents to maintain their own institutions from the primary level to the university. Yet they were already laying the foundations of the first Catholic "college" in the country, thus setting an example that was to be marvelously surpassed in the following two centuries.

The message to George Washington was signed on behalf of the clergy by one priest, John Carroll, who had recently been elected by his peers first bishop in the United States and was soon to be confirmed in that office by the Holy See and to be consecrated in England. It was signed on behalf of the laity by four prominent gentlemen. From the beginning lay people have assumed a heavy responsibility for the progress of the Church both as members of parishes and societies and as leaders in thought and action—writers, organizers, and administrators. It is not only since the Second Vatican Council that the role of the laity has been acknowledged in the United States, especially when faith and morality have impinged on political and social questions.

All these lines of development which were adumbrated by the Catholics' congratulatory address to the Father of their country have been drawn out in greater detail by the writers of the essays that follow in this book. Though these topics can only be sketched because of the necessary limitation of space, they are sufficient to delineate the rich religious heritage of which American Catholics can justly be proud in this Bicentennial year. The articles also reveal the failings and shortcomings that continue to admonish succeeding generations. Whether edifying and inspiring or sobering and mortifying, they can lead the reader to further study and provide useful lessons for those who will translate their faith into action during the third century of our nation's life.

Preface

Not only as Americans but also as Catholics do American Catholics have reason to celebrate the Bicentennial of the Revolution and the Declaration of Independence, for these political events brought about the granting of religious freedom. Previously in the English colonies and also subsequently in many countries from which they emigrated, Catholics had lacked such freedom, but with it they developed in the United States a new and in several remarkable ways a unique branch of the universal Church. Ecclesiastical historians, therefore, no less than their secular colleagues, have welcomed the opportunities that this celebration has afforded.

When the subcommittee on history of the National Conference of Catholic Bishops' Committee for the Bicentennial excogitated various ways of promoting knowledge of the Church's past in this country, it proposed, in addition to other undertakings, to produce a series of weekly articles on important topics and by different writers. The full committee under the chairmanship of His Eminence, John Cardinal Dearden, gave its approval, and the Shell Companies Foundation provided a grant from which each contributor could be modestly remunerated. The National Catholic News Service, moreover, decided to distribute the articles without charge to all its subscribing newspapers, beginning in July, 1975.

Before anyone was invited to write an article, the professional members of the subcommittee suggested topics and recommended experts to treat them. In order to include a large and representative number of scholars, it was agreed that no one would be asked to contribute more than two articles. The choice of topics was partially determined by the areas of special research of contemporary historians. Most of the contributors have published or are writing monographs which may not be or will not become known to general readers but which are condensed in these articles. It is regrettable that the names of several prominent authorities are missing from the list of contributors. The selection of topics was also partially dictated by the presumed interests of the prospective readers and by the theme of "Liberty and Justice for All" which the Committee for the Bicentennial had adopted for all its activities. It seemed to be advisable, however, to omit some subjects such as trusteeism and "Americanism" in spite of their obvious importance because of the difficulty of presenting them intelligibly in a thousand words.

The articles have been divided into fifteen sections under subject headings. It should be noted that with the exception of the first section consisting of a preliminary geographical survey, complete coverage of any subject has not been attemped. In the section dealing with the immigrants of different nationalities, for example, it would have been neither feasible nor desirable to devote a separate article to each ethnic group. The same principle has been observed in the case of national organizations. Biographical articles, moreover, have not been permitted to exceed a certain ratio. On the other hand, several articles which had been planned were, unfortunately, never written. In its final form, nevertheless, this collection provides a broad introduction to the history of American Catholicism.

Before being sent out to the newspapers, the articles were edited for style by Mr. Jerry Filteau of the National Catholic News Service. His improvements have been retained in this volume, but each author's literary style remains distinctive. The passages that Mr. Filteau was forced to delete in some articles in order to reduce their length to the prescribed wordage for newspapers have for the most part been restored here.

Reliable and readable, written by specialists but not pedantic, the articles were so favorably received by the editors and subscribers of many diocesan weeklies that the idea of making them available in a more permanently accessible form and at a low cost was readily accepted by the subcommittee and the full committee. The Most Reverend Robert E. Tracy, therefore, obtained from the Catholic Daughters of America a grant to aid in publishing them as a book.

To all the persons referred to above—to the contributors of advice, of articles, of funds, and of skills—I would like to express abundant thanks. I also wish to make known my gratitude to the chairman of the subcommittee, the Most Reverend Edward A. McCarthy, for supporting the efforts of the historians and for embellishing the book with a foreword, as well as to the other episcopal member, the Most Reverend Raymond J. Gallagher, and to the Honorable Judge Genevieve Blatt, a member of the full committee who participated also in the meetings of the subcommittee. I gratefully acknowledge, furthermore, the indispensable assistance of the executive director of the office of the Committee for the Bicentennial, Dr. Francis J. Butler, of the assistant director, Mr. Kevin R. Farrell, and of the administrative assistant, Mrs. Marguerite Repice Madigan, as well as of my secretary, Miss Anne M. Wolf. I am indebted likewise to Mr. Thomas Lorsung, formerly photo editor of the National Catholic News Service, who secured many of the illustrations used in the newspaper series and in this volume. Finally, I must compliment Mr. Gerard A. Valerio for the attractive design of this book.

R.T.

With a few exceptions the articles are followed by one or more titles for "recommended reading" on the topic. For the sake of brevity and of facility in locating, only books have been listed. Additional bibliography, especially of periodical literature, will gladly be supplied to any inquirer by the individual authors of these articles or by the editor of this book. The reader may also wish to consult the following general works:

A selection of primary source-materials: John Tracy Ellis, *Documents of American Catholic History* (Milwaukee: Bruce Publishing Company, 1956; 2d ed., 1962; 3d ed., Chicago: Henry Regnery Company, 1967 [2 vols., Logos 61L-721 and 722, paperback]).

General histories: John Tracy Ellis, *American Catholicism* (2d ed. revised, Chicago: University of Chicago Press, 1969). Thomas T. McAvoy, C.S.C., *History of the Catholic Church in the United States* (Notre Dame, Indiana: University of Notre Dame Press, 1969).

Background: John Tracy Ellis, *Catholics in Colonial America* (Baltimore: Helicon, 1965). Sister Mary Augustina (Ray), B.V.M., *American Opinion of Roman Catholicism in the Eighteenth Century* (New York: Columbia University Press, 1936; reprinted, New York: Octagon Books, 1974).

Collections of articles: *Roman Catholicism and the American Way of Life*, edited by Thomas T. McAvoy, C.S.C. (Notre Dame, Indiana: University of Notre Dame Press, 1960). *Catholicism in America*, edited by Philip Gleason (New York: Harper & Row, 1970).

Articles on all important topics may be found in the *New Catholic Encyclopedia* (15 vols.; New York: McGraw-Hill Book Company, 1967; Volume XVI, 1974). Current articles may be found in the *Catholic Historical Review* (Washington, D.C.: The Catholic University of America Press, 1915–).

National councils and pastorals: Peter Guilday, *A History of the Councils of Baltimore, 1791–1884* (New York: Macmillan Company, 1932; reprinted, New York: Arno Press & The New York Times, 1969). *Pastoral Letters of the American Hierarchy, 1792–1970*, edited by Hugh J. Nolan (Huntington, Indiana: Our Sunday Visitor, 1971).

General bibliographies: John Tracy Ellis, *A Guide to American Catholic History* (Milwaukee: Bruce Publishing Company, 1959; a new edition is being prepared). Edward R. Vollmar, S.J., *The Catholic Church in America: An Historical Bibliography* (2d ed., New York: Scarecrow Press, 1963).

FATHER TRISCO is a professor of church history in the Catholic University of America, editor of the *Catholic Historical Review*, and secretary of the American Catholic Historical Association.

CATHOLICS IN AMERICA

1776-1976

SAINT FRANCIS XAVIER CHURCH, NEWTOWN, SAINT MARY'S COUNTY, MARYLAND

The first mission was established at Newtown in 1640, and the first church was completed twenty-two years later. The present structure, built in 1766, is the oldest Catholic church in continuous existence in Maryland. (*Courtesy of the Reverend Robert O. McMain, historian of the Archdiocese of Washington*)

Catholics in Maryland

and Pennsylvania in 1776

THOMAS O'BRIEN HANLEY, S.J.

In 1776 Catholics in Maryland and Pennsylvania were prepared to play distinguished roles in the Revolutionary War for Independence declared that year. In the first state constitutions established by the end of that historic year came the great blessings of freedom to the Catholic Church.

Charles Carroll of Carrollton, a Marylander, and Thomas FitzSimons of Pennsylvania were prominent in the state conventions which led to decisive action committing their states to the formation of a new nation.

Two Irish-born Philadelphians, General Stephen Moylan, aide-de-camp to General George Washington, and Commodore John Barry, were among the more prominent Catholic military figures in the war. From the heavily Catholic St. Mary's County came a large number of soldiers in the famous Maryland Old Line contingent which averted the danger of surrender by Washington in New York City. In 1776 many from the area went to the defense of Boston.

Perhaps the culminating event for Catholics in both states in 1776 was the establishment of religious freedom through the adoption of constitutions which Carroll and FitzSimons helped establish. This was a cherished occasion for Catholics, particularly in Maryland. For until 1775 Catholics there were forbidden to worship in public and excluded from voting and holding public office. The situation was better in Pennsylvania. Old St. Joseph's in Philadelphia had been open to Catholic worship since the 1730s. But there was no more security for the future there than in Maryland. True, the fundamental laws of William Penn protected public worship. But the history of the colonies showed that the Crown and Parliament might at any moment change this toleration.

Maryland had seen such a change. A man of like mind with Penn, George Calvert, First Lord Baltimore and Proprietor of Maryland, won royal approval for a charter in 1632 which protected religious freedom in his province. After the Protestant Revolution of 1688 put William and Mary on the throne of England, all was soon changed and hostility to Catholics continued until 1776. The promise of an independent American nation, with Maryland and Pennsylvania as sovereign states, was great indeed, for it would secure the future of Catholic freedom in America.

It was understandable that a priest like John Carroll in 1776 would take an active part in bringing about American independence. He was willing to go with his second cousin Charles Carroll, Benjamin Franklin, and Samuel Chase on a mission to Canada for the Continental Congress, hoping to bring the French Catholics to support the American cause. Most of the twenty-five or so priests who ministered in the English colonies (largely in Maryland and Pennsylvania) wanted independence. Their ministry would be helped by success in the revolution. For as things were, chaos was imminent: The Society of Jesus, to which the priests had once belonged, had been suppressed in 1773 and could not provide them with orderly government; and the Catholic bishop in London, who was now supposed to direct them, was far away and aloof to their needs. With the status of an independent nation, a fully developed American Church with its own bishop would be possible and even required.

The needs of the Catholic population in 1776 were urgent, for their numbers were growing rapidly. In Maryland there were about 15,000. With the growth of Baltimore in the 1760s and 1770s, however, an influx of poor immigrants called for a corresponding growth in the supply of priests and churches. Missionaries to isolated Catholic families in the northern part of the state were needed. The number of Catholics in Pennsylvania was about half of that in Maryland. But there, too, there was a new growth from immigration before 1760, particularly from Germany. Fortunately, some German priests came with the immigrants, both to Philadelphia and to Lancaster, in the southern part of the state. A Wuerttemburg-born Jesuit, Father Ferdinand Farmer, did much at this time to serve the needs of the Catholic community. In 1763 St. Mary's Church was added to St. Joseph's in Philadelphia, while chapels began to appear in other parts of the state.

By 1776 the temper of toleration for Catholics in both states had improved as a result of the liberality in the patriot leaders of the revolution. Even the Tory Anglican clergyman, Jonathan Boucher, gave a dramatic sermon calling for a greater practice of toleration for Catholics.

But old prejudices were not entirely swept away with America's quest for political freedom from England. This was shown in New England, when Parliament passed the Quebec Act continuing the privileged position of the Catholic Church in Canada. In Carpenter's Hall, Philadelphia, there were outcries against the act, tainted with hatred of Romanism.

Yet Maryland and Pennsylvania Catholics were willing to risk the future, hoping that the spirit of liberty in the Revolution would transform even New England. Their immediate grounds for confidence, however, were their own state constitutions, which the constituency of New England could not disturb. The autonomy of individual states was a legal protection great enough to outweigh any hope that a victorious England might restrain discrimination in America. Moreover, such giants of independence as George Washington spoke out publicly against displays of bigotry toward Catholics.

Very soon the mood toward Catholics changed. Their fellow Christians and others plainly saw what John Carroll later pointed out. "Their blood," he said of his co-religionists, "flowed as freely in proportion to their numbers to cement the fabric of independence as that of any of their fellow citizens."

When the war was won, Father Joseph Mosley, an English-born Jesuit in Maryland who had seen the hard times before the liberation of 1776, rejoiced in the blessings of independence and the freedom found in the state constitutions of Maryland and Pennsylvania. "Toleration granted by the Bill of Rights," he wrote, "has put all on the same footing, and has been of great service to us."

When John Carroll returned from his consecration in England as the first Catholic bishop of the United States, he clearly saw the guidance of the hand of God in the trying days of the War for Independence. "Since the American Revolution," he said, "I have always thought that Providence was reserving an even more extraordinary revolution in the order of grace."

RECOMMENDED READING: Charles H. Metzger, S.J., *Catholics and the American Revolution* (Chicago: Loyola University Press, 1962).

FATHER HANLEY is the editor of the papers of John Carroll and of Charles Carroll of Carrollton and resident lecturer at Loyola College, Baltimore.

THE LOG CHAPEL AT CAHOKIA, ILLINOIS

This chapel was built by the French settlers in the late 1780s, when Father
Paul de Saint Pierre was pastor. Previously Father Sebastian Meurin had
been pastor here from 1768 to 1777.

᷌᷌᷌᷍᷍

2

The Church in the Middle West in 1776

RAPHAEL N. HAMILTON, S.J.

On the morning of Saturday, July 4, 1778, the Virginia-born George Rogers Clark stood in the shade at the edge of the forest and looked out across the lush bottom land of the Mississippi River. For weeks he had journeyed through a wilderness still unknown to the folk of his birthplace. He now gazed upon the object, which had led him to risk such a trip, and he was dumbfounded to find the reality so different from what he had imagined it would be.

Clark was twenty-six years old, a surveyor by profession, and in the practice of his trade he had spent the last five years along the Kentucky River in the "land of the westward flowing waters," where in 1773, Daniel Boone had led his family west of the Appalachian Range by way of the Cumberland Gap. On the Kentucky, Clark had familiarized himself with the standard type of English frontier village: a scattered group of cabin-clearings with a centrally located stockade whither, in time of danger, the settlers from the clearings might take refuge.

Now, two years after the Declaration of Independence, Clark was a lieutenant colonel in the Continental Army, sent by the Governor of Virginia, Patrick Henry, to seize the French settlements on the eastern shore of the Mississippi River which were now held by the British. Clark had expected them to be like the frontier towns of his experience. What he saw that fourth of July morning was Kaskaskia, a town with a thousand or more inhabitants, with comfortable dwellings marshalled round the common pasture and with a fine parish church a bit apart from the rest. This hamlet compared favorably with the Virginia capital of Williamsburg; and beyond Kaskaskia's town limits, what Williamsburg did not have, golden fields of wheat stretched away as far as the eye could see.

The account of Clark's infiltration of Kaskaskia on the night of July 4 with a tiny army of about 150 men is fairly well known. When the town's people obtained Clark's assurance that their Catholic religion would be respected and his avowal that the King of France was an ally of the Continental Congress, they lined up behind their parish priest, Father Pierre Gibault, and swore allegiance to the new Republic.

Less well known is the continued activity of Father Gibault, who brought influence to bear on other French towns—Cahokia, Prairie du Rocher, and St. Philippe along the Mississippi and Vincennes on the Wabash River—with the result that they too embraced the American cause. Probably very few have weighed the value of this Catholic priest's contribution to the ascendancy possessed by the representatives of the embryonic United States when, at the close of the Revolutionary War, they took their places at the peace table in 1783. Because of what Gibault and Clark had done, the American delegates could lay claim to the whole eastern half of the fertile Mississippi Valley, a prize without which the barren seaboard colonies would hardly have become a prosperous nation.

Gibault was in the position to accomplish what he did because of one hundred years of Catholic history which preceded 1778 in the Middle West of America. That history began on another Saturday, June 17, 1673. On that day with five companions in two canoes, Louis Jolliet, a Catholic trader from Sault Ste. Marie (now in Michigan), and Father Jacques Marquette, a Jesuit priest whose mission had grown into the settlement where Jolliet plied his trade, glided from behind a willow-covered island at the mouth of the Wisconsin River and drifted out on the smooth surface of the mighty Mississippi. White men had never come this way before. Marquette and Jolliet were the first to trace the river's course southward for nearly a thousand miles. As they went, they came to understand the valley's immense potentiality. They were surprised to observe that the land was very sparsely populated by widely separated tribes, so primitive that they could barely survive in spite of the bounty with which they were surrounded. Small wonder that the natives welcomed the peaceful intrusion of the French settlers who would later come with know-how and tools and ameliorate their living conditions.

In 1675 at the urgent request of the Illini, Father Marquette took the first step in satisfying the Indians' desire for European culture by founding Conception Mission just across the Illinois River from the present Starved Rock state park.

In 1679, the fur trader, Robert Cavelier de la Salle, with the Franciscan priests, Father Gabriel de la Ribourde, Zenobe Membré, and Louis Hennepin, and a troop of skilled artisans brought the first major supply of tools to the Illinois Valley. Near the present Peoria, Fort Crèvecoeur for the protection of the settlers, and a ship for conveying furs to Europe via the mouth of the Mississippi, began to take shape.

At once, Father Hennepin and two Catholic voyageurs, Accault and Auguelle, were sent to determine the navigability of the Illinois River. Hardly had their birch bark nosed its way into the current of the Mississippi when a flotilla of Sioux hunters surrounded it. The three white captives were conducted north to a site near the present city of St. Paul, Minnesota. The Falls of St. Anthony were named by Father Hennepin in 1680. The three prisoners were still adjusting to their unaccustomed life, when one of those strange coincidences of history took place. Sieur Daniel Greysolon Duluth, thinking himself to be hundreds of miles from the nearest European, beached his canoe at the Indian village to be met by the priest and his companions. Duluth demanded freedom for the hostages and conducted them through the Fox-Wisconsin River route to the ten-year-old Jesuit mission of St. François Xavier, where De Pere, Wisconsin, now stands. Thence, Hennepin made his way back to France and Duluth returned to the area, west on Lake Superior, where a flourishing Minnesota city now bears his name.

Disaster fell on La Salle's fort and ship when his carpenters deserted. His patent was running out; hence, with his lieutenant Henri de Tonti, with Father Membré, with the remaining white men of his party and a group of friendly Indians La Salle decided to complete the exploration of the Mississippi River. At its mouth, on April 9, 1682, by formal proclamation, he added the whole valley to the domain of Louis XIV, king of France. Returning to the Illinois country, La Salle set out for Paris and Tonti built Fort St. Louis on Starved Rock, where it was destined to remain until evacuated at the end of the French and Indian War. The Jesuits from Conception Mission, across the river, ministered to the garrison's spiritual needs.

By the close of the seventeenth century, the Chicago River with a short portage to the Des Plaines and the Illinois was being much frequented by western bound traders. There in 1696 Father François Pinet established the Jesuit mission of the Guardian Angel. Among his visitors, in 1699, was Father St. Cosme, of the Society of Foreign Missions, on his way to evangelize the Tamaroa tribe whose village lay opposite the mouth of the Missouri River. He went on to lay the foundation for Cahokia, the first farming settlement in the area. As soon as the Canadians heard of the fertile bottom lands to be had for the taking, Kaskaskia, Prairie du Rocher, and St. Philippe came into being. Vincennes, the last French farm community, owed its origin (1732–33) to François Buisson, Sieur de Vincennes, and the Jesuit Sebastian Louis Meurin was its first pastor.

Briefly, this is the story of the diffusion of French Catholic priests and laymen along the Marquette-Jolliet discovery route. They brought the prosperity and peace to the Mississippi Valley which Father Gibault offered to George Rogers Clark on that Saturday, July 4, in 1778.

Just before France ceded the east side of the Mississippi Valley to Great

Britain, she turned the west side, along with New Orelans, over to Spain. The two main towns north of New Orleans on the west bank of the great river were Ste. Genevieve, built beside the Ozark lead mines in 1734, and St. Louis, the emporium of the Missouri Valley fur trade, both in the present-day state of Missouri. In 1776 Father Genoveau was the pastor of Ste. Genevieve, and his parish boundaries extended over the entire triangle between the Mississippi and Missouri rivers. By then his parishioners numbered close to 4,000, and the miners at Ste. Genevieve were soon supplying bullets to the Continental army.

In 1776, probably the majority of Father Genoveau's congregation lived in St. Louis (Missouri), where Pierre Laclede and his fourteen-year-old stepson, René Auguste Chouteau, had cleared a site on the west bank of the Mississippi and founded a town (1763) to control the fur trade of the Missouri Valley. There, fifteen years later, the Italian-born Catholic, Joseph Maria Francesco Vigo, was one of the most successful managers of the trade. When George Rogers Clark took over Kaskaskia across the river, Vigo devoted his whole energy and fortune to the American cause. Clark soon discovered that the natives would not do business with him in exchange for Virginia paper dollars; Vigo converted the doubtful currency into cash. For this and other forms of assistance Vigo deserved to be called sharer with Clark in the conquest of the Old Northwest.

The Mississippi Valley suffered only one British campaign during the Revolution. It was aimed at St. Louis. Spain's formal declaration of war against England was made in April, 1779, and the English Lieutenant Govenor, Patrick Sinclair, from his fort on Mackinac Island immediately began planning a punitive expedition to be carried out largely by the Indian tribes of Canada. They were to fight under the supervision of their English-licensed traders.

Through the winter of 1779 the Indians assembled at Prairie du Chien (Wisconsin), and in May, 1780, by canoe and raft, the assailants took to the river confident of victory. Meanwhile, friendly American Indians had warned the St. Louisans. They had time to fortify themselves by constructing a series of earthworks, and when the northern Indians came to the attack, a withering fire from behind the ramparts killed one of their chiefs and spread terror among the attackers. The battle was over with the failure of the first charge. The British expeditionary force retreated up the Illinois River to Chicago, where the English were picked up by relief boats and the Indians disappeared into the wilderness. Next year, the disaster to General Cornwallis' army at Yorktown (Virginia) convinced the English Parliament that the continuation of hostilities with the thirteen colonies was to the disadvantage of the mother country. The Revolutionary War never returned to the Mississippi Valley, so its contribution to American Independence is almost entirely Catholic history.

RECOMMENDED READING: John Anthony Caruso, *The Mississippi Valley Frontier* (Indianapolis: Bobbs-Merrill Co., 1966). Joseph P. Donnelly, S.J., *Pierre Gibault, Missionary, 1737–1802* (Chicago: Loyola University Press, 1971).

FATHER HAMILTON is professor emeritus of American colonial history in Marquette University, Milwaukee, Wisconsin.

THE URSULINE CONVENT IN NEW ORLEANS, LOUISIANA

The Ursulines arrived from France in 1727 and erected this convent in 1745. It is the oldest building now standing in the city and the only French colonial structure in the French Quarter, as well as the first convent built within the area of the present-day United States. The school conducted here by the nuns was the first girls' school in the Mississippi Valley. (*NC Photos*)

3

The Church in Louisiana in 1776

Louisiana in the 1770s was a French colony trying to become Spanish—or, rather, trying *not* to become Spanish, at least not *too* Spanish. This Catholic neighbor protected the backdoor of the Thirteen Colonies, and aided the Revolution in a striking measure too little recognized in American textbooks.

Settled by the French in 1699, Louisiana included the Mississippi, Missouri, Ohio, and Red River valleys. In addition to Illinois country villages, the towns were Natchez, Natchitoches, Baton Rouge, and New Orleans. Biloxi and Mobile extended Louisiana eastward along the Gulf Coast. For several decades French Jesuits evangelized the Indians, and French Capuchins served as the pastors of the settlers.

At the end of the Seven Years' War (1763), when England asked her American colonies to pay new taxes for defense expenditures, a much more radical demand was laid upon the almost 8,000 French subjects in Louisiana. By treaty all of Louisiana east of the Mississippi was yielded to England. All of Louisiana west of the Mississippi, with New Orleans attached, was ceded to Spain.

Some Louisianians thought of declaring independence. Some united to send the first Spanish governor back home. Resistance, however, was futile. Independence for so small a population was impossible.

Without haste and without eagerness, Spain accepted Louisiana as a buffer to protect Mexico and her borderlands against the multiplying English colonists to the northeast. With a policy of easy trade and with respect for the local population, the Spanish monarchy set about absorbing this French-speaking region.

France had theoretically intended all colonists in Louisiana to be Catholics, but in reality a tolerant policy had admitted Protestants. Indeed the percentage of Protestants in French Louisiana (between 5 and 10 percent) was higher than the percentage of Catholics (one percent) in the English colonies on the Atlantic Coast.

The French government, motivated by a mixture of Bourbon absolutism, Gallican anti-Romanism, and Jansenist anti-Jesuitism, had recalled the Jesuits from the Indian missions and brought them back to France in 1764 to live as secular priests. This action cut Louisiana's Catholic clergy by half, and left only the Capuchins, who served in the French towns and outposts.

During the French regime (1699–1766) Louisiana had been a part of the vast diocese of Quebec which covered the St. Lawrence Valley, the Great Lakes, the Mississippi Valley, and the Gulf Coast between Texas and Florida. When Spanish civil authority replaced French, there was also a change in church jurisdiction. Louisiana passed under the Spanish king's patronage (*patronato real*), and in 1771 was placed under the bishop of Santiago, Cuba.

Spanish Capuchins began serving in Louisiana in 1772. Père Dagobert from Longwy in northeastern France was succeeded as vicar general and father superior of the Capuchins by Padre Cirilo of Barcelona in Spain. When old Father Dagobert died in May of 1776, an era came to an end: of the seven French friars present at the beginning of the Spanish regime, only two or three remained. The Spanish clergy, usually about ten, were assisted later by several Irish diocesan priests who catered for English-speaking settlers. The clergy traveled widely to minister to a population thinly scattered over a vast region.

The Ursuline nuns continued caring for orphans and teaching in the school founded in New Orleans in 1727. Meanwhile the Spanish government subsidized a school in which religion was taught along with other subjects—in Spanish. Attendance there was low, for the Creoles preferred French tutors and their academies.

The Church in Louisiana in 1776 was unusually polyglot and multi-ethnic for such small numbers. The French colonists, mostly males in the first two decades of settlement, had married Indian women in upriver posts, and also fathered children out of wedlock. German farmers had arrived in 1719. Simultaneously the black slave trade reached Louisiana. From the same era a population of "free persons of color" steadily developed.

In the 1760s Acadian refugees, scattered by the English genocidal expulsion (from present-day Nova Scotia) trekked and sailed their way to French Louisiana just when it became Spanish. Interestingly, the same Edmund Burke who defended the Anglo-American colonists' cause in the British Parliament condemned the "inhumane rooting out of this poor, innocent, deserving people," and insisted that England had "no sort of right to extirpate" them. Uprooted whites, uprooted blacks peopled Louisiana.

In the late 1760s some Maryland Catholic families, who observed the erosion of the religious liberty their ancestors had planted in America, petitioned Spanish authorities for permission to enter Louisiana.

Following Spanish civil and military officials, there also came immigrants from the Canary Islands who farmed, fished, and trapped in the coastal marshlands and waterways. Today, two hundred years later, their descendants still speak Spanish in localities twenty miles from New Orleans.

Present-day Louisiana is unusual in that the state's counties are called "parishes." The riverbank "civil parishes" (counties) bear the names of churches that in the eighteenth century served the settlements on either side of the Mississippi. In common speech on into the nineteenth century, these church parishes remained the easiest place references and became the official nomenclature for civil districts in the state of Louisiana.

Spanish Louisiana Catholics played a major role in the War of American Independence. Irish-born merchant Oliver Pollock had come from Philadelphia to New Orleans at the beginning of the Spanish regime. From the start of the American Revolution he persuaded the Spanish governor to lean to the colonists' side as far as he could without inviting British retaliation. Pollock, named agent of Virginia and of the Continental Congress, spent his own fortune, borrowed further sums from the Spanish governor, and went deeply into debt to other merchants in order to supply George Rogers Clark, who seized from the English the trans-Appalachian area north of the Ohio River. When Spain joined France in an alliance against England (1779), Governor Bernardo de Gálvez, with his Spanish regulars and heterogeneous local militia, boldly captured Baton Rouge, Mobile, and Pensacola. These military victories ended English presence on the Mississippi River and on the Gulf Coast.

Unusual Louisiana would in the future be attached to the United States of America, but her distinctive blend of faith and culture has to this day resisted homogenization—a testimony both to the locals and to the nation whose independence their ancestors helped win.

RECOMMENDED READING: Charles Edwards O'Neill, *Church and State in French Colonial Louisiana* (New Haven: Yale University Press, 1966). Roger Baudier, *The Catholic Church in Louisiana* (New Orleans: Chancery Office, 1939).

FATHER O'NEILL, a professor of history at Loyola University, New Orleans, is particularly interested in the French and Spanish history and culture of Louisiana.

THE CHURCH OF MISSION SAN JOSÉ IN SAN ANTONIO, TEXAS

This stone edifice was begun in 1768 and was completed in 1782. In the
1930s this and other buildings of the mission were restored. (*NC Photos
courtesy of the Research Library of San José Mission*)

4

The Church in Texas in 1776

MARION A. HABIG, O.F.M.

As the first rays of sunrise pierced the darkness of the eastern horizon on the morning of July 4, 1776, the Angelus bell of San José Mission in the Spanish province of Texas announced the dawn of another hot summer day.

About 275 Coahuiltecan Indians, who lived in stone apartments abutting the walls of the mission square, got up from their raised wooden beds covered with buffalo hides and gunny-sack sheets, and quickly assembled for morning Mass and instruction.

Franciscan Father Pedro de Ramírez, who had begun the building of a beautiful new stone church eight years before, was waiting for the mission Indians in the spacious triple-domed sacristy. Because the church proper was still under construction and was not completed until six years later, the sacristy was used for divine services and the overflow of the congregation stood in the arched hallway of the adjoining *convento* or priest's residence.

A year and a half later Father Juan Agustín Morfi (a Spanish phonetic spelling of the Irish "Murphy") visited San José Mission and found its new church to be "very beautiful, having a lovely cupola and a rich façade, decorated with statues and ornaments." It was nearing completion at this time, Father Morfi wrote in his *History of Texas, 1673–1779*, and he added that "the whole structure is admirably proportioned and strongly built of stone and mortar. . . . It is, in truth, the first mission in America, not in point of time, but in point of beauty, plan, and strength."

Founded in 1720 by Venerable Father Antonio Margil de Jesús, the saintly apostle of New Spain during a period of forty years, San José Mission was now reaping the fruits of the hard and patient work of the earlier missionaries. Father Ramírez, whose "dedication, zeal, and religious spirit deserved all praise" (as Father Morfi wrote), was the Father President of all the missions in Spanish Texas, and so San José served as the headquarters. In 1776 there were seven missions. Because it was necessary to protect them against the raids of hostile Apaches and Comanches, all of them were built like fortresses. For this reason, too, they were established close together in two groups, each of them near a presidio or fort at which there was a garrison of Spanish soldiers. Near each presidio there was also a villa or town of Spanish colonists.

One group included, besides San José Mission, the missions of San Antonio de Valero, Nuestra Señora de la Purísima Concepción, San Juan Capistrano, and San Francisco de la Espada. San José was always in the care of missionaries from the so-called Franciscan Missionary College of Guadalupe de Zacatecas, Mexico. The other four were founded by Franciscans of a similar college in Querétaro, Mexico. In 1773 the friars from Querétaro, because they had to take over the former Jesuit missions in Pimería Alta (northern Mexico and southern Arizona), surrendered their Texas missions to the friars from Zacatecas.

Mission San Antonio was founded in 1718, the same year as the Presidio of San Antonio de Béxar and the Villa de Béxar were established. Secularized in 1793, the mission became famous as the Alamo. Missions Concepción, San Juan, and San Francisco were originally founded in eastern Texas in 1716 and "moved" to the San Antonio River in 1731. In that year also a small group of fifteen families came from the Canary Islands and settled in the Villa de Béxar, which was henceforth known as the Villa de San Fernando.

Mission Concepción, which served for a time as the headquarters of the Texas missionaries from Querétaro, had a large and beautiful stone church with twin towers long before the San José church was built. It was dedicated on December 8, 1755, and is still standing intact today, the oldest unrestored stone church in the United States. The missions in the San Antonio group, except San Antonio de Valero, were not completely secularized until 1824. The Villa de San Fernando, in 1776, had a parish church of adobe (completed about 1750) with a transept, dome, and tower, "perfect and harmonious in every detail." The pastor was a priest of the diocese of Guadalajara until 1777, when Texas became a part of the new diocese of Linares (now the Archdiocese of Monterrey), Mexico. For a time the Presidio of San Antonio also had its own military chaplain. The population of the entire San Antonio area in 1776, including the Indians in the five missions, was about 2,000.

The second group, consisting of two missions in 1776, was also situated on the banks of the San Antonio River, about ninety miles southeast of San Antonio, near the present city of Goliad. Nearby was the Presidio of La Bahía with a company of soldiers and also a settlement of Spanish colonists. Originally the presidio and one of the missions, Nuestra Señora del Espíritu

Santo, were founded in 1722 on Garcitas Creek which flows into Matagorda Bay. Both were moved to the Guadalupe River in 1726, and from there in 1749 to the banks of the San Antonio River. Another mission, that of Nuestra Señora del Rosario, was founded near the La Bahía mission and presidio in 1754.

At the Espíritu Santo Mission a new stone church was under construction in 1776 and it was solemnly dedicated the following year on December 12, the feast of Our Lady of Guadalupe. Though the new church collapsed about twelve years later, the mission continued to exist until 1830. The Rosario Mission had practically come to an end in 1807 when most of its Indians were transferred to Mission Nuestra Señora del Refugio, which had been founded in 1793, the last of the Texas missions to come into existence. Like the Espíritu Santo Mission, that of Refugio was secularized in 1830.

The Presidio of La Bahía was a wooden structure in 1776. It was not until the 1790's that the stone fort with the chapel of Nuestra Señora de Loreto was constructed. Divine services for the soldiers and settlers were conducted by a diocesan priest who served as military chaplain of the presidio; but by 1829, when the La Bahía settlement changed its name to Goliad, the town had a little church of its own. The population of the La Bahía area in 1776, including the presidio, the Spanish villa, and the two Indian missions, was probably about 1,000.

The Spanish Province of Texas in 1776, of course, was not co-extensive with the present State of Texas, for it extended only from the San Antonio area northeastward to the Sabine River and beyond that into present Louisiana and southward to the Gulf coast. At that time the Rio Grande was not a political boundary, and three other provinces extended across this river into western Texas; these were Nuevo México, Coahuila, and Nuevo Santander (now Tamaulipas).

In what is now the state of Texas there were sixty-four Spanish settlements begun between 1632 and 1793 and lasting for at least a short time. This total includes thirty-seven missions (not counting different sites of the same mission separately, except the three which were moved from eastern Texas to the San Antonio River in 1731), nine presidios or forts, and ten villas or towns of Spanish colonists. The most successful missions were those in existence in 1776.

Today in the city of San Antonio there is still the original church of Mission Concepción as well as the restored churches of the other four missions (San José is now a State and National Historic Site, and the aqueduct of Espada Mission a National Historic Landmark). Near Goliad are the restored La Bahía presidio with its chapel (a National Historic Landmark) and the ruins and restored church of Mission Espíritu Santo (a State Park).

RECOMMENDED READING: Marion A. Habig, O.F.M., *The Alamo Chain of Missions: A History of San Antonio's Five Old Missions* (Chicago: Franciscan Herald Press, 1968). Carlos E. Castañeda, *Our Catholic Heritage in Texas* (7 vols.; Austin, Tex.: Von Boeckmann-Jones Co., 1936–1958; reprinted: New York: Arno Press, 1976).

FATHER HABIG is a leading Franciscan historian and author of twenty-four books and more than 200 articles. His latest book is *Saints of the Americas*, published by Our Sunday Visitor, Huntington, Indiana.

5

The Church in the Southwest in 1776

KIERAN McCARTY, O.F.M.

The momentous year of 1776 launched an era of new freedom and expanding horizons, not only in the Anglo society of our eastern seaboard but in our Mexican-Hispanic Southwest as well. Recent research has dispelled some of the black legends of royal oppression in the Spanish colonies of our borderlands, and it has also revealed sympathetic activity, promoted in the Southwest by the Spanish crown itself, aiding the cause of the American Revolution. The Catholic Church played an essential role in fostering this activity, in expanding frontier horizons, and in increasing frontier freedoms generally.

In May of 1776, two months before the Declaration of Independence, King Charles III of Spain granted local government to the frontier provinces of New Spain, and urgent appeals no longer had to go all the way to Mexico City. High-level decisions, pending royal approbation, could be made in the city of Arispe and would affect our borderlands from the Gulf of Mexico to the Pacific Ocean.

Arispe, in present-day Mexico near the Arizona border, and other Spanish settlements in the Arizona-Sonora desert, had also been hampered in Church matters by their distance from the episcopal see of Durango, which was 800 miles eastward on the opposite side of the Mexican Rockies. In May, 1779, three years after the designation of Arispe as civil capital of the northern provinces, Pope Pius VI declared Arispe the headquarters of a new and independent diocese.

The Southwest was mainly mission territory at this time, and would be for a long time to come. The new civil jurisdiction at Arispe listed some thirty-five Indian missions for Spanish Sonora, including Arizona, and

RUINS OF THE CHURCH OF MISSION SAN JOSÉ DE TUMACÁCORI
IN SOUTHERN ARIZONA

The Pima Indian village located on this site was first visited by the Jesuit
missionary Padre Eusebio Kino in 1691. Around 1772 Tumacácori became
the headquarters of the Franciscan missionaries in the district. This church,
made of adobe, was begun between 1796 and 1806, and though never completed, it was in use from 1822 on. (*NC Photos*)

twenty-eight for New Mexico, administered by Franciscans from Mexico City, Querétaro, and Guadalajara.

The dream of independence from Britain in the Atlantic-coast colonies coincided in the Mexican-Hispanic Southwest with dreams of new horizons and new beginnings. Catholic churchmen played an outstanding part in this heroic task of exploration and new settlement. Such were the Garcés-Anza colonizing expedition from Tubac (Arizona) and the Domínguez-Vélez de Escalante exploration trek from Santa Fe (New Mexico). Both were taking place in 1776, the year of our Declaration of Independence.

Father Francisco Garcés, Franciscan missionary at Mission San Xavier del Bac near Tucson, was pathfinder for the expedition that founded the first Spanish colony on the shores of San Francisco Bay. Earlier in the decade he had explored southwestern Arizona and southeastern California to establish the route for 240 men, women, and children to cross some of the harshest terrain on North America. In 1770 Captain Juan Bautista de Anza, commander of the royal Spanish fort at Tubac, had discussed with Father Garcés the old dream of an overland route to California. Word had reached them recently through the Indian grapevine of the arrival of Spaniards in Upper California.

Two expeditions resulted: the first an exploration in 1774 and the second a colonizing trip in 1775–1776. Father Garcés did not accompany the second expedition all the way to the coast. His restless nature was already seeking new horizons. Hoping to find still another route further north to connect Santa Fe, New Mexico, with the newly founded port of Monterey in California, he left the second Anza expedition on the lower Colorado river to head northward along its shores, then westward all the way into the San Joaquín valley of California, then eastward onto the Hopi rocks of present-day northern Arizona.

July 4, 1776, found Father Garcés at the Hopi village of Oraibi and at the end of his northern explorations. It also found an Acoma Indian, named Lázaro, hurrying eastward with a letter written by Garcés the day before at Oraibi to the Franciscan missionaries at Santa Fe. Neither knew that at the other end was a fellow explorer who was not only dreaming of but actively engaged in the same project, discovering a northern route from Santa Fe to Monterey.

Father Silvestre Vélez de Escalante and Father Francisco Atanasio Domínguez had planned their departure from Santa Fe for July 4, 1776. Circumstances delayed their leaving long enough for Lázaro to arrive with Father Garcés' letter, containing helpful information. Late in July, the two friars left Santa Fe with a handful of Spaniards and Indians and spent nearly four months on the trail. Though they did not reach Monterey, they brought back valuable information on the Great Basin country of the West, especially the present-day state of Utah.

But the Spanish empire in the New World was not acting in isolation from other world events. The important role of Spain and her colonies in the American Revolutionary War has long been underestimated. Without the Spanish offensive along our southern seaboard and her patrols up and down the Mississippi River, protecting the Thirteen Colonies from rearguard action by the British, the outcome of the war might have been very different. In addition, recent research has revealed a monetary contribution, a free-will offering, made by both Spanish and Indian settlements in the Southwest to defray Spain's expenses in the war.

In August, 1780, berating "the insulting tyranny of the English nation," Charles III of Spain appealed to his New World colonies for a *donativo* or free-will offering. The royal suggestion that each Spaniard should give two pesos and each Indian one peso was only a guideline, not a command. An instruction sent by the Viceroy of New Spain to the commissioners of the collection strictly forbade them to use any coercion whatsoever or even to show any sign of displeasure if the prospective donor gave nothing at all. The royal decree urged the Church's involvement by publicizing the collection from the pulpit and by giving good example through generous donations.

Perhaps the best example of church involvement in what is now the American Southwest was that of the Franciscans administering the missions in Pimería Alta (in present-day southern Arizona). First, they pledged their prayers for the success of the war effort through an official act of their mother college of the Holy Cross of Querétaro, dated January 14, 1780. Then, their Pimería Alta missions donated 641 pesos, over three times the amount collected in the wealthy capital of Arispe. The purchasing power of this sum is suggested by the price of an excellent riding horse at that time—from six to eight pesos. At the final tabulation in Arispe, the Spanish settlements and Indian missions of our greater Southwest were credited with a donation of 22,420 pesos to the war that won American independence.

RECOMMENDED READING: *Desert Documentary: The Spanish Years, 1767–1821*, edited by Kieran McCarty (Tucson: Arizona Historical Society, 1976). John L. Kessell, *Friars, Soldiers, and Reformers: Hispanic Arizona and the Sonora Mission Frontier, 1767–1856* (Tucson: University of Arizona Press, 1976).

FATHER McCARTY is Arizona state commissioner for the national Bicentennial, Franciscan priest, Indian missionary, and resident historian at Mission San Xavier del Bac in Tucson.)

6

The Church in California in 1776

MAYNARD GEIGER, O.F.M.

Several years ago I received a letter from a gentleman in New York saying he had heard that I had in the Santa Barbara Mission Archives a copy of a letter sent by Father Junípero Serra to General George Washington. He wondered if he could obtain a copy of it.

I was amazed. Had such a letter existed, it would surely have been published long ago. On July 4, 1776, Father Serra was sailing along the Pacific coast between Monterey and San Diego, totally oblivious to the events in Philadelphia. Neither Father Serra nor General Washington knew of the other or of the other's work.

The Atlantic and Pacific shores were both populated by non-Indians in 1776. But the differences between the two colonial areas in political viewpoints, religion, and language, and the vast physical separation by mountain ranges, deserts, and plains made their eventual union in an expanded United States seem to be inconceivable at that time.

Catholic Christianity in the present state of California took root on July 16, 1769, when Father Serra planted the cross on a hilltop above the harbor of San Diego. Contrary to a commonly held opinion, Spain did not come to California primarily to spread the Catholic religion. She moved in to create a buffer state for what was then known as New Spain (today Mexico) against the threat of Russian aggression or encroachment from the north. In the process, however, she also wished to propagate the Catholic faith among the natives and to civilize them on the Spanish pattern. This work was entrusted to the Franciscan missionaries of the College of San Fernando, Mexico City, who were already laboring in Lower California (the peninsula, which is still a part of Mexico).

The king of Spain and under him his American viceroys controlled the Church in all external affairs—a situation totally alien to our subsequent na-

MISSION SAN CARLOS BORROMEO, CARMEL, CALIFORNIA

In this sketch drawn in 1839, the Christian Indian village is seen on a hill to the right. This mission, the second in chronological order of foundation, was established by Padre Junípero Serra in 1770 at Monterey and was soon moved to Carmel. As president of the missions of Upper California Padre Serra made this his headquarters. His successor built the stone church shown here between 1792 and 1797. (*NC Photos*)

tional tradition of complete separation of Church and state. And missionaries had to conform to this arrangement. The governors were also military men. The Franciscan superior in California lived at Carmel near Monterey, close to the governor's headquarters. Each mission was guarded by a corporal and five soldiers, one of whom was in charge of the mission's economic affairs.

By the end of December, 1776, seven missions had been founded: San Diego, July 16, 1769; San Carlos, Monterey-Carmel, June 3, 1770; San Antonio, July 14, 1771; San Gabriel near present Los Angeles, September 8, 1771; San Luis Obispo, September 1, 1772; San Francisco, October 4, 1776, and San Juan Capistrano, November 1, 1776. There were no civilian settlements, but three presidios were founded along with the missions of the same name at San Diego, Monterey, and San Francisco.

From the very beginning there were misunderstandings and conflicts between the missionaries and the military. By 1772 these reached the point that Father Serra was forced to return to Mexico to obtain from the new viceroy, Antonio María Bucareli y Ursua, a freer hand for the missionary enterprise. He presented thirty-two requests, most of which were granted, and as a result, the missionaries had full control of the Indian converts except in high criminal cases.

Money from the Pious Fund, a fund established by the Jesuits in Lower California but after their expulsion in 1768 taken over by the government, was used for mission expenses in both Upper and Lower California. One thousand pesos were appropriated for the establishment of each mission and 350 pesos a year for the salary of each missionary. The missionaries' salaries were used to purchase items needed by the convert Indians. Ships brought supplies from Mexico each year for the presidios and missions. At times cattle and other animals were driven northward to Upper California from Lower California.

The early mission buildings were crude frontier establishments. The churches, living quarters, work shops, and storage rooms were built of unhewn timber with thatched roofs and hard dirt floors. Soon adobe began to replace the wood-and-dirt structures. Until the converted Indians could be taught the various trades, buildings could be erected only in the simplest fashion. These early missions stretched along 600 miles of coast from San Diego to San Francisco. The principal road connecting them was called El Camino Real.

The Indians of these missions were nomadic or marginal peoples with no literature or agriculture. They lived from the bounty of the land and the sea alone. Most of the time men went about entirely naked. There were six distinct languages spoken between San Diego and San Francisco.

The missionaries attracted the Indians from the native villages to the mission settlements by kind treatment and gifts. They gave rudimentary instruction in the Catholic faith before Baptism. There was daily Mass and instruction and the feasts of the Church were colorfully celebrated.

At the missions the Indians built their traditional huts. Only later could they be induced to build adobe houses with tile roofs after the Spanish manner. Simple woolen clothing was provided for them along with three regular meals a day, supplemented by food of their choice obtained by hunting, fishing, and seed and nut gathering.

The missionaries attended also to the spiritual needs of the soldiers and their families, for no diocesan priests had been supplied by the government. A doctor at Monterey was the sole physician in the area. By the end of 1776 at San Diego 461 Indians had been baptized and 115 Christian marriages performed, although some of the neophytes had rebelled in 1775, killing one of the missionaries and burning the buildings. The mission was re-established, however, and by the end of 1776 it had 498 live stock (cattle, sheep, goats, hogs, horses, and mules). Agriculture had been introduced, and ever more abundant crops of wheat, barley, Indian corn, beans, peas, and lentils were produced. The other missions gradually developed along the same lines both materially and spiritually.

The great Anza expedition of 1775–1776 brought soldiers and families from Sonora, Mexico, to found Presidio San Francisco and later the civilian pueblo of San José. Most of the 242 persons in this expedition remained in Upper California.

Exact statistics on the Catholic population in California by the end of 1776 cannot be given, because two mission registers are no longer extant. But available evidence suggests that the total number of Catholics by that time, both Indians and Spaniards, was about 1,900. When the American Revolution began, California was still pure mission territory with only seven years of missionary work behind it.

RECOMMENDED READING: Maynard Geiger, O.F.M., *The Life and Times of Fray Junipero Serra* (2 vols.; Washington, D.C.: Academy of American Franciscan History, 1959).

FATHER GEIGER has been archivist-historian at the Santa Barbara Mission Archive-Library in California since 1937.

7

The Carrolls in the American Revolution

THOMAS O'BRIEN HANLEY, S.J.

Charles Carroll of Carrollton, the Catholic signer of the Declaration of Independence, and John Carroll, founder of the American Catholic hierarchy, saw the American Revolution as not only a political event, but a religious one as well. Both took an official role in the action which created the American Republic.

By 1775 they had returned from Europe, and that was the last year they would live in a country where they had not been allowed public worship nor the right to vote and hold public office. They and their families before them had lived under the suspicion that a Catholic was somehow prone to sedition, and the statutes of Queen Elizabeth's time penalized them as if they were guilty by association with a small number of sixteenth and seventeenth-century Catholics who had collaborated with Spanish designs on England and her empire.

In 1688 Charles Carroll's grandfather had come to America with the hope that Maryland would continue to be a sanctuary for those persecuted in Europe for their religious beliefs. The father of his second cousin, John Carroll, later came to Upper Marlboro, Maryland, because his property in Ireland was threatened with confiscation. Maryland as founded by the Catholic Calvert family and initiated by the assembly of the first settlers, most of whom were Protestants, provided for religious freedom for all in its Toleration Act of 1639. But when William and Mary came to the throne in 1688 by overturning the Catholic King James II, the Church of England was established in the province and the statutes of Elizabeth were imposed. The Catholic proprietor, Charles Calvert, third Lord Baltimore, was removed. Both Carroll families lived in the hope that the original happy condition of the colony would one day return.

It was not until a new generation of young Marylanders discovered a

FATHER JOHN CARROLL

This portrait (oil on canvas) by an unknown artist was probably executed in 1774 or 1775. Born in 1735, John Carroll had returned from Europe in 1774 as a secular priest after the suppression of the Society of Jesus, to which he had belonged. At that time the missionaries wore lay attire because of the anti-Catholic sentiment in Maryland. (*Courtesy of the Kennedy Galleries, Inc., New York*)

deeper meaning of freedom that the hope seemed possible. These men, Samuel Chase, Thomas Johnson, and some others, turned to Charles Carroll for help in their defense of American liberty against the governor of Maryland and soon against George III, his ministers, and Parliament. In the pages of the *Maryland Gazette* in 1773 Carroll attacked the governor's attempt to tax Marylanders without their consent by the assembly. In 1774 and 1775 he went to the Continental Congress in Philadelphia as an adviser to the Maryland delegation, seeking to prevent Britain's unjust taxation and the application of her military force on the American colonies. By January of 1776, hope of conciliation was lost and a war for freedom became inevitable.

The British plan, after failing to stop Americans at Lexington, Concord, and Boston, called for a military buildup in the St. Lawrence River area for an advance southward to New York City. American forces were already taking forts in upper New York and ultimately Montreal. But the whole Canadian area needed to be stabilized. On the advice of John Adams and Samuel Chase, the Congress called for a Commission to Canada for this purpose. Because Canadians did not trust Protestant Americans, Charles and John Carroll were asked to join Benjamin Franklin and Chase in the mission. In March, 1776, the four men departed. By the time they returned in early June, the revolutionaries' position was considerably improved in the northern theater of war. The commission's work was ultimately rewarded when British Gen. John Burgoyne failed to advance toward New York City as planned.

Charles Carroll then led the way at Annapolis, where he successfully persuaded the revolutionary convention to declare independence from England. The convention also elected him a delegate to the Continental Congress where he signed the Declaration of Independence. Perhaps of even greater importance was his appointment to the committee which drafted the Maryland Constitution. His draft, with few exceptions, was passed as the basic law of the new state. It provided religious freedom for Marylanders. Carroll served, in addition, on other important committees necessary for the success of the war effort. In the Congress he was a member of the Board of War and proved a great support to the command of Gen. George Washington when the general was under criticism during the dark days at Valley Forge.

In the life of the American Church, John Carroll was no less creative than Charles. He suffered in mind and heart when the Society of Jesus, to which be belonged, was suppressed in 1773. He saw the twenty-five priests of that order, on whose ministry American Catholics depended entirely, adrift as the war went on. The bishop (vicar apostolic) in London, who had jurisdiction over American Catholics, did not see how he could continue his role after American independence. A new nation, John Carroll believed, called for an American Church free from foreign control.

Hardly had the Treaty of Paris been signed in 1783 when Father Carroll came forward with a plan to provide for the discipline and support of the priests in the new nation. He drafted a "Form of Government" for the clergy and other rules and regulations for their temporal affairs, and their deputies adopted his proposals in 1784. Meanwhile the Holy See was preparing to establish a more normal kind of ecclesiastical jurisdiction in the United States. Once it was assured that the American Congress would not object to the appointment of a bishop, the Holy See had the apostolic nuncio in Paris consult Benjamin Franklin about the choice of an individual, and Franklin, who esteemed Carroll highly ever since their difficult mission to Canada, recommended him warmly. Carroll's age (forty-nine), family connections, excellent education, and gifts of leadership also distinguished him among his fellows. On June 9, 1784, therefore, the Holy See named him "superior of the missions" in the United States, that is, the local head of the Church, intending to make him a vicar apostolic (a titular bishop) in the near future. The American clergy, however, wanted an ordinary bishop with a see located in an American city, and eventually the Holy See allowed them to designate the city and elect the first bishop. Thus in May, 1789, the general chapter of the clergy selected Baltimore as the see city and elected John Carroll as the bishop. After the Holy See confirmed these decisions, Carroll was consecrated in England on August 15 of the following year.

At this time Bishop Carroll told his cousin Charles that he, more than anyone else, was responsible for the winning of religious freedom for American Catholics in the Revolution. But both were remarkable for their involvement in both civil and religious life during these historic times. None could doubt that their religious faith fortified their service to their country. Their friendly relations with Protestants whose forebears had suspected and oppressed Catholics testified to the magnificent achievement of these two great American Catholics.

RECOMMENDED READING: Thomas O'Brien Hanley, S.J., *The American Revolution and Religion: Maryland, 1770 to 1800* (Washington, D.C.: Catholic University of America Press, 1972); Thomas O'Brien Hanley, S.J., *Charles Carroll of Carrollton: The Making of a Revolutionary Gentleman* (Washington, D.C.: Catholic University of America Press, 1970); Ellen Hart Smith, *Charles Carroll of Carrollton* (Cambridge, Mass.: Harvard University Press, 1942); Peter Guilday, *The Life and Times of John Carroll, Archbishop of Baltimore (1735–1815)* (reprinted, Westminster, Md.: Newman Press, 1954); and Annabelle M. Melville, *John Carroll of Baltimore. Founder of the American Catholic Hierarchy* (New York: Charles Scribner's Sons, 1955).

FATHER HANLEY is the editor of the papers of John Carroll and of Charles Carroll of Carrollton and resident lecturer at Loyola College, Baltimore.

8

French Contributions to the Church

in the New Republic

ANNABELLE M. MELVILLE

Frrench clergy and lay persons deserve no small part of the credit for laying the solid foundations of the Catholic Church in the early years of the Republic. Indeed, for half a century after 1775 American Catholicism was permeated by the spirit of French piety and promoted by the arduous labors of bishops and priests who came from France. It was also strengthened by close ties with that country and supported by generous financial aid from French Catholics.

French contributions to American Catholicism began during the Revolution, particularly after France became the active ally of the United States by the treaties of 1778. French naval chaplains gave many American seaports their first glimpses of Catholic ceremonies. In Newport, Rhode Island, the military funeral of Admiral De Ternay aroused great public interest. In Boston, Masses in the French military and naval hospitals led to regular Catholic services. When the Revolution ended, some of these chaplains—such as the Franciscan Seraphim Bandol in Philadelphia, Father Paul de St. Pierre in Illinois, and the Capuchin Sebastian de Rosey in Maryland—remained in the United States and joined the permanent clergy.

The wartime alliance with France also produced other results. Intermarriage between Frenchmen and American women averaged seven a year after 1778. The French consul in Boston, Joseph de Valnais, for example, married Eunice Quincy; Louis Baury de Bellerive, who served with D'Estaing, married Mary Clarke of Middletown, Connecticut. Baury, who was one of the wealthiest of the postwar French-Americans, was a moving force in starting

33

THE FIRST BUILDING OF MOUNT SAINT MARY'S COLLEGE,
EMMITSBURG, MARYLAND

The college was founded in 1808 by John Dubois with the aid of Louis
William Dubourg and was also long served by Simon Gabriel Bruté de
Rémur. All three were French priests who later became bishops in the
United States. (*NC Photos courtesy of Mount Saint Mary's College*)

a church in Boston. In fact, these French-American marriages were responsible for many an infant congregation in New England.

A third effect of the French assistance to American independence was the benefit to Catholicism among the Indians, particularly the Penobscot and Passamaquoddy tribes in Maine. These Indians, who were very loyal to the American cause, went to Boston after the Declaration of Independence to request that the new nation secure a Catholic priest to serve them. Through Admiral d'Estaing's influence a French Augustinian, Hyacinthe de la Motte, was sent to Maine. There he became the first in a succession of French clergy who nourished the religious faith and political loyalty of the Indians both during and after the war.

French Canadians contributed to the success of American arms in the Northwest. For example, Father Pierre Gibault, a native of Montreal who was serving in Illinois, came to be called "The Patriot Priest." Through his influence over the French people living in Illinois Father Gibault enabled George Rogers Clark to bring the Northwest Territory under American control. Father Gibault's flock furnished supplies to the American military forces, and the priest even enlisted a company to aid in the recapture of Vincennes from the British. This led to the permanent acquisition of the territory by the United States at the peace settlement in 1783.

It was in the postwar era, however, that French influence became a major factor in the development of American Catholicism. When the first bishop of Baltimore, John Carroll, decided to begin a seminary for the training of priests he turned to France for assistance. The first band of French Sulpicians embarked from St. Malo in 1791. The story of their trip is preserved in the *Voyage en Amérique* by Chateaubriand, who accompanied them. Thus, during President Washington's first administration, St. Mary's in Baltimore became the first Catholic seminary in the United States.

This first nucleus of French education soon produced other benefits. In Baltimore itself a French Sulpician, Father Louis William Dubourg, began a college for Catholic laymen. In Emmitsburg, Maryland, Father Dubourg helped Father (later Bishop) John Dubois found Mt. St. Mary's, which came to be known as "The Cradle of Bishops" for its many graduates who eventually reached episcopal rank. It was French Sulpicians, too, who directed St. Elizabeth Seton toward educating young women, first in Baltimore and later in Emmitsburg. The names of French-American priests and bishops— Dubourg, Dubois, John Baptist David, Simon-Gabriel Bruté, Benedict Flaget —are all linked with the work of this first native saint of the United States.

Besides initiating much of the Catholic educational activity in the new Republic, the French founded new parishes and dioceses as well, particularly in New England and in the west. The success of the Church in Massachusetts and Maine during the Federalist era was largely due to émigré priests fleeing from the French Revolution. Fathers François A. Matignon and Jean

Lefebvre de Cheverus worked together in such harmony and zeal in this center of anti-Catholicism that when Boston's new Church of the Holy Cross was undertaken, some 140 Protestants' names, headed by that of President John Adams, appeared on the subscription list of contributors. It is not surprising that when new dioceses were created in 1808, Boston was among them and Father Cheverus became its first bishop. When he was recalled to France in 1823, many prominent Bostonian Protestants petitioned King Louis XVIII to let him stay, calling the Catholic bishop "a treasure ... we cannot part with."

In the Northwest Territory and the frontier regions spreading out from Kentucky and Louisiana the French were equally important. Father Michel Levadoux, who came with the first Sulpicians in 1791, did much to wean the French in the Northwest Territory away from their former allegiance to Canada and to inspire them with loyalty to the new Republic. Father Gabriel Richard, who fled France a year after Father Levadoux, not only founded centers of learning in the Detroit area, introducing the first printing press and giving Michigan its first printed book; he also became the first priest to sit in the United States Congress as the territorial delegate from Michigan in 1824.

The French Ursulines were already conducting schools in the Diocese of Louisiana when that area became part of the United States. After Father Dubourg became Bishop of Louisiana he brought numerous priests and Sisters from France, including Mother Philippine Duchesne, who began many schools—even one for Indian children—along the Mississippi. Bishop Dubourg also induced many Vincentians to come to the West, where they assumed pastoral duties and educated candidates for the priesthood. To support his efforts financially, Bishop Dubourg aroused the zeal of lay friends in Lyons, where the Society for the Propagation of the Faith was founded in 1822. This organization, always under lay control, contributed unstintingly to the American Church for the rest of the nineteenth century.

The Church in Kentucky was virtually synonymous with the name of Bishop Benedict Flaget, perhaps the greatest gift France ever gave to American Catholicism. This "Bishop of the Wilderness" served for forty years in humility, virtue, and incredible vigor, beloved both at home and abroad. Reluctant to accept episcopal rank when the Diocese of Bardstown was created in 1808, but finally consecrated by Archbishop Carroll in 1810, he tried to resign at the end of his first twenty years of service. But Rome insisted on reappointing him, and he died as Bishop of Louisville in 1850, long after the frontier had passed beyond Kentucky.

No other bishop or diocese in America was followed with such interest in France. In his fatherland Flaget became the "legendary Bishop of Kentucky" whose periodic visits to seek recruits for the clergy and religious orders and money were triumphal journeys. French Catholic newspapers reported in detail every development in his diocese from the building of his cathedral to the deaths of his priests. As a result of his "begging trip" through France in 1837, contributions to the Society for the Propagation of the Faith were increased by a million francs, and Kentucky continued to be a most favored recipient of subsidies from the Society. To Bardstown were also sent paintings of the great masters—Van Eyck, Murillo, Rubens, and Van Dyck—which were donated by the King of France himself.

Although the predominance of French influence waned as succeeding waves of Irish and German immigration reached American shores in the nineteenth century, the United States remains to this day the beneficiary of the French clergy and laity who did so much for the Church in its early years. The impetus they gave to combining sound theology with intellectual élan produced a tradition in priestly training which flourished not only in the eastern cities but even on the frontier long after French bishops and priests became a minority. With few exceptions, they were imbued with a devotion to American political principles, and they inculcated a respect for law and order in those around them. They notably added to the cultural life of their time with their splendid libraries and works of art. Never hesitating to enter the arena of apologetics or defense of the faith, they promoted a better understanding of the Catholic religion and earned the respect of their Protestant neighbors.

Upon the departure of Bishop Cheverus the Boston *Commercial Gazette* commented, "The amenity of his manners as a gentleman, his accomplishments as a scholar, his tolerant disposition as a religious teacher, and his pure and apostolic life have been our theme ever since we have known him." This tribute could well be paid to the French Catholic leaders in the United States as a body. Their civility, learning, ecumenism, and piety left an indelible stamp on the Church in this country.

RECOMMENDED READING: Annabelle M. Melville, *Jean Lefebvre de Cheverus, 1768–1836* (Milwaukee: Bruce Publishing Company, 1958). J. Herman Schauinger, *Cathedrals in the Wilderness* [a biography of Bishop Flaget] (Milwaukee: Bruce Publishing Company, 1952). Frank B. Woodford and Albert Hyma, *Gabriel Richard, Frontier Ambassador* (Detroit: Wayne State University Press, 1958).

ANNABELLE M. MELVILLE is professor emeritus of history at the State College at Bridgewater, Massachusetts.

THE FIRST AMERICAN CARMELITE CONVENT

The convent was established at Port Tobacco in southern Maryland in 1790
by three American and one English nun who had been professed in Belgium. (*NC Photos courtesy of the Carmelite Monastery of Baltimore*)

9

The First Nun Professed in the

Original United States

ROSE L. MARTIN

Freedom to embrace a religious vocation was one of the liberties won by American Catholics through the War of Independence. On the veiling day of the first nun to be professed in the original United States, Father Charles Neale declared that it was "by the happy Revolution of the Government in America" that God "has drawn us out of our bondage and restored us to our just rights, both Civil and Religious."

The symbol of the liberty hailed by Father Neale was Elizabeth Carberry, who on May 1, 1792, became a Discalced Carmelite nun, Sister Teresa of the Heart of Mary. The place was the white-walled chapel of the small convent of Jesus, Mary, and Joseph, at Port Tobacco, Maryland, at that time the only convent in the United States.

Before the Revolution Catholics and Jews were barred from public office in Maryland, and public celebration of the rites of the Roman Church was prohibited. For generations the Mass had been offered only in private homes behind drawn curtains by a handful of Jesuit missioners, who carried the Host in their saddlebags. Suspected and sometimes harassed by the colonial authorities, they kept the faith alive in cooperation with the people they served.

In spite of such discouraging circumstances, Elizabeth Carberry had decided at the age of twenty that she wished above all things to become a nun. Pretty, popular, and courted, she had already refused several offers of marriage. She was born into a large and devout Catholic family and was apparently the favorite child of John Baptist Carberry II, a prosperous farmer in St. Mary's County (southern Maryland).

Since there was no convent in the colonies, she begged her father to send her to Belgium where other Maryland girls had gone to be professed—and had never returned. John Carberry, however, would not hear of it. So there was nothing for Elizabeth to do but wait and hope to take her vows some day in her native land. Her wait lasted twenty-seven years.

Meanwhile Maryland was caught up in the struggle against Great Britain. Records at the National Archives in Washington, D.C., reveal that at least three of Elizabeth Carberry's brothers—Henry, Joseph, and Peter—served as soldiers in the Revolutionary War. One of them, Captain Henry Carberry, was mentioned in George Washington's letters.

With her father deceased and her brothers away at war, Elizabeth Carberry stayed home and helped manage the family farm. The experience of running a Maryland plantation would prove useful in later years, after she had entered a convent attempting to subsist on its own agricultural products.

When peace came and with it a Constitution assuring religious freedom, Catholics of southern Maryland were prompt to avail themselves of the new opportunities. Repeatedly "several in Charles County" petitioned the bishop of Antwerp, Belgium, to send nuns to establish a convent in the United States. After more than six years those efforts were successful, and in April, 1790, four Discalced Carmelite nuns left Hoogstraeten, Belgium, for Maryland.

Three of them were Maryland-born: their superior, Mother Bernardina, who had been Anne Matthews, and her two nieces, Sisters Mary Aloysia and Mary Eleanora Matthews. The fourth was an English nun, Sister Clare Joseph Dickenson, from a neighboring convent in Antwerp. Escorting them were Father Neale, who was Mother Bernardina's nephew, and Father Robert Plunkett, soon to be the first president of Georgetown College.

Because it was dangerous to wear religious garb in public while Belgium was in a state of revolt, the four nuns were obliged to travel in secular dress. Carrying luggage which included a host-baker and chapel fittings and wearing fashionable clothing contributed by well-wishers, the four women boarded a small vessel at Amsterdam, the Netherlands. After a storm-tossed voyage lasting several months, early in July they debarked at Port Tobacco in Charles County, where they were guests for a time at the Neale family residence. Elizabeth Carberry was among the first to welcome them.

Acreage for a monastery was soon found on a secluded green hillside surrounded by fertile farmland near Port Tobacco. Father Neale donated his entire patrimony to buy it for the nuns. Several tiny clapboard buildings adjoining a small chapel were hastily erected, and the convent was dedicated on October 15, 1790, the feast day of St. Teresa of Avila, mother and foundress of the Discalced Carmelites.

One week later the convent's first postulant arrived. She was, of course, Elizabeth Carberry, bringing with her a bedstead, farm implements, kitchen utensils, and for a dowry 150 British pounds left to her by her father. Eighteen months later, she became the first nun to be professed in the convent and the nation.

As Sister Teresa of the Heart of Mary, she stayed at Mt. Carmel in Maryland the rest of her life. She died in her sleep January 18, 1814, at the age of sixty-nine.

Concerning her, the original handwritten Book of Professions and Deaths of the Discalced Carmelites states: "She was our first religious in this country and was remarkable for her gratitude to God and to us for entering religion."

By 1831 the nuns were obliged for economic reasons to leave Port Tobacco. The little convent buildings fell into ruins and were almost forgotten. In our own time, however, there has been a serious movement to restore them. The site has been declared a National Shrine, and it has become a place of pilgrimage. In May, 1976, six nuns returned to Port Tobacco, and on October 1 the rebuilt Carmel was solemnly dedicated.

RECOMMENDED READING: Charles Warren Currier, C.SS.R., *Carmel in America. A Centennial History of the Discalced Carmelites in the United States* (Baltimore: John Murphy Company, 1890).

MRS. MARTIN is an author and historian. She has compiled the life of Elizabeth Carberry from a family Bible, government records, and other original sources.

SAINT ELIZABETH BAYLEY SETON TEACHING

This relief by the sculptor John Angel is located in the tympanum in the south wall of the Charity Porch (west side) of the National Shrine of the Immaculate Conception, Washington, D.C. (*Reni Photos*)

Mother Seton: All Things to All Men

JOSEPH I. DIRVIN, C.M.

Elizabeth Ann Bayley Seton was born August 28, 1774, just a few days before the first Continental Congress met in Philadelphia to talk about social justice. She was nine years old when the colonists had done something about it by wresting their independence from Great Britain. Many other social injustices remained, even in the idealistic young nation, such as slavery, poverty, and inequity of income, but they were either not recognized as such or ignored. It was too early a point in history.

Elizabeth acquired early, however, a spirit of social compassion—which is a great step toward social justice—and her efforts to alleviate human misery and ignorance were steps leading inevitably to the present common concern with uprooting their causes.

Her first lesson was the example of her grandfather, Reverend Richard Charlton, who as a young curate of New York's Trinity Episcopal Church was catechist to all the black slaves of the city and truly their friend. He was even an early practitioner of integration, instructing his black and white converts side by side in the same class.

Then there was the example of her father, first health officer of New York, who tended the poor more than the rich and actually laid down his life for the sick poor, dying of yellow fever contracted from Irish immigrants.

In 1797 she founded, along with other charitable Protestant matrons, the Widows' Society in New York, to sew for and feed and nurse poor widows and orphans. She and her sister-in-law Rebecca Seton became so identified with good works that they were fondly and prophetically nicknamed "Protestant Sisters of Charity."

She had married William McGee Seton, a wealthy young merchant, in 1794, and had five children by him before he died in 1803. When Elizabeth's

43

father-in-law died in 1798 she unhesitatingly added his six young orphan children to her own growing brood, and at times took in the large family of an ailing sister-in-law with a ne'er-do-well husband. When relatives or friends fell ill, Elizabeth was the first called. She sat long hours by many a sickbed, closed many a dying eye, prepared many a corpse for burial. Charity indeed began at home for her, a charity and compassion that would, in God's good time, reach out across the years to all.

She became a Catholic in 1805, largely as a result of her contacts with the Filicchi family in Italy with whom she stayed for several months after her husband died.

Her first public social concern was with moral ignorance. The school she founded in Baltimore in 1808 was not just a refuge from the ostracism of New York because of her conversion, nor a means of livelihood for herself and her five fatherless children. She told her pupils that her object was "not to teach you how to be good nuns or Sisters of Charity but . . . to fit you for that world in which you are destined to live: to teach you how to be good . . . mothers of families." Her unique purpose was articulated by her sponsor, Father William Dubourg, in these words: "There are in the country, and perhaps too many, mixed schools, in which ornamental accomplishments are the only objects of education; we have none that I know where their acquisition is connected with, and made subservient to, *pious* instruction—and such a one you certainly wish yours to be."

The establishment of her religious community in Baltimore and later at Emmitsburg, Maryland, was the time-honored means for giving stability and permanence to this practical apostolate and to the others that called her. The scope of her compassionate vision was evident in a letter to a Philadelphia friend, Julia Scott: "To speak the joy of my soul at the prospect of being able to assist the poor, visit the sick, comfort the sorrowful, clothe little innocents and teach them to love God!—there I must stop!"

It was not, therefore, by accident that Mother Seton adopted the rule of St. Vincent de Paul, the great Father of the Poor, for her infant community, since her ideals were truly Vincentian. These ideals were not realized at once. She was forced by financial circumstances, for example, to shift the emphasis of her school from poor to paying pupils, although as many non-paying pupils were admitted as the budget could afford, and the little knot of pupils who came daily from St. Joseph's parish in the village of Emmitsburg formed in reality the first free parochial school in the United States, the cell of the future far-flung parochial school system. But Elizabeth Seton was a patient woman who always waited on the will of God.

She had not long to wait. From the beginning she had "the entire charge of the religious instruction of all the country round" and made sure that the sick were visited. In 1814 she sent three Sisters to take charge of an orphanage in Philadelphia, and three more to staff a second orphanage in New

York in 1817. These were the only foundations made outside Emmitsburg in her lifetime, but they began the pattern of universality in charitable social works which she so much desired. From them sprang the bewildering network of hospitals, child care centers, homes for the aged, clinics, social welfare centers, mental institutions, etc., that her thousands of religious daughters maintain today.

This universality of works is the reflection of Elizabeth Seton's universality of mind and soul. She strove like St. Paul to be all things to all men. Thus she could advise her son William: "Love your country, yet also all countries, ..." and, making a choice of Sisters for the New York orphanage: "So much must depend, as say the good gentlemen who write about it, on who is sent to my 'native city,' they say, not knowing that I am a citizen of the world." But the sincerity of her all-embracing love is perhaps best stated in a letter describing her daily life to her friend Eliza Sadler:

"You know I am as a mother encompassed by many children of different disposition, not all equally amiable or congenial; but bound to love, instruct and provide for the happiness of all, to give the example of cheerfulness, peace, resignation, and consider individuals more as proceeding from the same origin and tending to the same end than in the different shades of merit and demerit."

Such a universal love of neighbor, if widely practiced, would make social justice inevitable.

RECOMMENDED READING: Joseph I. Dirvin, C.M., *Mrs. Seton: Foundress of the American Sisters of Charity* (New York: Farrar, Straus and Cudahy, 1962; revised edition, 1975). Annabelle M. Melville, *Elizabeth Bayley Seton, 1774–1821* (New York: Charles Scribner's Sons, 1951; reprinted, 1976).

FATHER DIRVIN is Vice-President for University Relations and Secretary of the University, St. John's University, New York.

The Arrival of Mother Philippine Duchesne and Her Companions
in Saint Louis

In this scene the Religious of the Sacred Heart are shown being escorted
on August 21, 1818, by Captain Reed of the steamboat *Franklin*, on which
they had traveled from New Orleans, and being greeted by the Bishop of
Louisiana, Louis William Dubourg, who had invited them from France. (*NC
Photos*)

❧❦❧

Mother Philippine Duchesne,

French Nun With an American Dream

WILLIAM BARNABY FAHERTY, S.J.

Philippine Duchesne had an unusual kind of man trouble on her arrival in the American Midwest. She had to deal with two zealous but unpredictable clergymen: Bishop Louis William Dubourg of New Orleans, who had invited her to America; and Jesuit Superior Charles Felix Van Quickenborne, her reluctant spiritual director. Those totally different personalities played a significant role in the life Mother Duchesne faced setting up the first convent of the Religious of the Sacred Heart outside of France and the first free school west of the Mississippi.

A colonial aristocrat educated in Paris, Bishop Dubourg felt more at home dining with President Washington than running a frontier diocese. Rugged Father Van Quickenborne found his place riding the mission trails or moving up the wild Missouri. A flamboyant promoter, Bishop Dubourg could enlist many missionaries for the new world but never stopped to think how they would feed, house, or clothe themselves. The more practical Father Van Quickenborne took up his axe and led his Jesuit novices into the forests to build their own log cabin novitiate.

Bishop Dubourg had promised Mother Duchesne that the nuns could begin a school in St. Louis, the future metropolis of the Midwest, but sent her to the then thriving but eventually quiet town of St. Charles on the Missouri, twenty miles west-northwest of St. Louis. He had promised that the Jesuit superior would serve as the nuns' spiritual director, but he neglected to notify Father Van Quickenborne, who had neither the previous experience nor the present desire to support Mother Duchesne in her difficult work.

Philippine had been born in August, 1769, the daughter of a prosperous,

47

progressive, and prominent lawyer in Grenoble, France. She was sent to a boarding school conducted by the Visitation nuns, and against her father's wishes, she decided to become a nun-missionary and joined the Visitandines in Grenoble at the age of nineteen.

In the French Revolution the government closed the convents. Eventually the Reign of Terror ended, and Philippine went back to Grenoble with several other nuns to work among the poor and the orphaned. When her group could not reopen the old Visitation convent, they joined a new congregation, the Religious of the Sacred Heart. In 1818, after working for eleven years in Grenoble and three in Paris, Philippine heard Bishop Dubourg speak of the American West and begged the mother foundress, Madeleine Sophie Barat, to let her go to his vast diocese. Having received permission, she sailed for America with three other nuns in her charge.

Although several prominent French families wanted her to open a school for girls in St. Louis, Bishop Dubourg sent her to tiny St. Charles on the Missouri, expecting the village to grow more rapidly than it did. The school barely lasted through the first hard winter. The following year, the nuns moved across the Missouri to a farming community called Florissant. Four years later two Jesuit priests and seven seminarians opened a combined Indian school and Jesuit seminary three miles from the village. Sisters of the Indian boys at the Jesuit school attended the nuns' school along with the white pupils from St. Louis and southeastern Missouri.

As several American-born girls joined Mother Philippine's growing band of nuns, she opened four convents and two schools in west central Louisiana. Supported by the prosperous French-speaking plantation owners, these schools succeeded in the bayou area, while the Florissant foundation barely staggered along.

Shortly after Bishop Joseph Rosati succeeded Bishop Dubourg in 1827, he invited Mother Philippine to staff a school in St. Louis in a building donated by a prosperous businessman, John Mullanphy. A few years later, Mother Duchesne retired as head of the American venture and went back to Florissant and engaged in a variety of charitable activities.

A decade after her return to Florissant, Father Pierre Jean De Smet, whom she had befriended as a Jesuit novice in Florissant years earlier, needed nuns to teach Indians farther west. Mother Duchesne, then seventy, was weak. But she had dreamed of working among the Indians. Now the chance came, and she left for the Jesuit mission among the Potawatomi in Kansas.

She lived in an Indian hut all summer. A log house was ready by winter, but it was crude, with no fireplace and only a ladder to sleeping quarters in the loft. She visited the sick and elderly and responded with a smile when the children greeted her, since she had little facility with the Indian language. After one year in Kansas, her superiors recalled her to St. Charles, where they had built a new school and convent.

Even during her busiest years prayer had consumed much of her time. Now she had plenty of time for prayer, for writing to relatives and nuns in France and mending clothes for the girls in the school. Brought up in class-conscious French society, she had always dealt formally with adults, but children found her easy to approach. A dear friend, Jesuit Father Peter Verhaegen, pastor of the parish, gave her Viaticum on November 18, 1852. In the funeral sermon two days later he spoke of her sanctity.

Mother Philippine Duchesne had seen Missouri grow from a frontier territory into the largest state of the West. The editors of the *Dictionary of American Biography* recognized her contribution to the building of the state and the nation, one of the few women of her time in the trans-Mississippi region so honored. The Church beatified her in 1940.

RECOMMENDED READING: Mother Louise Callan, R.S.C.J., *Philippine Duchesne—Frontier Missionary of the Sacred Heart, 1769–1852* (Westminster, Md.: Newman Press, 1957; abridged edition, 1965).

FATHER FAHERTY is a professor of history in St. Louis University and author of ten books.

FATHER SAMUEL MAZZUCHELLI, O.P.

This portrait was painted in Italy in 1825, when he was only nineteen years of age. Three years later he arrived in the United States, and after being ordained a priest in 1830, he began his missionary career. (*NC Photos*)

❦

12

Father Mazzuchelli,

Apostle to the Winnebagos

JAMES B. WALKER, O.P.

In 1833 the local Indian agent at Fort Winnebago, John Kinzie, sent to Governor George Porter of the Michigan Territory a message addressed to President Andrew Jackson by Chief Whirling Thunder "in behalf of the Winnebago Nation of Indians."

The message showed the degree of trust the Winnebagos placed in a new missionary priest working among them, Dominican Father Samuel Mazzuchelli. Chief Whirling Thunder was asking the President to change the site of a planned school for the Winnebagos from Prairie du Chien (on the western border of present-day Wisconsin) to the Baraboo River about 100 miles to the east where most of the Winnebagos lived.

Noting that "many of us have lately joined the Catholic Church and have become Christians," the chief said:

"We therefore hope that our prayers may be granted by our great Father the President; we will then be able to have our children educated among us and in the Catholic persuasion. We have never had any one until lately to teach us the word of God. We begin to see the light, and we wish to know more of the great Father above. We want Mr. [Father] Mazzuchelli to remain with us and the school established among us. We intend to be good people, and it is in the power of our Father, the President, to render us much aid."

It is not known whether the message ever reached the President, but Kinzie's successor, Captain Robert M. McCabe, wrote several times during 1834, warmly endorsing the Indians' request. Although the government knew the Indians' preference, it proceeded with the school near Prairie du Chien as planned, and the Indians refused to attend it. It was 120 miles from where most of them were then living.

Father Mazzuchelli had come to America from Italy in 1828. After his ordination in Cincinnati in September, 1830, he was given care of a few thousand souls on the fringes of civilization in the Michigan Territory. The center of his mission, Mackinac Island, was the hub of trade with the Indians. Though ever increasing numbers of Americans were moving into the Northwest, the inhabitants were still largely of French-Canadian origin, nominally Catholics, of whom many had contracted civil marriage with Indian women.

For four years the sole chapel in Father Mazzuchelli's vast parish was at Mackinac. To minister to his flock, he had to travel up to Sault Sainte Marie, down the Lake to Green Bay, and across the wilderness south and west to the Father of Waters, the Mississippi, at Prairie du Chien. His ministry was primarily to the white settlers, but he visited the Indians in their villages, for they were eager to hear the word of God.

He at once began to build a church in Green Bay. There in June, 1831, he established a free Indian school for the Menominees. By 1834 half of the thousand or so Menominees in the area had become Catholics.

In July, 1831, he received an invitation to visit the Winnebago Indians at the portage between the Fox and Wisconsin rivers. They had the reputation of being the most cruel and intractable in the Northwest; yet Father Mazzuchelli made an attempt to reach them before the ink was dry on the Treaty of September, 1832, which brought an end to the inhuman Black Hawk War. In May, 1833, a son of the esteemed Chief Decari came from the portage to contact and guide Mazzuchelli to Fort Winnebago. During that first visit of about six weeks, he won over the hearts of these "children of the forest," as the message of Whirling Thunder clearly indicates.

On three subsequent visits in 1833 and 1834 he was able to instruct and baptize more than 300. In the fall of the latter year, having been replaced at Sault Sainte Marie, Mackinac, and Green Bay, he established a little school on the west bank of the Wisconsin river near the fort with nineteen or twenty full-blooded Indians and some half-breeds. Without money and unable to obtain support, he had to abandon the Indian mission in February, 1835, and move on to Prairie du Chien, although the school struggled on until April. On May 10, during a trip back to Ohio at his superiors' request, he wrote a vigorous appeal to the President, seeking redress for the injustices to the Winnebagos and the discrimination toward a foreigner and a priest, saying he believed the President desired "to give equal encouragement to all Christian denominations so that none of them should predominate, especially against equity and justice."

Bishop Joseph Rosati of St. Louis had asked the Dominicans in Ohio for the services of Father Mazzuchelli for the missions on the upper Mississippi where a priest was desperately needed. When the priest reached St. Louis, a letter from C. A. Harris, Acting Secretary of War, was awaiting him. In it he was informed that no change could be made regarding the location of the school and that no change would be made in its supervision.

Father Mazzuchelli did not accept defeat. He repeatedly communicated his grave concern for the Winnebagos to his friend, General George Wallace Jones, congressman from the newly created Territory of Wisconsin, but without success. In fact, in 1835 and 1836 the Winnebagos were moved across the Mississippi to lands along the Turkey River, and there a few years later the injustice and discrimination mushroomed into a national scandal. Then the protagonist of the Indians was the future first bishop of St. Paul, Father Joseph Cretin, who was supported in his efforts by a host of the most prominent men in Iowa. Father Mazzuchelli, in his *Memoirs*, written in 1844, predicted:

"It will be their [the Indians'] fate to continue in their wild, roving, and uncivilized state until the day when the civilized population of European origin will have filled the entire continent. Then the Indian will have left scarcely a trace of his existence in the land."

Despite this unhappy initiation into life on the American frontier, Father Mazzuchelli was unflagging in his praise for our form of government and for the quality of its laws. He never missed an opportunity to speak such sentiments at patriotic gatherings and assorted civic celebrations. His ministry to the settlers moving into the Midwest and across the upper Mississippi has made of his name a household word which is still, after more than a century, held in benediction and veneration in Wisconsin, Illinois, and Iowa. He designed no less than five public buildings, built at least twenty churches, and singlehandedly for four years laid the foundation of the Church in an area now comprising seven dioceses. One of his more durable accomplishments was the founding of the Congregation of Dominican Sisters at Sinsinawa, Wisconsin.

Those who knew him personally believed that he was a saint. The cause of his beatification, opened in Rome in 1967, is making slow but steady progress. On January 16, 1976, the Sacred Congregation for the Causes of Saints, after mature deliberation, decreed that "nothing hinders proceeding further."

RECOMMENDED READING: Jo Bartels and J. Michael Alderson, *The Man Mazzuchelli, Pioneer Priest* (Madison: Wisconsin House Ltd., 1974); and *The Memoirs of Father Samuel Mazzuchelli, O.P.*, translated by Sisters Maria Michele Armato and Mary Jeremy Finnegan (Chicago: The Priory Press, 1966).

FATHER WALKER is archivist and historian of the Dominican Province of St. Albert the Great, River Forest, Illinois.

Bishop Frederic Baraga

13

Bishop Baraga, Missionary to the Indians

DAN RUPP, O.S.A.

Mackinac Island, Sault Sainte Marie, and the Apostle Islands are names long revered in the Catholic missionary history of the United States. These remote settlements of northern Michigan conjure up recollections of the great seventeenth-century Jesuits: Fathers Isaac Jogues, Charles Raymbault, René Ménard, and Jacques Marquette. But almost 200 years later this same area was the scene of yet another edifying chapter in American history. Another missionary toiled there whose heroic, exciting, and holy life is now proposed for beatification.

His name was Frederic Baraga. Born in Slovenia, now part of Yugoslavia, in 1797, he had the benefit of a fine education in Ljubljana and at the University of Vienna. But after completion of his law degree in 1821 he broke off his marriage engagement, renounced his substantial inheritance, and entered the seminary. Ordained in 1823, he became a renowned and beloved parish priest in his native Slovenia.

Through the Leopoldine Society, founded in Vienna in 1829 to aid the American missions, Father Baraga volunteered to work among the Indians of Michigan. His first efforts at the Ottawa mission of Arbre Croche near present-day Petoskey were very successful and within twenty-eight months he had baptized 547 Indians and transformed the deteriorating mission into a model Christian community. But he grew restless in the missions of lower Michigan and in 1835 began to search for souls in long-neglected Upper Michigan. His first mission was LaPointe (Apostle Islands). He arrived there alone, with only three dollars in his pocket, without even his winter clothes, which had been lost in transit, without a church or even a place to live. In 1841 he moved to L'Anse, Keweenaw Bay. A letter he wrote to his sister while he was there reveals much about this man.

"L'Anse is an unpleasant, sad, sterile place which cannot compare with

LaPointe," he wrote. "Solely the desire to help these poor Indians attain eternal happiness keeps me here. I have here . . . no comforts, often times barely the necessities of life; but what consolation . . . for me when, on the Day of Judgment . . . my good children in Christ will surround me and give their testimony before the stern Judge. 'He was the first to announce to us Thy divine word . . . to tell us of Thy mercies. . . .' Oh, how I thank my God for calling me to the laborious but highly consoling missionary state."

How did this educated, refined, and intellectual man spend his time in the wilds of an isolated forest? Baraga's diary gives us a hint. Every morning no matter how cold or uncomfortable, he rose at four o'clock for his meditation and prayers. During the summer months he was constantly caring for the spiritual needs of his people. Mass, Baptisms, marriages, confessions, and instructions; not just at his own mission post, but for years he was the only priest in the whole Lake Superior area. During the winter months he taught school, continued his travels no matter the distance or the weather, and spent the long nights writing an Ojibway dictionary, grammar, catechism, and other religious books.

Because of the government threat to remove the Indians to reservations west of the Mississippi, he purchased lands for the Indians with his own limited funds, thus allowing them to remain in their ancestral territory. His concern for the Indians required constant vigil against the continued efforts of the fur traders to get them drunk. By 1845 the nascent communities of European immigrants around the newly discovered copper mines of Keweenaw Peninsula required his spiritual attention, and he added them to his regular circuit of visits. Thus even in the north woods, Father Baraga spoke French, German, English, Slovenian, and Italian, as well as Ottawa and Ojibway, for the salvation of souls.

In 1857 he became Upper Michigan's first bishop. But this honor did not alter his lifestyle. Even as bishop, he still traveled to his far-flung outposts. A companion priest describes Baraga in 1862:

"—The bishop was then 64 years of age and his health had greatly failed. The winter was extraordinarily severe and we had about six feet of snow. Newly arrived from France, I would scarcely go out of the house myself on account of the cold. But the bishop . . . the longest time he spent in his residence during that winter, was two weeks. The rest of the time he went from one wigwam to another, visiting his Indians. After having come home again for a little rest . . . he started out alone . . . for new conquests. It was far from the Sault [Sault Sainte Marie, where Bishop Baraga was living], but when it was to rescue a soul he never counted the distance.

"At last he arrived, after having slept many nights in the snow. He assembled them [the Indians] and told them the good tidings that he was bringing to them, and after a few days he baptized the chief and all the tribe and came home again happy. . . . The bishop, half frozen, was sitting on a little sleigh about two inches higher than the ground, dragged by a small Indian dog.... Our Lord in his travels used to ride an ass but our bishop was perfectly satisfied to have a dog for riding."

In 1866 Bishop Baraga transferred his See from Sault Sainte Marie to Marquette. During the fall of the same year he suffered a stroke in Baltimore while attending the American bishops' Second Plenary Council. Though critically ill, he insisted upon returning to Marquette to die among his beloved Indians.

"When Bishop Baraga was in his last sickness," his companion wrote, "only a few days before his death Father Terhorst called on him.... The bishop pointed to a tin box on a library shelf and requested him to hand him the box, which was done. Then he asked him to take the key of the box from under his pillow and give it to him. With his weak, trembling hand the bishop opened the box and told Father Terhorst to take the money in it, which was $20. Upon Father Terhorst's remark that it was all the money he [the bishop] had, and that it was not right to take it, the sick prelate answered: 'I don't need any more money—take it [for the Indians].'"

And so to the very last Bishop Frederic Baraga completely dedicated all his talents, energy, money, indeed his whole life, to the missionary effort. On January 19, 1868, the worn-out missionary commended his soul to the Lord.

RECOMMENDED READING: Joseph Gregorich, *The Apostle of the Chippewas. The Life Story of the Most Rev. Frederick Baraga, the First Bishop of Marquette* (Chicago: Bishop Baraga Association, 1932). Bernard J. Lambert, *Shepherd of the Wilderness. A Biography of Bishop Frederic Baraga* (L'Anse, Michigan: The Author, 1967). Maksimilijan Jezernik, *Frederick Baraga* (New York, Washington: Studia Slovenica, 1968).

FATHER RUPP, an Augustinian priest, studied theology and church history for nine years in Rome and is currently writing his doctoral dissertation on Bishop Baraga while serving as associate pastor in Holy Rosary parish, Kenosha, Wisconsin.

FATHER PETER DeSMET, S.J., AND THE INTERIOR CHIEFS

This photograph was taken during the Jesuit's peace mission to General Harney in 1859. (*Courtesy of the Jesuit Historical Archives, Oregon Province, Spokane*)

14

Father Peter DeSmet,

A Peripatetic Bookkeeper

WILLIAM N. BISCHOFF, S.J.

Jesuit Father Peter John DeSmet, renowned apostle among the Oregon Country native tribes in the 1840s, never was a resident missionary there. This frequently consulted authority on frontier survival was a priestly bookkeeper, fundraiser, and pious public relations man who filled various office jobs during his mature years, 1848–1873, while living in St. Louis.

Father DeSmet spent less than four years in the Pacific Northwest, where he never learned an Indian language. He moved about ceaselessly, visiting tribes and transacting mission business along the Columbia River and as far as Ft. Augusta (now Edmonton, Alberta). After his return to St. Louis in December, 1846, his superiors never again assigned him to the Rocky Mountain missions.

Although in his repeated visits with the natives Father DeSmet did sit around many a campfire, officially his post was that of treasurer of the Missouri Province of the Society of Jesus for the last twenty-five years of his life. During part of this time, in a ten-year period ending in 1862, he served also as assistant to the superior of the province. Rightly famed as friend of the Indian, Father DeSmet was in fact, a patient, painstaking accountant, a skillful financial manager, dependable secretary, promoter, money-getter, and press agent. Several close associates agreed with his self-analysis that he was "fitted rather for making excursions by which he opens the way for the missionaries and prepares the field than for staying permanently in some one or other station." Yet it was to be a missionary that he had come from Belgium in 1821, at the age of twenty, and entered the Society of Jesus in Missouri.

The name DeSmet stands today for missionary zeal and work in behalf of American Indians because he made the Indian cause known in Europe and America through his enormous correspondence, countless public lectures, and published works. Besides the priest's immensely successful begging trips in their behalf, probably his most noteworthy role was that of peacemaker to the tribes. Donald Mitchell, Superintendent of Indian Affairs at St. Louis, invited Father DeSmet to participate in the mammoth council of 10,000 Plains Indians convened near Ft. Laramie, September 12–23, 1851. His persuasive talks with the natives contributed substantially to the meeting's marked success. Father DeSmet's unusual ability to instill confidence in and elicit agreement from the Indians was revealed again in 1858–1859 when he accompanied General William Harney to the Pacific Northwest and persuaded the interior tribes to transform the uneasy calm prevailing between Indians and whites into a firm peace.

One of Father DeSmet's major accomplishments was his peace mission to Sitting Bull and other warring Hunkpapa Sioux in June, 1868. Resentment, bitterness, fury long festering over the irritation of manifest white encroachments, finally erupting in retaliatory attacks on white settlers, peaked on August 17, 1862, in the massacre of 700 Minnesotans. The years following this savage onslaught were stained by innumerable ambushes, killings, and burnings, which were repaid in kind by relentless punitive attacks by United States troops. The plains over which Father DeSmet searched for Sitting Bull's camp on the Yellowstone River had been bloodied and charred by six years of war.

Along with eighty friendly Sioux, Charles Galpin as interpreter, and Galpin's Hunkpapa wife, Father DeSmet left Ft. Rice, near present-day Bismarck, North Dakota, on June 3, 1868. Through rain, mud, heat, fog, and torturing mosquitos, they pushed to the west and south for sixteen days. The nearer they approached to the rumored site of the hostile natives' camp without being met by the expected messengers from Sitting Bull, the more nervous and anxious they became. Finally, on Friday morning, June 19, they were loudly welcomed by a 500-man escort dispatched from the main camp on the Yellowstone (about thirty-five miles from Miles City, Montana).

Father DeSmet's spirits were lifted, even before the council, by Sitting Bull's volunteered avowal, "I rose tomahawk in hand, and I have done all the hurt to the white that I could. Today thou art amongst us, and in thy presence my arms stretch to the ground as if dead. I will listen to thy good words, and as bad as I have been to the whites, just as good am I ready to become toward them."

The next afternoon Father DeSmet made his appeal to the council: "Bury *all* your animosities against the whites . . . forget the past . . . and accept the offering of peace which is now kindly sent you." The 400 braves present stolidly recounted their grievances, but before the meeting ended, they concurred with Black Moon's hope "that these things past will be forgotten from this day." To Father DeSmet the forthright Sitting Bull declared, "I will thank you in the hearing of the chief [Four Horns] and braves for your kindness and willingly accept the tobacco as a token of peace ... and whatever is done by others, I will submit to, and for all time to come be a friend of the whites."

Eight Hunkpapa deputies, thirty families (160 persons), his escort, and the faithful Galpins returned with Father DeSmet to Ft. Rice, where they signed a treaty with the United States Peace Commissioners on July 2, 1868. Father DeSmet's hazardous mission had paid off handsomely. Three ranking generals who served as commissioners (William Harney, John Sanborn, and Alfred Terry) acknowledged the priest's dominant role, assuring him, "but for your long and painful journey into the heart of the hostile country, and but for the influence over even the most hostile of the tribes which your labor among them have given to you, the results which we have reached here could not have been accomplished."

It was a deserved tribute for the fruitful exertions of the peace-loving nomadic account-keeper.

RECOMMENDED READING: *Life, Letters, and Travels of Father Pierre-Jean DeSmet, S.J. 1801–1873*, edited by Hiram M. Chittenden and Albert T. Richardson (4 vols.; New York: Harper, 1905). E. Laveille, S.J., *The Life of Father de Smet, S.J., 1801–1873*, trans. Marian Lindsay (New York: P.J. Kenedy & Sons, 1915). Gilbert J. Garraghan, S. J., *The Jesuits of the Middle United States* (3 vols.; New York: America Press, 1938).

FATHER BISCHOFF is professor of history at Seattle University, Seattle, Washington.

BISHOP FREDERICK RESE

As a priest of the Diocese of Cincinnati, Father Rese promoted the establishment of the Leopoldine Foundation at Vienna in 1829, and as the first bishop of Detroit (and the first bishop of German birth in the United States), he persuaded King Ludwig I of Bavaria to found the Ludwig Mission Society in 1838. (Portrait in the residence of the Archbishop of Detroit, courtesy of *The Michigan Catholic*)

15

Financing the Frontier Church

BENJAMIN J. BLIED

Money may be filthy lucre but even God's work needs it. That's why it's gathered in churches. Originally the few Indian converts had next to nothing to drop into the collection box, and later, when veritable waves of impoverished immigrants inundated America, God's work stood in even greater jeopardy. They had needs, not assets. Yet disaster was warded off. People elsewhere spared and shared. If France could help Americans in war, could she not also help them in peaceful pursuits?

In the early 1820s, when the fears that were to culminate in the Monroe Doctrine were waxing strong, a seminary student in Paris, Philéas Jaricot, was writing glowing letters about the missions to his sister Pauline, whom he had left in Lyons. She in turn breathed his spirit into her friends and acquaintances whom she marshaled into groups of ten, then into ten groups of ten (centuries), and finally into ten groups of a hundred. They began to pray for the missions and to contribute at least a *sou* (a penny) a week.

Pauline Jaricot and her associates were not particularly concerned about the infant Church in the United States, but its urgent needs were not unknown in Lyons, because one of the citizens, Madame Petit, had been collecting funds for Bishop Louis William Dubourg. He had befriended her and her children in Baltimore when they were refugees from Santo Domingo (his birthplace). Needing more aid than she could send for his vast diocese of Louisiana, which included all the territory purchased from France in 1803, Bishop Dubourg dispatched his young Italian vicar general, Father Angelo Inglesi, to Europe to organize more regular and productive means of support. Inglesi's extensive itinerary brought him into contact with a galaxy of prestigious persons and included a visit to Lyons.

A slippery character with winning ways and the knack of advertising, Inglesi printed a pamphlet on the Louisiana mission. In Lyons he called a meeting of all the mission-minded people on May 3, 1822. Pauline Jaricot was represented by some friends, and Madame Petit by her son Didier. Father Inglesi would have liked to convert Miss Jaricot's organization to his own purposes exclusively, but he had to compromise. Some of those at the meeting were opposed to expanding her operation while others propounded the universal goal of assisting missions everywhere. The latter viewpoint prevailed, and the lay people kept control. Out of the meeting came the Society for the Propagation of the Faith.

That same year the Society made its first distribution of funds. The sum of $4,583 was divided in three ways, one-third going to Bishop Dubourg, another third to the Seminary of the Foreign Missions in Paris, and the remainder to Bishop Benedict Flaget of Kentucky. The first American bishop to call in person at the Society's headquarters in Lyons was Bishop Edward Fenwick of Cincinnati. He was followed over the years by a long procession of American bishops and their agents, and they did not depart empty-handed. In its first hundred years the Society provided six million dollars for the Church in the United States.

When Bishop Fenwick went to Lyons, he was accompanied by one of his new recruits, Father Frederick Rese. Several years later this same German priest, by then a seasoned missionary, returned to Europe seeking volunteers and funds for Bishop Fenwick's diocese, which included the Michigan Territory as well as the whole State of Ohio. With recommendations from Rome he obtained an audience with the Emperor of Austria, Francis I. Sensing that the French society might be somewhat out of place on the Danube and unwelcome to the government, he suggested organizing a similar one specifically for the Hapsburg domains. Like Inglesi, he compiled a brochure about the Diocese of Cincinnati, and thanks to his efforts a new mission society made its debut in 1829.

Taking a personal interest in this venture, the Emperor decided to name it the Leopoldine Society in memory of his daughter who had recently died as Empress of Brazil. The general structure of the society was similar to that of Lyons, but all the funds were earmarked for North America. Though Austrian generosity declined after several decades, the society survived until World War I. By then it had outlived its usefulness, but only after the Church in the New World had received $700,000 from its coffers.

After Austria, Father Rese had also visited Bavaria, expecting to form another society there, but he was unsuccessful at that time. In 1838, however, he returned to Munich. Now he was the first Bishop of Detroit and the first German bishop in the United States. Since his previous visit, conditions had changed in the little kingdom of four million people. A grass-roots interest in the missions had developed, and the king feared lest the French society obtain too much influence over his subjects. To this worry

Bishop Rese added his own misgivings about the proliferating Protestant Bible societies.

Such considerations moved the king to consent to the formation of a mission society within his realm. More than that, he gave it his own name; it would be called the Ludwig Mission Society. The funds, which were raised almost exclusively in this one German state, were distributed largely in North America and Asia. Like the Leopoldine Society, this organization lasted until World War I. By then it had sent $900,000 across the Atlantic, not counting donations which the king made directly to projects which appealed to his German spirit as well as to his Catholic faith.

The total contribution of these three societies to American Catholicism, less than $8 million, might seem slight by today's standards. But in their day the purchasing power of money was vastly more than it is today. Moreover, the donations arrived in an era when America offered many unusual opportunities. And help from abroad, far from making the recipients supine, spurred them on to make a greater effort themselves. Besides cold cash, these societies stimulated the flow of chalices, vestments, altar pieces, and other equipment to the struggling parishes and institutions. More important still, the publications of the societies inspired European priests and religious communities to settle in the New World. So striking was the progress of the Church on the frontier that suspicious spectators, duly bewildered, took to the offensive in Nativist or Know-Nothing groups.

Curiously enough, the generosity of the Society for the Propagation of the Faith proved to be self-rewarding for, while receiving gifts, the United States concurrently sent contributions to France for other mission countries. The first ones were, indeed, negligible. But by the time the society celebrated its centennial it had received eleven million dollars from that once impoverished land that it had started out to help.

RECOMMENDED READING: Theodore Roemer, O.F.M. Cap., *Ten Decades of Alms* (St. Louis: B. Herder Book Company, 1942). Benjamin J. Blied, *Austrian Aid to American Catholics, 1830–1860* (Milwaukee: The Author, 1944).

FATHER BLIED is a professor at Marian College of Fond du Lac, Wisconsin.

BISHOP AUGUSTIN VEROT

Born, educated, and ordained in France, Father Verot had taught at Saint
Mary's College in Baltimore for twenty-three years and had done parochial
work in the same archdiocese for four years before he was consecrated in
1858. He was vicar apostolic of Florida until 1870 but also bishop of Savannah from 1861. In 1870 he became the first bishop of Saint Augustine. (*NC
Photos*)

16

Bishop Verot and the Slavery Question

MICHAEL V. GANNON

On January 3, 1870, during the course of the First Vatican Council, a stocky, five-foot-two bishop who presided over the Church in Georgia and Florida, mounted the speaker's platform in front of the assembled bishops of the world to deliver an impassioned defense of the black population in the American South. His name was Augustin Verot. French-born, he had taught as a member of the Society of St. Sulpice at St. Mary's College in Baltimore from 1830 to 1858, when he was consecrated bishop and appointed vicar-apostolic of Florida. Georgia as well as Florida would come under his jurisdiction during the difficult years of the Civil War.

Now, five years after the close of that conflict, he had something to say to the other Fathers of Vatican I. "I come from a diocese," he said, "in which there are many Negroes, more than a half-million Negroes, in fact. . . . We condemn the inept error of those who dare to assert that Negroes do not belong to the human family, or that they are not endowed with spiritual and immortal souls." He went on to observe that "errors of this kind are more deserving of condemnation" than are the abstract doctrines of obscure theologians.

Among his own people, Bishop Verot had practiced what he preached, providing priests, sisters, and schools for the freed black populations of Georgia and Florida. In fact, he took the part of the Freedmen, as they were called, with a vigor and eloquence that was unmatched elsewhere in the southern Church. It would be difficult to point to a southerner of any persuasion, religious or political, in the postwar years, who interested himself as deeply in the moral, intellectual, and material welfare of the blacks—in the necessity, as Bishop Verot said, of "enlightening, civilizing, and ennobling a race that has suddenly emerged from bondage to the enjoyment of civil rights and the blessings of liberty."

Yet, just a few years before, Bishop Verot had been one of the staunchest Southern voices raised in the defense and vindication of the institution of slavery. On January 4, 1861, for example, a day set aside by President James Buchanan "for humiliation, fasting and prayer," Bishop Verot mounted another speaker's platform, the pulpit of the parish church of St. Augustine, Florida, to deliver a sermon excoriating the "false and unjust principles of abolitionism," the movement in northern states to emancipate the slaves. The institution of slavery, he said, did not offend any of the sanctions of natural law, divine positive law, ecclesiastical law, or civil law. Nowhere in the Bible could there be found any condemnation of it; indeed, the New Testament books, especially the writings of St. Paul, contain, "on the contrary, plain and evident approbations of it."

In this position, the reader may be surprised to learn, Bishop Verot did not differ from the other American bishops, North or South, or from most of the Protestants in the South and many in the North, before the Civil War. The classic Catholic argument was that the state of involuntary servitude was not necessarily evil, and that it ought to be tolerated until a better social order could be secured. Wherever circumstances permitted the slave to achieve better conditions on his own, the Church encouraged manumission (setting him free). But the institution itself ought to be abolished gradually, the bishops maintained, by careful stages, as feudalism had been abolished in Europe.

Bishop Verot went further in the defense of slavery, however, than did any of his colleagues in the episcopacy. He asserted that it was no worse a form of life than that of the average wage earner in the industries of the North. "It is truly remarkable how gay, cheerful and sprightly are the slaves of the South. I do not hesitate to say that they seem to be better contented than their masters; assuredly more so than the sullen and gloomy population found in the work shops and factories of large cities." What particularly nettled Bishop Verot was the fact that many of the abolitionist voices belonged to bigoted members of the Know-Nothing party, whose "unholy attacks" had only recently been directed toward the Catholic Church. "But the South," the bishop warned, "has not been, and will not, as a nation, be as patient as the Catholic Church." These words electrified his audience, and were afterwards published and disseminated throughout the South as a Confederate tract. In the North they earned for Bishop Verot the opprobrium of being a "rebel bishop."

What very few noticed then, either in the North or in the South, was the second half of that sermon. By 1865, less sure of the moral grounds on which the Confederacy fought, Southern newspapers would be quoting the second half rather than the first. For Bishop Verot had gone on to say that slaveholders had certain duties as well as rights, and that not all had observed those duties. Some masters had cruelly abused their slaves, treating them as animals instead of as their fellow human beings. Thus they had proven themselves unworthy of their own rights. He gave a number of examples, in the course of which he declared:

"I am a sincere and devoted friend of the South, to which Divine Providence sent me, and I am ready to undergo any hardship—to make any sacrifice—for the true welfare of the people among whom I live; still I must say it for conscience sake—... The Southern Confederacy, if it should exist must rest on morality and justice, and it could never be entitled to a special protection from above, unless it professes to surround slavery with the guarantees that will secure its morality and virtue."

In this connection, Bishop Verot argued that to deny blacks religious instruction "would be the sure way to render slavery an untenable and ruinous institution, deserving the contempt of men, and the malediction of God."

This was the first such code governing slavery proposed in the South. As the Civil War ran its course, similar demands for slavery reform were heard in other quarters of the Confederacy. In 1865 the Southern Protestant and secular press alike was supporting all the same conditions that Bishop Verot had laid down in 1861 as necessary for a just and lawful slavery.

By the time of his death, in 1876, the one time "rebel bishop" had proven his pro-black convictions in many and ample ways. School enrollment figures show the extent to which he succeeded in assisting young Florida blacks, Catholic and non-Catholic—often in the face of strong white opposition. Six black schools were in operation: at St. Augustine, with one hundred pupils; Jacksonville, forty pupils; Fernandina, eighty-three pupils; Palatka, fourteen pupils; Mandarin, eleven pupils; and Key West, for which no figures are available. No other Southern diocese put forth so great an effort, and none enjoyed the same success. True, the number of blacks under instruction in the immediate postwar years was small by comparison with the school systems sanctioned by federal bureaus and religious agencies endowed from the North. Given the small resources at his command and the shortness of accomplishment elsewhere in the Catholic South, however, Bishop Verot's black schools deserve history's notice. And readers of his 1861 sermon would know that it was the latter half of it that counted.

RECOMMENDED READING: Michael V. Gannon, *Rebel Bishop: The Life and Era of Augustin Verot* (Milwaukee: Bruce Publishing Company, 1964). Madeleine Hooke Rice, *American Catholic Opinion in the Slavery Controversy* (New York: Columbia University Press, 1944). Maria Genoino Caravaglios, *The American Catholic Church and the Negro Problem in the XVIII-XIX Centuries* (Rome: The Author, 1974). Joseph D. Brokhage, *Francis Patrick Kenrick's Opinion on Slavery* (Washington, D.C.: Catholic University of America Press, 1955).

DR. GANNON is a professor of religion and history at the University of Florida, Gainsville.

A ROMAN CATHOLIC MISSION FROM ENGLAND TO THE "HEATHENS" OF AMERICA.—[SEE PAGE 1220.]

DR. MANNING. "Of all the Nations on the Earth, England has been the most Guilty in regard to Slavery, and it was most fitting that the Reparation to the new Liberated Slaves should proceed from England."

THE HEATHEN AMERICAN. "No, thank you. We have just been Emancipated, and if England is responsible for Slavery in the United States, I don't care to jump from the English Frying-Pan into the English Fire."

A Cartoon by Thomas Nast Impugning the Motives of the
Mill Hill Fathers' Mission to the Negroes

Appearing in *Harper's Weekly* for December 30, 1871 (Volume XV, Number 783, page 1221), this cartoon depicts Henry Edward Manning, Archbishop of Westminster, in whose diocese the missionary society had been founded by Father Herbert Vaughan in 1866. The first band of four priests, accompanied by the founder, had arrived in Baltimore on December 8, 1871. (Reproduced from the collection of the Library of Congress)

17

The Early Apostolate Among

the Emancipated Negroes

EDWARD J. MISCH

The hottest debate among the American bishops at their Second Plenary Council of Baltimore in 1866 was over proposed decrees relating to the recently emancipated Negroes. With harsh words and raised voices, Catholic bishops argued over the extent to which the American Church could aid the impoverished blacks. They were not debating theology, but the very practical question of what should be done for the blacks. It is a question that continues to be asked today.

The destitute condition of the freed slaves just after the Civil War deeply moved a number of Southern bishops. In calling the Plenary Council for 1866, Archbishop Martin Spalding of Baltimore wrote that it was the bishops' most urgent duty to discuss the future status of the Negro: "Four million of these unfortunates are thrown on our charity, and they silently but eloquently appeal to us for help."

In the draft decrees Archbishop Spalding made several recommendations, among them the providing of Catholic schools and orphanages and shelter and clothing assistance. To carry these out he suggested the appointment of a priest administrator who would find staff, raise money, and organize projects.

Archbishop Spalding's suggestions included the possibility that the priest administrator could become a missionary bishop for the blacks. As the field expanded, other bishops could be appointed, and the archbishop envisioned a distinct black Catholic Church, following the example of the Eastern-rite groups in the Middle East. He also brought up the question of ordaining American blacks as priests. (Black priests were a rarity, although black women had helped to found two religious communities before the Civil War. The mulatto Healy brothers from Georgia, ordained abroad, worked with whites in the North and were never directly involved with the Negro apostolate.)

The idea of ordaining blacks in this country was rejected even before the formal debate began. And after protests from several bishops the plan for a priest administrator was dropped, lest problems of jurisdiction arise. Since so few Negroes were Catholic, most bishops were opposed to specific programs on their behalf. (Among blacks in the United States, about one out of fifty was Catholic; they made up only one or two percent of the Catholic population.) Archbishop John McCloskey of New York, whose diocese was faced with caring for increasing numbers of Catholic immigrants, spoke against general fund-raising for the blacks, since "this obligation did not weigh on the consciences of the bishops of the North" where few blacks lived.

In the course of voting, the bishops reduced the proposed decrees concerning the blacks to general exhortations. Each bishop was left to decide what to do in his own diocese. The major emphasis was on uplifting the blacks morally and providing for their spiritual needs. While individual bishops did become involved in projects such as black parishes in Charleston, South Carolina, and Louisville, Kentucky, orphanages in New Orleans, schools in Florida, and a small Benedictine monastery in Georgia, these were all on a small scale and often in dire need of funds.

In 1883, writing a report on the American Church for officials in Rome, a high Vatican official, Cardinal John Franzelin, noted that a vast program was needed to break down the "barrier which exists between the blacks and the whites in order to bring it about . . . that they may be brothers in Christ Jesus." Following the advice of his fellow German Jesuit, Father Francis Weninger, who was a missionary in the United States, Cardinal Franzelin urged the bishops to order an annual national collection for both Negroes and Indians. In 1884 the American bishops decreed this mission collection after some discussion at the Third Plenary Council of Baltimore.

In 1887, the first annual collection was taken up for the Negro and Indian missions. An episcopal commission, established to supervise and distribute the funds, also became a clearing house for information. In the first five years about $361,000 was collected; this was equivalent to a little less than one cent per Catholic per year.

Judging from the commission's reports, earlier Catholic mission efforts among blacks had resulted in few converts. Over the years following the Civil War, the bishops concentrated less and less on adults, and turned their attention to the children. Catholic schools were considered the best way to aid and convert blacks. Considering the cost of education even then, it is not surprising that one of the chief complaints was a lack of money.

Not until 1889 did black American Catholics get together as a distinct group, in what was called the Negro Catholic Congress. From then until 1894 a congress met annually and issued statements expressing hopes and disappointments.

One of their main complaints was the color line within the churches. At their first congress, the black Catholics showed confidence that their Church would dispel the prejudice of a misguided people. And Archbishop John Ireland, in a sermon in Washington in 1890, publicly attacked the color line and raised black expectations. Yet the blacks noted that they were barred from Catholic industrial schools and that virtually no Catholic school was open to blacks over twelve years of age.

Another problem was the attitude of the clergy toward black demands. Whites showed discomfort at black independence and outspokenness. Bishops and priests did not encourage or support the blacks who spoke up; rather they cautioned them to go slowly, to wait for public opinion to change.

Certain conclusions can be drawn from a study of this period. On the positive side, the Northern bishops moved from a general disinterest to some concern. The national collection, statements at the councils, and the annual reports fostered some awareness of the plight of the blacks. On the negative side, they often saw the problem as the blacks' own fault, with education being the means of uplifting them morally.

To the blacks the problem appeared to be one of white prejudice. This the Catholic Church made no attempt to change. Bishops recognized the existence of enmity between the races and tried to circumvent it by separate facilities, protecting the feelings of the whites. The color line continued to be a problem both in the North and in the South, and few Catholics spoke up against it.

Certain priests such as the Josephites, and congregations such as the Sisters of the Blessed Sacrament, did work with black communities, but their efforts did not alter the blacks' social plight or remove the prejudice within the Church. The blacks observed that the Church did not use its moral force to strike at the anti-Negro bias of its own people. Even in the cathedral in Baltimore, blacks had to sit on the backless benches at the rear. Such accommodation to white prejudice made the Catholic teaching on equality meaningless for many blacks.

RECOMMENDED READING: Thomas W. Spalding, *Martin John Spalding: American Churchman* (Washington, D.C.: Catholic University of America Press/Consortium Press, 1973). John T. Gillard, S.S.J., *The Catholic Church and the American Negro* (Baltimore: St. Joseph's Society Press, 1929) and *Colored Catholics in the United States* (Baltimore: Josephite Press, 1941).

DR. MISCH is a professor at Simon's Rock College, Great Barrington, Massachusetts.

MOTHER KATHARINE DREXEL

(*American Catholic Historical Collections*)

18

Katharine Drexel: Woman of Action

SISTER CONSUELA MARIE DUFFY, S.B.S.

The story of Katharine Drexel, 1858–1955, daughter of the millionaire banker, Francis Anthony Drexel, is unique in American history. She was an American woman whose maternal ancestors came to Pennsylvania four years after William Penn founded the colony. She dedicated her life and her fortune of $21,000,000 to right a great wrong done to blacks and Indians. She knew their story; she learned from personal contact the agony of their situation.

Katharine Drexel was thrust into an awareness of Indian problems after the sudden death of her father in 1885. The publication of his will of $15,500,000 touched off a long line of appeals. Two missionaries to Indians, Bishop Martin Marty, Vicar Apostolic of Northern Minnesota, and Monsignor Joseph Stephan, director of the Bureau of Catholic Indian Missions, crossed the country to present to the three Drexel daughters the dire needs of the Indians. They were more than interested, and Katharine began consulting contractors and calculating costs. Soon boarding schools were being erected on the reservations. The cost would spiral into millions.

In the fall of 1887 and again in 1888, the Drexel sisters accepted the invitation of Bishop James O'Connor of Omaha and Monsignor Stephan to visit the reservations and see for themselves. They saw many of the raw realities of reservation life. At Immaculate Conception Mission in Stephan, South Dakota, they noted a lone wooden cross marking the grave of a Benedictine nun, Sister Wilhelmina, who had been caught in a violent blizzard before she could reach a building. The Sisters had found her pinned against a wire fence, frozen to death. Katharine realized the high price some people paid to serve the Church in early America.

With the measured keenness of a banker's daughter Katharine spanned the great West with donations to Indians from Wyoming to Wisconsin, from

South Dakota to New Mexico, from Arizona to California. She grasped the challenge to the Church in extensive churchless areas. Checks and recommendations flowed from her home. In addition she was deeply concerned about another matter—her religious vocation. The desire to be a sister intensified with her father's death. At first her director, Bishop O'Connor, former rector of St. Dominic Church, Holmesburg, Pennsylvania, opposed the idea. But finally he recognized it as from God. When Katharine and her sisters were going on a European tour he asked Katharine to try to find priests willing to come to the aid of the Indians. This she did in a private interview with Pope Leo XIII on January 27, 1887. He simply answered: "My child, why not become a missionary yourself?" She was stunned. Not only did she become a religious, but at the insistence and promise of help from Bishop O'Connor and Archbishop Patrick Ryan of Philadelphia, as well as the words of Leo XIII, she founded a new congregation in the Church.

Alongside her efforts to fund education for Indians arose an eventually widespread assistance for blacks in both the North and the South. The Reverend Jean Girault, a priest of noble French lineage serving in the back areas of the lower Mississippi, called her attention to the lack of educational opportunities for the black children there. As she traveled with him by boat through bayous and along the banks of the Mississippi, she learned of the miserable situation firsthand. She went into immediate action and wrote Bishop Jules Jeanmard of Lafayette, Louisiana, asking his direction. He arranged a visit there and accompanied her. She built twenty-four rural schools immediately. Her zeal intensified daily. She went on with the erection of schools North, South, East, and West and crowned her educational efforts with the building and maintenance of Xavier University in New Orleans, the first (and still the only) Catholic college for blacks on the continent. Her intention here was to provide educated leaders for the race, and it has been abundantly realized.

At her death in 1955, her congregation was active in twenty states. In the midst of this expansive activity she was a woman of deep prayer. Every time she contributed to or built a church she rejoiced that this was a place where Mass had never been offered before.

She was a very wealthy woman, heir to millions, but she allied herself to the poor and the downcast, gave away her fortune of $21,000,000 to victims of poverty and hate, offered herself to God as a living gift of love, and led hundreds of other women to follow her in a new congregation in the Church, the Sisters of the Blessed Sacrament for Indians and Colored People. How is her life to be explained? The answer lies both in the grace of God filling her with a flaming desire to draw souls to knowledge and adoration of Christ in the Holy Eucharist and also in her keen understanding of human dignity and her strong sense of justice.

She loved America deeply, but her love of God and the Church was a consuming fire in her life. To it she gave her life's service and her entire fortune. Her whole contribution to the cause of the Church and to America has not been fully recorded yet.

On February 27, 1964, Cardinal John Krol of Philadelphia announced the beginning of the ordinary process toward the cause of the beatification of Mother Katharine Drexel. The cause is in progress. Knowledge of the remarkable life of Katharine Drexel is spreading throughout the country. Hope rises high among many that some day soon this great American woman may be enrolled among the saints of the Church.

SUGGESTED READING: Sister Consuela Marie Duffy, S.B.S., *Katharine Drexel, A Biography* (available through Sisters of the Blessed Sacrament Motherhouse, 1663 Bristol Pike, Cornwells Heights, Pennsylvania 19020).

SISTER DUFFY, formerly associate professor of theology at Xavier University, New Orleans, is the biographer of Mother Katharine Drexel and resource person on her life and works.

THOMAS D'ARCY MCGEE

Born in Ireland in 1825, McGee fled to the United States in 1848 after the
failure of the revolt against England in which he had been active. In New
York he published the *Nation,* a liberal weekly, in which he devoted a regular column to the uplift of the immigrants, but Bishop John Hughes denounced and banned the newspaper because of its revolutionary ideas on
Irish politics. Having moved to Boston, he published the *American Celt*
from 1850 to 1857 in a more conservative vein. To preserve the Irish in their
Catholic faith, he thought it necessary to make them aware of their distinctive character as a people; the spirit of the Celt, he maintained, was iden-
tical with that of Catholicism. During these years he also defended the
Irish against the Know-Nothings and organized night schools for adult immigrants. To save them from the moral blight and grinding poverty of the
slums of Eastern cities, he promoted a scheme to establish Irish Catholic
settlements in selected rural districts of the western United States and
Canada; this colonization project, however, never materialized.

19

Irish Catholics in America

THOMAS N. BROWN

A hundred years ago the celebrators of the centennial had a lot to cheer about. In the massive parade through Boston on Bunker Hill Day, June 17, 1875, more than half a million people watched Generals William Sherman of the Union Army and Fitzhugh Lee of the Confederate Army parade together. On the platform erected beneath the towering Bunker Hill obelisk on Charlestown Heights, the two warriors spoke of the union of hearts forged in the fires of the Civil War. An entire division of the parade was composed of Irish Catholic fraternal and temperance societies. The divided states had become a nation once again and the once despised Irish had become a part of it.

We bicentennial celebrators make a brave show of it but we don't find much to cheer about. The present seems menacing and the past seems dubious. The Bunker Hill monument today towers over an Irish community embittered by busing. In the streets of Charlestown, where John Kennedy was cheered in his first race for Congress, Senator Edward Kennedy has a bad name. The 1975 Bunker Hill Day parade was a Charlestown neighborhood affair.

Concern about the present has encouraged new views of the past, and in the process we may expect revision of the conventional view of the Irish in the American Catholic Church.

The conventional story, dramatized with some important matters omitted, goes something like this: In the early years of the Republic the Church was weak in institutions, feeble in numbers. But it was respected, even liked, in the tolerant years following the American Revolution. Its leaders were aristocrats like John Carroll, the first bishop of Baltimore, or men of presence and learning like Bishop John England of Charleston. The best Protestants of Boston helped Bishop John Lefebvre de Cheverus build the first Cathedral of the Holy Cross on Franklin Street.

Then came the shock waves of the Irish. They came by the thousands in the 1830s and by the tens of thousands in the 1840s. They were refugees from hunger. They were poor, illiterate peasants, militantly Catholic, intensely conservative. They came in the midst of a Protestant Evangelical revival when Catholicism was no longer a comfortable persuasion. Conflict and recrimination replaced the good manners of an earlier day. The Ursuline convent at Charlestown (now Somerville), Massachusetts, was burned to the ground in 1834. Catholic churches in Philadelphia and New York were attacked. Nativist hostility toward Irish Catholics became part of the national history in the decades before the Civil War.

The new situation brought forward new leaders: Irish and aggressive. Bishop Cheverus, a Frenchman, had been known as the gentle bishop. No one so described Archbishop John Hughes of New York, Irish-born and symbol of the new leadership. He fought tenaciously for Catholic rights, most notably in the public schools. Lay Catholics who disagreed with him suffered. The new style was heavily authoritarian.

By the conclusion of the Civil War the Irish had established their supremacy in the American Church. But Catholic participation in the war had softened animosities. In the improved atmosphere of the post–Civil War period, the Irish demonstrated new abilities. They became Americanizers. They, or at least those among them who are the heroes of conventional history, were determined to demonstrate that Catholicism and democracy were compatible. In this work they had to deal gingerly with an American public and an Italian Vatican that, for different reasons, had serious reservations about the proposition.

Cardinal James Gibbons of Baltimore urged restraint to Vatican authorities critical of American working-class efforts to improve the conditions of labor. Others took the lead in organizing Irish temperance and fraternal societies that would make of their members more congenial citizens. Archbishop John Ireland of St. Paul argued with conservatives in the Church, at home and abroad, that American democracy provided unique opportunities for the Church. He and other liberals opened up cooperative ventures with the public school system and opposed the so-called Cahensly movement, which they feared would establish divisive German-speaking enclaves in the American Catholic Church. Among laymen, John Boyle O'Reilly, editor of the Boston Catholic paper, *The Pilot*, was the prominent voice for sweetness and light.

The Americanizers had their enemies in the Church but the work went on. By directing the Church toward social action, they made their most important contribution: saving the working classes from the atheism that had overcome their brethren in Europe.

The Irish were builders, and they erected an elaborate set of institutions: churches, schools, hospitals, charitable agencies, colleges, and universities. Despite the separatist character of these institutions, they would in time win acceptance as an integral part of American life.

The work, still under Irish leadership, would continue in the twentieth century. The American Church would loyally support the American state in two World Wars. In the Cold War, under the leadership of Cardinal Francis Spellman of New York, Catholicism would become an important prop of American policy. By the middle of the century, the Church was a power in the land.

Critics from without complained about Catholic power. Critics from within lamented the low status of Catholics in the nation's intellectual and cultural life. Irish leadership was under challenge and the time seemed ripe for a new leadership.

The Irish had done their job and, on the whole, it appeared to be a success story. And then it came undone. The elaborate edifice that was the American Church collapsed as though from an implosion.

Explanations have poured from the presses, topical and confessional most of them. But to understand the disarray of the Church today, we will have to go back to history.

The conventional story of the Irish in the Church is only half a story; the other half remains to be written. Even the conventional account must be revised. Emmet Larkin of the University of Chicago has told us that pre-famine Ireland was not the intensely Catholic country we once thought, and David Doyle of University College, Dublin, has shown that the post-famine immigrants were not the impoverished and unskilled people we once thought.

The half that remains to be written concerns the dissenters, those who resisted Americanization, who for one reason or another rejected the chauvinism of an Archbishop Ireland. This history may demonstrate that the Berrigan brothers and their fellows are not unique in American Catholic history.

Irish immigrant Catholicism has always been ambivalent about American culture and the claims of the American state. Conventional history has ignored the "outsiders" or has assigned to them the minor roles of conservatives or radicals.

One can imagine Thomas D'Arcy McGee, that man of intelligence and sensitivity whom Archbishop Hughes drove from New York, taking a stand during the Vietnam War with the dissenters.

Had we today that other half of Irish Catholic history, perhaps the Irish of Charlestown could take comfort from it. For they too are standing in opposition to what McGee called the American "juggernaut."

RECOMMENDED READING: *The United States of America:* "The Irish Clergyman," by Thomas T. McAvoy, C.S.C.; "The Irish Layman," by Thomas N. Brown ("A History of Irish Catholicism," Volume VI, Fascicle 2 [Dublin: Gill and Macmillan, 1970]). William V. Shannon, *The American Irish* (revised edition; New York: Macmillan Company, 1966).

DR. BROWN is a professor of history in the University of Massachusetts at Boston, Harbor Campus.

20

German Catholics in America

COLMAN J. BARRY, O.S.B.

The Catholic Church in the United States has been in large measure an immigrant institution. The tide bringing millions of settlers to American shores was a phenomenon unparalleled in the Church's history. Peoples of different races, nationalities, traditions, and prejudices came to establish new homes in a strange country. Among these the German people occupied a leading place.

Immigrant German Catholics of the nineteenth century had a firm loyalty to their religion, sound organizational techniques, and a strong community pattern of worship, culture, and social action. From the time of their first Pennsylvania settlements in the mid-eighteenth century, German Catholic leaders had insisted on separate treatment and recognition as an ethnic group. Their demands in the following century for language rights, national parishes, and proportional representation in the hierarchy were, they maintained, defenses against attack by liberal German Americans after 1848, as well as insurance that their religious faith would be preserved intact.

Simultaneously, other leading Catholic churchmen and laymen were working to instill devotion to American constitutional and political ideals among all segments of immigrant Catholics. Toward the end of the century these robust Americanizers came into open conflict with German Catholics over procedure and practice. German Catholic leaders and newspapers, supported by a large number of French, Polish, and Spanish representatives both in the United States and abroad, accused the Americanizers of striving to break down precipitately all the native traditions and customs of the Catholic immigrants. The Americanizers were also accused of causing a loss of religious faith and creating an undue attachment to American secular trends.

Peter Paul Cahensly, an active Catholic lay leader in Germany and one of the founders of the St. Raphael's Society for the protection of emigrants,

HOLY TRINITY CHURCH, PHILADELPHIA

Built by German Catholics in 1789, this was the first national parish church in the United States.

was joined by other leaders of the Society in seven European countries in taking the whole question to Rome. Cahensly was the pioneer in the defense of the human and spiritual rights of the immigrant.

On their side the Americanizers, following especially the principles of Orestes Brownson and Isaac Hecker, were wedded to the vision of traditional Catholicism formed in an American democratic mold and based on a fusion of all national groups. Led by many of the country's most prominent Catholic bishops and teachers, they maintained that free political institutions can be secure only when the people are imbued with religious ideals, that without religious sanctions the moral solidarity which makes democratic government possible would be broken. They wanted to show the necessity of the Catholic religion to the modern world and to impress on Catholics the necessity of their being in tune with the age.

This task of creating a religious and national unity among the Catholic immigrants reached a climax between the Civil War and World War I. German immigration to the United States was given a new impetus after 1865, and Catholics made up more than thirty-five percent of the total German immigration of that period. They totaled around 700,000 from 1865 to 1900, becoming the largest Catholic immigrant group arriving in the United States. By 1865 the Germans equalled the Irish influx, and from 1870 to 1890 they led the field until Italian immigration began in earnest in the last decade of that century.

Germans who came after 1865 generally settled in the same regions as their predecessors. As in the eighteenth and early nineteenth centuries German settlers had chosen the best farming land they could find, so in the second half of the nineteenth century they congregated in agricultural areas and towns which in time came to be known as "the German belt." This zone lay between the northern boundaries of Massachusetts and of Maryland, spread westward through the Ohio River basin to the Great Lakes, and extended out into the prairie states beyond the Mississippi River. Germans settled in the Mohawk Valley, in Pennsylvania, along the shores of the Ohio and Great Lakes, and down the Mississippi to New Orleans. But it was in the triangle formed by lines joining Cincinnati, Milwaukee, and St. Louis that the German population was especially dense. In some places they established exclusively German colonies, sometimes spontaneously but more often under the direction of a German priest or missionary.

German Catholics were concerned not only with their material well-being in the New World, but primarily with their spiritual life. Among their first interests was the erection of a church and a parish school. Fresh from Europe and feeling isolated in American society because of their different language, the German Catholics from the outset insisted that churches of their own were absolutely necessary. In these separate churches their traditional religious observances and customs could be carried out; they could hear sermons in their mother tongue, go to confession as they had learned to confess from early childhood, and take an active part in parochial life through their favorite societies. They wanted the order and discipline of parochial life as they had known it before coming to the United States. This German attachment to the customs of the fatherland was often misunderstood by their co-religionists in America. But the German immigrants held that since the English-speaking Catholics had no language problem of their own, they could not properly understand the close bond which existed in the German consciousness between the practice of their faith and these traditional customs which were deeply rooted in the centuries-old Catholic culture of their fatherland.

During the nineteenth century the German Catholic leaders in the United States were insistent upon these special arrangements because the immigrants, they said, were joining German associations or societies (*Vereine*) in which they felt themselves to be more at home and could hear their mother tongue spoken. Editors of the German American press, liberals and freethinkers of the "'48er" type, as well as influential German *Vereine* were conducting a concerted campaign to preserve German language and culture in the New World. German Catholics, both in Germany and in the United States, who were judged to be hyphenated Germans because of their allegiance to Rome, realized that they would be open to cynical attack if they should diminish their efforts to preserve *das Deutschtum* in the New World. Many of the common people among the German Catholics, timid and homesick in a new environment, would be essay prey to such charges.

The German Catholics eventually came to accept the position of the Americanizers, as did the other immigrant groups. Their mother tongue was dying out; American national habits were being assimilated; they were beginning to recognize the United States as a nation instead of a mere collection of European nationalities. No more protesting memorials were sent to Rome, since German parishes gradually became mixed parishes, national parishes slowly gave way to territorial parishes, and the German parishes became distinguished only by a spirit of German Catholicism as practiced by American citizens of German origin. Interest in the appointment of bishops of German ancestry and language became an academic question as the American Germans took their place in national life as one of the many elements that went to make up one people.

At the same time, the Americanizers, seeing their program being accomplished and their ideals being fulfilled by this process, ceased their intemperate charges about a conspiracy. Their aims had unquestionably been progressive, but their means were sometimes questionable. In time, however, they came to realize the valuable contribution of Germans to religious and social life in the United States. The parochial school system, so vigorously defended by German Catholics, was accepted as a policy of the Church. Several points of the program urged by Cahensly and the St. Raphael

Society, such as colonizing projects and care for immigrants and displaced persons, were also incorporated into American Catholic practice. From the German examples of a strong press and vigorous society activity much was learned. The use of the English language was left to time and environment rather than forced by stern admonitions which were open to misrepresentation and suspicion by immigrants not fully at home in American life. Perhaps, as more and more educators are now saying, the pluralistic linguistic and cultural values contributed to American life by the immigrant groups were recognized and respected too late, and the values which individual ethnic groups could contribute from their heritage to the enrichment of American life were not appreciated soon enough.

It is interesting today to watch growing demands for the teaching of foreign languages on all levels of the Catholic education system. We have been going through a vigorous analysis of the quality of American Catholic intellectual life, and searching questions have been asked about our proportional contribution to cultural life and ethnic leadership. The record of German Catholic contributions has been limited, and a rewarding study could be made as to whether too hasty Americanization was a serious cause. Another area that awaits investigation is the nature and character of American Catholic spirituality, or interior life, which has not been touched as yet. Why has there been a slow and reluctant response to the ideals of community worship, of the liturgical movement, of a respect for the Catholic traditions of participation, singing, and a Scriptural-centered life? Were immigrant groups such as the Germans swept into the dominant current of the "American" secular cultural patterns? What happened to the ancient Catholic tradition of the arts and crafts in American Catholic life and educational institutions? Such aspects of a Christian culture could have developed and received real impetus from immigrant groups like the Germans if they had not been uprooted and shorn of their true identity so rapidly and completely.

Apart from these considerations, the leaders of the Catholic Church in the United States who had encouraged Americanization made a contribution to the nation. Some nine million Catholic immigrants from over twenty countries had come to American shores in the century from 1820 to 1920. This vast number of settlers, almost half of the total net immigration to the United States of that period, was encouraged to understand and practice American democratic ideals by their new spiritual leaders. Divergent groups of people, like the Germans, were encouraged to amalgamate and adapt themselves. As a result a significant number of Catholic immigrants from Europe learned to live together as Americans.

RECOMMENDED READING: Colman J. Barry, O.S.B., *The Catholic Church and German Americans* (Milwaukee: Bruce Publishing Co., 1953).

FATHER BARRY, author of numerous books on Catholic history, is dean of the School of Religious Studies in the Catholic University of America.

BISHOP PAUL RHODE

The first bishop of Polish birth in the United States, he was auxiliary to the archbishop of Chicago from 1908 to 1915 and then bishop of Green Bay until his death in 1945. (*Courtesy of* The Spirit, *diocesan newspaper of Green Bay*)

21

Polish Catholics in America

ANTHONY J. KUZNIEWSKI, S.J.

"**B**etween the Poles and the Roman-Irish Church in America there can be no more understanding than between a lamb and a wolf. Sooner or later we [Poles] will become the victims of the crafty, greedy power...of the church dignitaries." With these words, part of an appeal addressed to Polish immigrants in May, 1904, Francis Hodur of Scranton, Pennsylvania, attempted to attract new members to the Polish National Catholic Church which he had organized in the United States. Having reached a membership of at least 10,000 in its first seven years of existence, the movement was already well established as the one large schism to affect immigrant Catholics in America.

Throughout the 1890s such independent groups had broken with local bishops in Chicago, Cleveland, Buffalo, and Scranton. Hodur eventually united them after receiving episcopal consecration from bishops of the Old Catholic Church in the Netherlands. Wherever disputes arose, the issues were the same: the reluctance of some Poles to deed church property to their bishop and the desire to have a bishop who could deal with them in their own language.

Even the leaders of the overwhelming majority of Polish-Americans who remained loyal to Rome admitted the attractiveness of the independents' arguments. "The schismatics have the popular side of the affair," members of the Polish Catholic Congress meeting in Buffalo in 1901 warned in a memorial to the American hierarchy. "They have so-called Polish bishops, whereas they accuse the Polish Roman Catholic clergy of treason to their nation when holding allegiance to Irish and German bishops, as they say." For, despite the heavy immigration from Catholic Poland dating from the 1870s, the first bishop of Polish descent in the United States was not con-

89

secrated until 1908. By that time, the issue had exasperated Polish and non-Polish Catholics alike.

At least the controversy indicated that the Poles were taking religion seriously. Beginning with their first settlements in Texas and Wisconsin in the mid-1850s, the building of a church had been a high priority. Later, as Polish immigrants favored cities north of the Ohio River and east of the Mississippi, cross-topped spires marked their districts. Parishes were often large: St. Stanislaus Kostka congregation in Chicago numbered 50,000 at the turn of the century, and St. Stanislaus parish in Buffalo included 30,000. Both were larger than many dioceses. The church structures, reflecting the ancient understanding of reserving the best things for God, sometimes became monumental edifices. A report sent to the Vatican by the Archdiocese of Milwaukee in 1923 included four Polish churches among the seven singled out as exceptional in construction and furnishing.

The Poles, like others, faced a shortage of priests when they began life in America. Part of the need was met by the Resurrectionist Fathers, who began work in America in the 1860s. Under the leadership of Father Vincent Barzynski, Chicago became the headquarters for their work among Polish immigrants and for an apostolate in the Southern states.

The suppression of Catholic monasteries decreed in the Russian section of Poland in 1864 caused a number of Franciscans to come to America. A group of Friars Minor founded a monastery on donated land in northeastern Wisconsin in 1887, and the first Conventual Franciscans of Polish origin established a mission in upstate New York about fifteen years later. Other victims of the suppression immigrated as secular priests and attached themselves to many dioceses containing Poles.

Concern with community affairs led several priests to the field of Catholic journalism, among them Fathers Jan Pitass of Buffalo, Boleslaus Góral of Milwaukee, and Lucjan Bójnowski of New Britain, Connecticut. Another priest, Father Wenceslaus Kruszka of Wisconsin, began publishing the first substantial history of America's Poles in 1905, a task carried forward today in part by Father Joseph Swastek of Orchard Lake, Michigan.

The pioneers among the Polish-American religious women were the Felician Sisters, who came from Cracow to Polonia, Wisconsin, in 1874. Limited by the poverty of the people among whom they worked and beset by two disastrous fires in the first year, these hardy women persevered to become a harbinger of future growth. As the number of Polish Catholic elementary and high schools grew to over 600, several Polish orders of nuns or orders with Polish-American members such as the Bernardines, the Sisters of Nazareth, the Sisters of St. Joseph of the Third Order of St. Francis, the Sisters of the Resurrection, and a number of Franciscan groups provided generous service. In addition, hospitals, orphanages and retirement homes staffed by these and other orders benefited the entire community.

Among the first lay people contributing to the quality of Polish life in America were the parish organists. These unknown heroes of the first generation of immigrant life often conducted the first parish school in addition to their liturgical duties. Polish historians such as Mieczyslaus Haiman and journalists such as Anthony Paryski, Stanislaus Osada, and Karol Wachtl served as recorders and guides to the immigrants. Peter Kiolbasa of Chicago and Michael Kruszka of Milwaukee represented Polish and Catholic viewpoints in the civil government well before the turn of the century. Finally, the Polish Roman Catholic Union, the Polish National Alliance, and other organizations have aided cultural activities and such educational enterprises as St. Mary's College in Michigan and Pennsylvania's Alliance College, which is nonsectarian.

Despite the appearance of success, the process of immigration brought insecurity to many of these individuals and groups. In Europe, Poles had courageously defended their faith and nationality during the century following annexation into the Russian, German, and Austrian Empires. In America they wanted assurance that the Church would continue to be their mother and would allow them freer expression than had been possible under difficult conditions in the Old Country. But the American hierarchy in those days was struggling to defend the faith against nativism and grappling with the issue of unifying a suddenly diverse membership. Thus the American bishops appeared to some of the Poles as unsympathetic. Misunderstandings arose. Thousands eventually joined independent churches, chiding the Catholic Poles about the lack of a Polish bishop in America.

Therefore, the effort to secure the appointment of a Polish bishop became crucial. A series of Polish Catholic conventions appealed to the American bishops. In 1903, a delegation petitioned Pope Pius X personally in the matter. In 1905, a papal representative came to examine the condition of America's Poles. Three American archbishops traveled to Rome in part to request Polish auxiliaries. In 1907, Archbishop James Quigley of Chicago was successful, and he allowed the Polish priests of his diocese to elect one of their number as auxiliary. They chose Father Paul Rhode, who was then consecrated amid general rejoicing. He was later named bishop of Green Bay, Wisconsin, where he remained until his death in 1945.

Bishop Rhode was followed by about fifteen additional episcopal appointments from the Polish ethnic community, mostly in the Midwest. In recent times, the appointment of John Krol as archbishop of Philadelphia, his prominent role at the Second Vatican Council, his elevation to the cardinalate, and his election to the presidency of the National Conference of Catholic

Bishops and United States Catholic Conference have been a source of pride to many Americans of Polish descent.

RECOMMENDED READING: *The Contribution of the Poles to the Growth of Catholicism in the United States*, edited by F. Domanski, S.J., *et al.* ("Sacrum Poloniae Millennium," Volume VI [Rome, 1959]). *The Poles in America, 1608–1972*, edited by Frank Renkiewicz (Dobbs Ferry, New York: Oceana Publications, 1973). Daniel S. Buczek, *Immigrant Pastor. The Life of the Right Reverend Monsignor Lucyan Bójnowski of New Britain, Connecticut* (Waterbury, Connecticut: Heminway Corporation, 1974).

REV. MR. KUZNIEWSKI, who holds a Ph.D. degree from Harvard University, is a Jesuit scholastic and an assistant professor of history in the College of the Holy Cross, Worcester, Massachusetts.

ᵞᶜᵚ᛫ᚷᵚᶜᵞ

Italian Catholics in America

SILVANO M. TOMASI, C.S.

On a Saturday afternoon in September, 1876, an Italian-American nun named Sister Blandina Segale fixed her gaze into the steel-blue eyes of Billy the Kid. "Billy," Sister Blandina wrote in the journal of her life in the Southwest, "was young, ... one would take him to be seventeen—innocent-looking, save for the corners of his eyes, which tell a set purpose, good or bad." The meeting took place in Trinidad, in the Territory of Colorado, where Sister Blandina, at twenty-six years of age, had been working as a Sister of Charity since 1872. Born Rosa Maria Segale in the Ligurian Hills of Italy in 1850, at age four she emigrated to America with her family in search of a better future. They landed in New Orleans and settled in Cincinnati, where she joined Mother Seton's Sisters of Charity in 1866 and took the name Blandina.

Chance had nothing to do with Sister Blandina's encounter with Billy the Kid and his gang. On the westernmost frontier she had been busy with Indians, settlers, and Mexicans, teaching, building, and caring for the sick. A wounded Methodist member of Billy's gang was patiently nursed by Sister Blandina for weeks. Since the four local doctors had refused to take the bullet out of the wounded man's thigh, the gang decided to scalp all of them. The courage and tact of Sister Blandina, who went to meet the gang, prevented disaster. She even extracted from the Kid the promise to protect the Sisters of Charity.

Her humanizing touch led this insightful and tireless woman to stop the lynching of outlaws. Her missionary activities and accomplishments, such as the opening of new schools, match those of an extraordinary band of Italian missionaries and educators in the American West in the nineteenth century. In the Southwest Jesuits of the Neapolitan Province such as Fathers Gasparri, Bianchi, Leone, Personné, and Gentile were pioneers with Bishop

AN ITALIAN RELIGIOUS PROCESSION IN THE STREETS OF NEW YORK

This picture was taken in Baxter Street around 1930. (*Courtesy of the Center for Migration Studies, Staten Island, New York*)

John Baptist Lamy of Santa Fe in serving the Catholic communities of Las Vegas, Albuquerque, Santa Fe, and other towns in New Mexico as well as of the Territory of Colorado. As Sister Blandina called them in her letters, they were vanguards of the Church.

Before the period of mass immigration, Italians in the United States were mostly known as missionaries among the Indian tribes of the Northwest or builders of Catholic educational institutions such as Gonzaga University, the University of San Francisco, and St. Bonaventure University. There were also some Italian artists and literati in the United States and some Catholic but anticlerical political refugees from different states of the Italian peninsula which through a long struggle were being unified into a single nation. But in 1870, when the unification finally resulted in the new Kingdom of Italy, the political and economic upheaval that shook the provinces of the old Kingdom of Naples and Sicily caused an unprecedented wave of emigration to the Americas.

Four and a half million Italians arrived in the United States from 1880 to 1920. Although a little more than 500,000 went back, their impact on the schools, parishes, and urban neighborhoods of the new country was dramatic. For the first time New York, Boston, Philadelphia, Cleveland, Chicago, San Francisco, and the smaller cities of the Northwest, the Middle West, and the Far West were confronted with Latin peasant traditions. The highly industrialized cities of America witnessed the violent and often dehumanizing change of farmers into factory workers. The neatness and puritanical reserve of the New England village stood in strong contrast to the boisterous processions of the Italian immigrants as they paraded statues of saints adorned with dollar bills and concluded with a feast of food of exotic smell and taste. The stiff austerity of the Irish clergy, in whose parishes most of the newly arrived settled, the language barrier, the long hours of work and the embarrassing poverty which kept them even from Church services, created what became known as the "Italian problem" in American Catholicism. The question is still debated, however, whether the Italian immigrants created more of a problem for the American Catholics than the way in which the Church was organized and administered in the United States did for the Italians.

Italian immigrants arrived when the organization of the American Church was already institutionalized, and they had to carve a niche for themselves in constant confrontation and cooperation with Irish and German Catholics and mostly Irish pastors and bishops. The turn of the century became a testing time for human relations. Unaware of the debate between Americanizers and conservatives among Catholic leaders, the Italian immigrants and their priests went quietly their own way within the Church. They could not relinquish their patron saints, good lobbyists before God, or their loyalty to the unity of the Church in spite of its seeming intransigence toward an alternative cultural expression of the faith. The way out of the immigrants' predicament was the ethnic, or national, parish.

By 1918, 580 Italian churches and chapels were functioning for an Italian population of 3,028,000. From a store front in the center of the Italian neighborhood or the basement of an Irish parish church or the courtyard of an immigrant settlement where the first religious services were held, the Italian parish would emerge as a focal point of the immigrant neighborhood. Its shortcomings notwithstanding, it became the place where the newcomers, who were on the religious and social periphery of the country, could fulfill their religious needs, find opportunity for self-expression, preserve their sense of identity in an unknown social environment. Like Sister Blandina on the Western frontier, the *contadini* (peasants) from the Italian South injected a dimension of humanness in the urban frontier. Their piety and devotion, love and sacrifice for the family, the earthy enjoyment of neighborhood life overspilled on their attitude to religion and dispelled Jansenistic residues, a process which is still at work. Occasionally encouraged by leaders such as Archbishop Michael Corrigan of New York, and more often just tolerated, the Italian parishes were perhaps a slower, but certainly a healthier road into American society—much as the two saintly leaders in the pastoral care of Italian immigrants had envisioned, St. Frances Xavier Cabrini and Bishop John Baptist Scalabrini, founder of congregations of priests and sisters for migrants.

Today's third-generation Italian Americans are proud of their background. If they no longer feel the need, however, to drop the vowel at the end of their names, neither are they very sanguine about ethnic associations as a way of participation in American life.

The flow of newcomers from Italy continues. More than 500,000 Italian immigrants have entered the country since 1950. They come from the same regions of Sicily, Campania, Calabria, and Abruzzi which supplied the bulk of arrivals during the period of mass immigration, and they constitute a challenge for their American cousins in terms of Christian thinking on hospitality and international responsibility.

Italian Catholics in America are not a homogeneous community. Some are Catholic Americans, others, Italian-American Catholics or Italian immigrant Catholics, all with different agenda.

As they celebrate the Bicentennial, they may want to rethink conventional Catholic history. Historians have largely overlooked the contribution of Italian immigrants to the institutional growth of American Catholicism before the period of mass immigration. They have also left unexplored the role of the immigrants' popular piety, which was one of the main conditions of survival in their urban setting often dominated by dehumanizing values. The Latin sense of measure, tolerance, and realism in human relations, which traditional Catholic peasant immigrants brought with them into urban

America, could be preserved, now that the old neighborhood is vanishing, amid conditions of pluralism in the country and the Church.

RECOMMENDED READING: Sister Blandina Segale, *At the End of the Santa Fe Trail* (Milwaukee: Bruce Publishing Company, 1948). Giovanni Schiavo, *Italian-American History*, Volume II: *The Italian Contribution to the Catholic Church in America* (New York: Vigo Press, 1949). *The Italian Experience in the United States*, edited by Silvano M. Tomasi and Madeline H. Engel (New York: Center for Migration Studies, 1970). Silvano M. Tomasi, *Piety and Power: The Role of Italian Parishes in the New York Metropolitan Area, 1880–1930* (New York: Center for Migration Studies, 1975).

FATHER TOMASI, author and editor of several publications, is director of the Center for Migration Studies of New York, Inc.

OUR LADY OF SILUVA, PATRONESS OF LITHUANIA

Created by Vytautas Kasuba, this statue stands outside the chapel of the American headquarters of the Lithuanian Sisters of the Immaculate Conception of the Blessed Virgin Mary in Putnam, Connecticut. (*NC Photos*)

23

Lithuanian Catholics in America

WILLIAM WOLKOVICH

Evidence of individual Lithuanians in America dates from the Revolutionary War. But it was peasants who made up the mass Lithuanian migration to the United States after the Civil War. Factors in their exodus were easier mobility arising from the end of serfdom in 1861, the insurrection of 1863 (Lithuania was under Russia, 1795–1915), the famines of 1867–1868, flight from military conscription, and the quest for economic and civil liberty.

The industrious Lithuanians usually embarked from German ports, paying their own way with modest spending money in hand. They were met at the New York harbor by agents of railroad and mining companies, who recruited them along with other immigrants.

The Pennsylvania anthracite region lured the first settlers to towns like Pittston in 1867 and Plymouth in 1869. Soon other colonies dotted the eastern and midwestern states: Chicago in 1892, Brooklyn and Worcester, Massachusetts, in 1894, Cleveland in 1895, Baltimore in 1897.

A quarter-million Lithuanians arrived from 1899 to 1914—mostly Catholics and laborers. But the prejudicial "national origins" quota of 1924 slowed subsequent immigration from Lithuania to a small trickle. The 1924 quota limited immigration to two percent annually of the residents from each nationality in the United States in 1890—thus eliminating the heaviest Lithuanian influx from consideration in the selection of newcomers.

Once here, the Lithuanians found heartaches along with their new-found freedoms. They came from a part of Europe little known to their English-speaking neighbors. People of a strange, ancient tongue, these immigrants were at times despised by fellow townsmen and frequently ignored by unsympathetic bishops and clergy.

They established mutual benefit societies which gave priority to founding parishes by purchasing land, building a church, and recruiting a priest. The first such undertaking was St. Casimir Church, Shenandoah, Pennsylvania, in 1872. At first the Lithuanians affiliated with Polish parishes and societies, but soon their traditional rivalry flared up into violence and court litigation, providing a strong impetus for the two groups to go their separate ways. Lithuanian newspapers promoted the campaign against fraternization with Poles, preaching the twofold message: Keep your faith and your ethnic heritage.

Much of Lithuanian Catholic life in America has been characterized by intermittent skirmishes between the Catholics and socialists and other anti-religious groups. A leading socialist spokesman was the physician, Jonas Sliupas, indoctrinated in secret cells of Russian university campuses. Anti-religious invective in lectures and writings provoked the Catholic clergy and laity. Mutual hostility fractured a nationwide fraternal benefit alliance in 1906, and over the years court dockets were sprinkled with civil and criminal cases arising from the conflicts. The most sensational involved charges of blasphemy, sedition, robbery, and murder.

Within Catholic parishes, another type of conflict arose—between trustees and pastor. For instance, in 1913 at Brockton, Massachusetts, the parish committee rejected the pastor appointed by Cardinal William O'Connell, locking both church and rectory. The Boston archdiocesan chancery promptly added its own set of locks, and there ensued an eighteen-month impasse. In the same parish the trustees warned the pastor that they would deduct five dollars from his salary for each mention of the devil during a sermon.

Disputes with local bishops over legal title to church property led to ten schismatic churches that were embraced by the Polish National Church which had been founded in 1897. Such separated Lithuanian communities were short-lived, and there are only a few survivors today.

Lithuanians valued Catholic education. Two decades before nuns were available for it, the first parochial school of St. George in Chicago was staffed by laity in 1894. A scholarship society was begun in 1900 by the clergy. Beneficiaries were sent abroad, especially to Fribourg, Switzerland. In 1907 the Sisters of St. Casimir were started at Mt. Carmel, Pennsylvania, for teaching and later nursing. In 1913 Lithuanian Marian Fathers came from Europe to Chicago to teach.

This dual apostolate was taken up by other American communities of Lithuanian Franciscan Sisters at Pittsburgh in 1922, and the Sisters of Jesus Crucified at Elmhurst, Pennsylvania, in 1924.

Women among Lithuanians took a greater part in community affairs than did their native American counterparts. Besides joining national fraternities for insurance and social goals, Catholics began a Women's Alliance in 1916, while their dissident socialist sisters formed the Women's Progressive Alliance the same year. Both these groups had their own publications, as did almost every Lithuanian-American society.

The Lithuanian Catholic press in this country dates from 1879. Though many publications had brief lifespans, others have continued to this day. There is *Draugas* ("Friend"), a daily newspaper of the Marian Fathers, conceived in 1909 by the Lithuanian Priests' League, the *Darbininkas* ("Worker") of 1915 origin, sponsored by the (Catholic) Workers Alliance, now produced by Franciscan Fathers. In addition, a large number of Lithuanian books were published—often through the generosity of private sponsors, since the small size of the potential readership meant that most such publications were unprofitable.

The Displaced Persons Act of 1948 brought some 30,000 Lithuanians to the United States. Though one in faith and ethnic origin, the DP's were socially distinct from the older immigrants and their American-born offspring. Misunderstandings erupted. The new parishioners transplanted organizations of their homeland, setting up youth camps, Scouts, professional societies, and Futurists ("Ateitininkai"), as well as their own publications.

While the several generations have gone mostly separate ways in social and cultural spheres, the press, radio programs, patriotic observances, and Lithuanian Days (festivals) have preserved a degree of unity.

Small in numbers, Lithuanian Catholics offer the Church several examples of long-standing collegiality. Long before diocesan priests' senates, the Lithuanian Priests' League of America had its first annual convention at the Astor Hotel in New York on May 5, 1909. The American Lithuanian Roman Catholic Federation originally assembled in 1906 at Wilkes-Barre, Pennsylvania. In 1931 this amalgamation of lay groups became affiliated with the National Catholic Welfare Conference through the National Council of Catholic Men.

RECOMMENDED READING: Antanas Kucas, *Lithuanians in America* (Boston: Lithuanian Encyclopedia Press, 1975). Victor Greene, *For God and Country. The Rise of Polish and Lithuanian Ethnic Consciousness in America, 1860–1910* (Madison: The State Historical Society of Wisconsin, 1975). Also many articles (in English) in the *Encyclopedia Lituanica*, edited by Simas Suziedelis (six volumes of which four are now in print).

FATHER WOLKOVICH, or Valkavicius, is a priest of the Archdiocese of Boston and a freelance writer specializing in Lithuanian-American themes.

FATHER MATTHEW JANKOLA

Father Jankola served Slovak communities in Pennsylvania, New York, and Connecticut and founded the Sisters of Saints Cyril and Methodius to teach in parochial schools and perform works of mercy. (*Courtesy of Jankola Library, Danville, Pennsylvania*)

24

Slovak Catholics in America

SISTER M. MARTINA TYBOR, SS.C.M.

It is not surprising that once the people of Slovakia became aware of the opportunities available to them in America, they began to emigrate in proportionately large numbers. For centuries they had been economically exploited and culturally repressed by their Hungarian rulers. Most Slovak children could obtain only the rudiments of an education in their homeland. Exceptions to this rule were students for the priesthood. It is understandable, then, that clergymen became the natural leaders of the Slovak people not only in spiritual matters but also in professional, intellectual, and political affairs.

Before 1880 fewer than 7,000 Slovaks immigrated to the United States. By 1921, however, there were 827,720 Slovak immigrants in America, and more than 500,000 of these decided to remain there. Nine out of ten were Catholics of the Roman or Greek (Uniate) Byzantine rite. It has been conservatively estimated that there must be at least 2,000,000 persons of Catholic Slovak origin in the country at present.

Strangers in a new land, the early Slovak immigrants were naturally drawn into closely knit communities in those localities that assured them a means of livelihood. The mines and industries of the East attracted many to Pennsylvania, New Jersey, Connecticut, New York, West Virginia, and Ohio. Other prospects brought Slovaks to Colorado, Wyoming, Montana, and Washington. Some who intended from the beginning to remain in the United States settled on farms in Arkansas, Michigan, Illinois, Wisconsin, and Minnesota.

Difficult adjustments to their new environment were compounded by language differences and hostilities from the "old immigration." But the Slovak pioneers were endowed with native traits that served them well in these circumstances. Such were their faith in God, loyalty to the family, and the long-tested ability to endure adversity. Their personal life was simple, devout, and religious. Spiritual exercises enriched their average day, but they felt the need for parish churches in which they might worship and hear the word of God in their own language. At first they attended whatever churches they found in their neighborhoods—Polish, Irish, German, or Czech—but they understood that they were merely tolerated by these other nationalities and were never really welcomed by them.

In the 1880s Slovak immigrants began to found local lodges to obtain some social and economic advantages. Members of lodges would have assurance of aid in times of need, caused by accidents, strikes, illness, or death; they would have the privilege of wearing a uniform and badge, of marching with fellow members on feasts and special occasions, and perhaps even of playing in the band; they could participate in discussions of topics of common interest. Before long, therefore, such fraternal and benevolent societies became very common, and membership in them became a status symbol.

In many instances one of the prime functions of a local lodge was to provide a church for Slovak Catholics. The initiative for such projects came from the laymen themselves if they were in an area lacking a priest. It was their responsibility to secure a suitable building for a church and at least temporary quarters for a priest. Once these preparations were completed, they endeavored to find a priest either in America or in Slovakia, Slovenia, Moravia, or Croatia. When they were assured of a prospective pastor, they applied for the local bishop's approval to establish a parish.

Part of the new experience in organizing a parish was to teach the immigrants their duty to support it financially. In the Old World their churches had been endowed and maintained by wealthy patrons, but in America the parishioners had to learn to bear these expenses.

Some Slovak priests came in the early years of immigration. Outstanding among them for their zeal and service were the Reverend Stephen Furdek, Matthew Jankola, Alexander Dianiska, and Andrew Pavco, as well as the Reverend Joseph Murgas, who was a scholar, scientist, artist, and inventor in wireless telegraphy and radio. Dedicated priests did not limit their ministry to those in their immediate charge. Father Jankola, for example, who became pastor of St. John the Baptist Church in Pittston shortly after his ordination, served the Slovaks in seven other adjoining settlements as well and periodically even visited the Slovak communities in Binghamton, New York, and in Wilkes-Barre and Maltby, Pennsylvania. In the twenty years of his priesthood Father Jankola was involved in the building of five churches, two schools, and a rectory. He and other active pastors understood the missionary aspect of their situation and strove to increase their priestly ranks. They appealed for volunteers to join them and even visited their homeland and neighboring Slavic lands, recruiting priests and seminarians especially from areas where prevailing conditions hampered Slovak clergymen in their ministry. Father Furdek induced many to come to America. Among them was Father Jankola, and he, in turn, persuaded eight priests and four clerical students to work among Slovak immigrants in America.

The first Slovak Catholic churches in America were completed in 1885— St. Joseph's in Hazleton, Pennsylvania, and St. Stephen's in Streator, Illinois. By 1903 there were approximately seventy-eight Slovak Catholic churches and fifty-five priests. Today there are more than 300 parishes and 200 parochial schools throughout the country.

At the outset some pastors were fortunate in obtaining sisters to staff their schools, but the existing communities in the United States could not furnish enough teachers to satisfy the demand created by the many immigrant groups competing for their services. The young and resourceful Father Jankola made many fruitless attempts to secure sisters both in this country and abroad. Finally, Mother Mary Cyril accepted several applicants for a formation program with the Sisters Servants of the Immaculate Heart of Mary in Scranton, Pennsylvania. This core group developed into the congregation of Sisters of SS. Cyril and Methodius with a generalate in Danville, Pennsylvania. This congregation of Slovak-American origin was approved by Pope St. Pius X in 1909 and today numbers approximately 400 sisters engaged in teaching and works of mercy in seven states. Seven other congregations of sisters also serve the Slovak Catholics in America.

The local Slovak societies or lodges multiplied so rapidly that by 1893 there were 277 in the United States. For greater economic stability and security (especially for their insurance funds), the independent lodges wished to be federated in a national organization. Thus in 1890 the National Slovak Society was founded with headquarters in Pittsburgh, but this was a nationalistic and secularistic movement attracting Slovak Catholics into a company of mixed membership including freethinkers, masons, indifferentists, and atheists. (Later it became a nonsectarian organization unobjectionable to Catholics.) This situation led to bitter debate and public controversy. Recognizing the need of Slovaks for a national Catholic organization, Father Furdek led the movement which culminated in the founding, in the same year of 1890, of the First Catholic Slovak Union (Jednota). Two years later the First Catholic Slovak Ladies Association was organized, and in 1905 the Slovak Catholic Sokol. These major Catholic fraternals have continued to flourish even to the present day and for a common cause they can pool their resources and rally formidable strength.

When secularism and liberalism began to threaten the wholesomeness of Slovak Catholic life early in the twentieth century, a conference was held at Wilkes-Barre to study these dangers. On the recommendation of Father Murgas the assembled bishops, priests, and lay delegates established the

Slovak Catholic Federation in 1911. This is an organization of laymen working with the clergy on behalf of faith, morality, education, publication, and charitable undertakings. It is a federation of all Slovak Catholic societies in the United States. During the two World Wars it provided extensive relief services in connection with the National Catholic Welfare Conference.

The press also played a very important role in the life of Slovak American Catholics. Although most of the early immigrants were illiterate and considered newspapers a luxury of the rich and leisured upper class, many of them were taught to read as adults and were soon convinced of the value of the printed page. The first Slovak newssheet, which was merely hectographed, was begun in 1885. Four years later the first church-oriented paper, *Katolicke noviny* (Catholic News), was started in Hazleton. The most influential Slovak Catholic newspaper was and continues to be the *Jednota*, the official weekly organ of the Jednota, which Father Furdek launched in Cleveland in 1891. Currently it is a bilingual publication with a circulation of more than 38,000. Another large Slovak Catholic bilingual weekly is the *Katolicky Sokol* published in Passaic, New Jersey. Slovak American Catholics also have four monthly bilingual publications, one bimonthly, and a children's monthly.

With the recent awakening of interest in ethnic groups, some note is being taken of the contributions of Slovak American Catholics to Church and State in America. A full account of their accomplishments, however, still remains to be written.

SISTER M. MARTINA TYBOR, author, translator, and literary critic, is director of Jankola Library, a center for Slovak and Slavic resource materials and archival reserves, in Danville, Pennsylvania.

Mexican-Americans in the Southwest

MATT S. MEIER

In 1848 the United States acquired, as one of the results of the Treaty of Guadalupe Hidalgo, about 75,000 citizens of Mexican origin. Living in rugged and isolated frontier conditions, these new citizens benefited little from the improving quality of life in urban America as the second half of the nineteenth century wore on.

The United States government had no program of acculturation for these new Spanish-speaking citizens, and the various social institutions of the country did little to relieve economic and social discrimination against them. At the end of the Mexican War there were approximately 60,000 Mexicans in New Mexico, 10,000 in California, 2,000 in Arizona, and perhaps 4,000 in Texas. In New Mexico, Mexican-Americans remained the numerical majority until about 1930 and during that time participated to a degree in the state's political, social, and economic life. In the other three areas—California, Arizona, and Texas—the much smaller Spanish-speaking populations were soon overwhelmed by the Anglo majority.

During the second half of the nineteenth century immigration from Mexico was extremely small, especially in comparison to the large number of Europeans then arriving. Noticeable immigration from Mexico to the United States did not begin until after 1900, and the movement became heavy only after the outbreak of the 1910 Mexican Revolution.

As the nineteenth century approached its end, some Christian leaders began to develop increasing awareness of the need for social justice for their followers and especially for the poor and minorities among them. Their concern was reflected in the initiation of the Social Gospel movement, settlement work, and similar activities; and in the Catholic Church it was evidenced especially in the 1891 encyclical of Pope Leo XIII, *Rerum Novarum.*

THE CHURCH AT LAS TRAMPAS, RIO ARRIBA COUNTY, NEW MEXICO

This late nineteenth-century social concern of the churches was most strongly expressed in the industrial East and Midwest, and largely centered on urban immigrant minority groups. Mexicans, unlike their European counterparts, were not seen as an urban proletariat in need of social justice because the Southwest, to which they were largely limited, was an area notable for its relatively small settlements with great distances between.

The physical reality of the Southwest's scattered and isolated villages tended to obscure social needs of Mexicans. It made social work among them quite different from similar work in large industrial centers and made such work virtually impossible in terms of late nineteenth-century social concern. Great distances and small community size made it difficult for American churches to fulfill their primary objectives of pastoral function in the Southwest; and as long as these were not fully met, secondary goals such as social welfare were unlikely to receive consideration.

At the time of the Treaty of Guadalupe Hidalgo there were only a few clergy in the entire area of the Southwest. The famed Archbishop Jean Baptiste Lamy (of Willa Cather's novel, *Death Comes to the Archbishop*), appointed as bishop of Santa Fe in 1851, was able to expand the number of priests in his huge diocese by bringing in missionaries from his native France; and a handful of Protestant missionaries labored in the area, especially in Texas.

However, most clergymen in the Southwest were just about as poor themselves as the Mexicans among whom they worked; and Mexican social amelioration, when it entered their minds at all, was apt to be expected as a natural byproduct of Americanization.

The Southwest, as a frontier area, remained essentially a missionary province with a relative shortage of clergy, and many priests were deeply concerned about the more relaxed Latin attitudes of a folk Catholicism. One missionary wrote about the offer of a group of Mexican musicians to play (a concert) at his church dedication, "I felt too great a repugnance to allow people who are so often the life of diabolical gatherings to take part in a religious ceremony."

While Catholic activities among Mexican-Americans centered around frontier missionary work, it also included the usual charitable and teaching activities of various religious orders. In 1866 Bishop Lamy reported that "almost all of our missionaries have at least one school under their direction, some have more...." A decade before the Civil War the Brothers of Mary established in San Antonio what is today St. Mary's University, with classes taught in both Spanish and English; and the Ursuline nuns opened an academy for girls at the same time. Subsequently, the Ursulines established a number of other schools in Texas as well as the first Catholic-operated hospital in that state. The Ursuline nuns also operated a free day school in San Antonio, principally for poor Mexican children. In New Mexico and Arizona the Sisters of St. Joseph and the Sisters of Loretto established a number of schools and five small hospitals by the 1890s. The Christian Brothers began the College of Las Vegas (New Mexico) in 1888 on land donated by one Félix Martínez; and Bishop Peter Bourgade established an orphanage near Tucson, as did the Sisters of St. Vincent de Paul in Santa Fe.

In the Southwest a major shift in orientation from the pastoral goals of a mission Church to the expanded social concerns of the modern Church began to occur just after the turn of the century. The first decades of the twentieth century saw the Catholic Church establishing diocesan bureaus of charity for social services as well as settlement houses in the Southwest. These new activities were, of course, largely limited to the urban Church; the Church in rural areas remained essentially pastoral in its goals.

In 1905 the first Catholic settlement houses began to appear in the Los Angeles area, and a decade later Bishop Anthony J. Schuler of El Paso, aided by the Catholic Extension Society, was organizing day nurseries, clinics, and hospitals. By 1919 the Bishops' Program of Social Reconstruction embodied many advanced socio-economic ideas and led to the founding of a Social Action Department headed by Father John A. Ryan in the National Catholic Welfare Conference. With this kind of encouragement, the National Council of Catholic Women established the San José Clinic in Houston in 1924.

A survey made in Los Angeles in 1920 indicated heightened levels of social concern for Mexican-Americans by the churches. It showed that the area had about seven Catholic social service centers, approximately an equal number of Protestant centers, as well as St. Vincent de Paul Societies, a Goodwill Industries, a Clothing Bureau, and several dispensaries and clinics. Social Christianity had begun to reach the Mexican-American.

RECOMMENDED READING: Matt S. Meier and Feliciano Rivera, *The Chicanos. A History of Mexican Americans* (New York: Hill & Wang, 1972). Paul Horgan, *Lamy of Santa Fe: His Life and Times* (New York: Farrar, Straus and Giroux, 1975)—winner of the 1976 Pulitzer Prize for history.

DR. MEIER is a professor of history in the University of Santa Clara in California.

26

Anti-Catholic Nativism
Before the Civil War

ROBERT F. HUESTON

On the evening of May 8, 1844, a huge mob in the street shouted encouragement as incendiaries gained access to St. Augustine's Catholic Church
in Philadelphia. Within minutes the building was engulfed by smoke and
flames. Frenzied shouts of approval rose from the crowd as the large cross
atop the steeple crashed to the ground. Within hours nothing remained but
charred ruins.

The burning of St. Augustine's culminated three days of anti-Catholic
rioting in the Philadelphia area, leaving several Catholic churches, other
church property, and more than forty homes (mostly owned by Irish
Catholics) in ashes. More than fifty people were killed or wounded, and
hundreds of homeless refugees wandered about the suburbs of the city.

The Philadelphia anti-Catholic riots of 1844 (another followed in July)
were a dramatic manifestation of a generally more subtle phenomenon in
American life known as "nativism"—hostility to aliens and, especially in the
nineteenth century, hostility to Catholics. Hatred of Rome had its roots in
colonial America when, with the embittered feelings of the Reformation
still running deep, the overwhelmingly Anglo-Protestant colonials lived in
recurrent fear of their French and Spanish Catholic neighbors in North
America.

The most serious outbreaks of anti-Catholic nativism occurred in the
three decades before the Civil War. The Philadelphia riots, the destruction
of an Ursuline convent in Charlestown, Massachusetts, in 1834, and the
spectacular growth in the mid-1850s of a secret political party called the

THE PHILADELPHIA RIOTS OF 1844

In the upper engraving a mob is attacking Irish Catholics; in the lower, Saint Augustine's Catholic Church is being burned to the ground by nativists. (*NC Photos courtesy of the American Catholic Historical Society of Philadelphia*)

Know-Nothings attracted the widest attention. But other less publicized anti-Catholic activity flared up sporadically throughout the young American republic. Catholic churches were damaged, priests were harassed, and Catholics were discriminated against in public institutions and excluded from some state offices. Lurid "No-Popery" publications, the most famous being *The Awful Disclosures of the Hotel Dieu Nunnery of Montreal* by Maria Monk (1836), streamed from the presses.

There is no easy explanation for the intensification of nativist bigotry during this era. To indict blind hatred, as many Catholics did, begs the question. It was only when Catholicism threatened established ways of life that nativism became widespread. And the "Romish" Church did become more imposing. A minuscule institution at the turn of the nineteenth century, it mushroomed after 1830. Churches, for example, multiplied from eighty in 1808 to more than 200 in 1830 and almost 2,400 by 1860.

This hitherto insignificant institution, now gaining in strength and influence, confronted an American society which, though theoretically secular, was actually permeated with Protestant values and customs. Protestantism, in fact, was considered essential to republicanism. When Catholics exerted pressure to gain respect for their creed in the army, the public schools, and other governmental institutions, they stirred up beehives of nativist resentment. The 1844 Philadelphia riots, for instance, were ignited by a local attempt by Catholics to have their children excused from compulsory reading of the Protestant Bible in the public schools. The Know-Nothing movement of the 1850s arose, in part, from a widespread Catholic crusade to acquire state funds for parochial schools.

Immigration, which accounted for most of the Church's growth, compounded anti-Catholic nativism. The American Church found the most controversial of the pre-Civil War newcomers, the Irish, within its fold. These Hibernians, who arrived by the hundreds of thousands in the 1840s and 1850s (especially after the famine in their native land), antagonized established society by clustering together in the cities, filling local jails, and utilizing public welfare institutions in disproportionately high numbers, voting in political blocs, working for low wages, and maintaining an irritating identification with the fortunes of the "old sod." Orestes Brownson, though a convert to Catholicism, reflected Yankee sentiments when he referred to the Irish as the "most drunken, fighting, thieving, lying and lascivious class of our population." Animosity toward Celts blended with that toward Catholics, and the "Irish Papists" became the prime targets of pre-Civil War nativism.

Nativism also drew sustenance from psychological factors buried deep in the spirit of the age. Strife and dislocation grew in the pre-Civil War decades as the country urbanized rapidly and as it fought a divisive war with Mexico and acquired gigantic stretches of new territory, thus raising the emotional question of the future of slavery in the West. What was happening to the older, simpler America? Into this unstable picture marched unprecedented hordes of foreign-born with their alien customs and religion. Many Northern reformers also objected to the Celtic immigrants because the latter opposed the abolition and temperance movements. Here, indeed, were perfect scapegoats. Restrict their influence, it was thought, and American society could be restored.

These various forces converged most completely in the middle 1850s, resulting in the creation of the Know-Nothing (or American Party) movement. At its core Know-Nothingism was a secret society dedicated to the exclusion of Catholics from all public offices. Startling outsiders with their ability to organize electoral victories clandestinely, the Know-Nothings and their allies soon controlled about seventy-five Congressional seats and a half-dozen state houses, and they were looking confidently toward the 1856 presidential election.

The American Party vanished almost as rapidly as it had appeared. Always a minority, soon riven by internal dissent and humiliated by ineffectiveness in office, the organization dwindled rapidly after 1855, as the slavery issue superseded all other political considerations.

Pre-Civil War nativism left no significant legislation on the statute books, but it did make its mark on American history. It forced Catholics, especially immigrants, to define their attitude toward America. Despite some bitterness, most responded with affirmations of loyalty (although a certain "siege mentality" in religious matters gained strength—evidenced, notably, in the proliferation of parochial schools). At the same time, Catholics invoked the Constitution in support of their claims, and they lined up votes in local elections. Among natives prejudice persisted. Yet, the more thoughtful, surveying the ashen ruins of St. Augustine's and similar scenes, reflected on the chasm between American ideals and practice.

From all this, the notion that the United States was a "Protestant nation" received an irreversible shock, and some discriminatory barricades began to fall. Thus American institutions edged a bit closer to the promise of the founding fathers.

RECOMMENDED READING: Ray Allen Billington, *The Protestant Crusade, 1800–1860* (New York: Rinehart & Company, 1952). Michael Feldberg, *The Philadelphia Riots of 1844. A Study of Ethnic Conflict* (Westport, Connecticut: Greenwood Press, 1975).

DR. HUESTON is an assistant professor of history at the University of Scranton, Pennsylvania.

27

Catholic Children and Bible Reading in Nineteenth-Century Public Schools

VINCENT P. LANNIE

It was spring, 1859, and the city of Boston was in a state of tension. A court case over the use of the Bible in the public schools was in progress, and it drove Protestants and Catholics into opposite camps. A great deal was at stake, and both sides knew it.

The Boston public schools required that all pupils read the Protestant King James Bible and recite Protestant prayers and hymns. Catholic parents objected and insisted that their children be excused from such devotional exercises. Some even forbade their children to take part in them. One Catholic youngster, Thomas J. Wall, obediently following the wishes of his father and parish priest, was beaten unmercifully for refusing "to join the religious exercise of repeating the Protestant version of the Ten Commandments as found in the King James Bible."

The boy's parents brought suit against the teacher, McLaurin F. Cook, charging that he had maliciously beaten their child with a heavy rattan stick. In its decision, the court ruled that no injustice had been done because as soon as the child complied with the law, the punishment ceased. Any other view, argued the court, would undermine the power of the state and subject the will of the majority to the conscience of the minority. This verdict made it possible for school authorities to force Catholic children to read the Protestant Bible, and it remained the leading case on the subject for much of the nineteenth century. The severity of the Boston case was unique, but Protestant-Catholic disagreement over public school Bible read-

CARTOONS BY THOMAS NAST DEPICTING THE ALLEGED HOSTILITY
OF CATHOLICS TO THE BIBLE

These drawings illustrate the book *Miss Columbia's Public School* by
Charles Henry Pullen (New York, 1871). (*Courtesy of the Mullen Memorial
Library of the Catholic University of America*)

ing remained constant in America for many decades preceding and following the Civil War.

Most Americans favored religion in the public schools. But since the country was religiously pluralistic, educators opted for a nondenominational Christianity in schools by using the Bible without note or comment. In practice, however, this nondenominational Christianity emerged as nondenominational Protestantism, for the Bible employed in the schools was usually the Protestant King James Version. Catholics denounced this formula as nothing more than a Protestant basis for public education and prohibited their children from reading the King James Bible.

Catholics emphasized, however, that they did not oppose the Bible in the public schools nor the use of the King James Version for Protestant children. They simply wanted Catholic children excused from reading a biblical version not authorized by their Church. Even when the Catholic Douay Bible was not allowed (it always included notes and comments), some bishops accepted the situation so long as Catholic children were not forced to participate. They felt that this request was a matter of fair play and involved no special concessions. Would not Protestant parents likewise object to the use of the Catholic Bible for their children? Of course they would and with good reason.

Catholics rarely succeeded in getting this point across to their Protestant fellow citizens, however. Perhaps they never could have in a nonecumenical century that featured frequent occurrences of Protestant-Catholic animosity.

Most Protestants viewed America as a Protestant country with a Protestant educational heritage. In their view, since the public schools prepared children for their moral, social, and civic responsibilities, those schools were in a unique position to inculcate the religious and political principles that gave birth and sustenance to this Protestant nation. This did not mean that the schools should admit sectarian creeds in their instruction. But the Bible, a religious and patriotic symbol of the highest order, incorporated those moral and spiritual lessons necessary for the pupils' proper conduct in an American Protestant republic. Since all Christians believed in the Bible in one way or another, it was important that the future citizens of this country come to understand and respect its message.

The Bible was the word of God and needed no annotations to explain its meaning, the Protestants felt. The King James Version, therefore, was not sectarian since it contained the essence of the Christian faith and not papist superstition. Indeed, Protestants conjectured that the attack on the King James Version was nothing more than a Jesuitical ruse by Catholics who wished to exclude the Bible completely from public schools. Large numbers of usually tolerant Americans were thus aroused and felt compelled to stand firm in opposition to Catholic demands over the Bible.

And firm they stood. Bloody riots broke out in New York, Philadelphia, and other cities over Bible reading in the public schools. Catholic teachers were threatened with dismissal if they hesitated to "read the Protestant Bible to their pupils" and some were actually fired. Some Catholic children were whipped before the class for refusing to read the King James Bible (the Boston incident was just the most outrageous); others were kept after school as punishment; in still other cases, teachers humiliated Catholic pupils in front of their fellow students because of their religious faith and ethnic background. Try as they did, Catholics were never able to convince the Protestant majority of their legitimate objections.

Attempts to minimize Protestant-Catholic friction by eliminating public school Bible reading drew the wrath of both religious groups. Protestants viewed such action as detrimental to American society and religion, while Catholics judged that Protestant public schools were being transformed into secularist and godless institutions.

Within this religiously hostile milieu, many Catholic clergymen concluded that the ultimate purpose of public schools was to undermine and destroy the religious faith of Catholic children. It was not long before they abandoned public education and made strenuous efforts to establish diocesan parochial school systems. Many bishops decreed that schools should be built before churches, and in 1884 at the Third Plenary Council of Baltimore the Catholic hierarchy legislated the parochial school system as an indispensable part of American Catholicism. Bishops, priests, and laity got on the parochial school bandwagon, and it set the course for Catholic educational endeavors for the rest of the nineteenth century and the first half of the twentieth.

RECOMMENDED READING: Vincent P. Lannie, *Public Money and Parochial Education. Bishop Hughes, Governor Seward, and the New York School Controversy* (Cleveland: Press of Case Western Reserve University, 1968). Robert H. Lord, John E. Sexton, and Edward T. Harrington, *History of the Archdiocese of Boston in the Various Stages of Its Development, 1604 to 1943* (3 vols.; New York: Sheed & Ward, 1944).

VINCENT P. LANNIE is professor of education in the University of Notre Dame and editor of the *Notre Dame Journal of Education*. The field of his special interest is the history of American Catholic education.

28

Alphabet of Hate: The APA and the KKK

JOHN L. MORRISON

It began in Pulaski, Tennessee, when half a dozen young men, ex-Confederate officers, decided to have some "fun." Donning ghostly disguises, they rode around town at night frightening the newly freed slaves. They called themselves the Ku Klux Klan, taking their name from the Greek word "kuklos" or circle.

Their idea spread rapidly throughout the South. It was one way to defend the old social order that was being turned upside down by the "Radical" Republicans in Congress. The Radicals had imposed Carpetbagger-Scalawag-Negro governments on the former Confederate states. Those Radical regimes, many felt, must be resisted if Southern "civilization" were to be preserved.

In April, 1867, the Klan convened in Nashville to adopt a constitution and elect General Nathan Bedford Forrest as its first imperial wizard.

The Klan's preferred tactic was terror, directed against blacks who supported the Radical regimes by voting or joining the Union League. White-sheeted night riders, surrounding the cabin of a black family, chanted:

> Niggers and Leaguers, get out of the way
> We're born of the night and we vanish by day
> No rations have we but the flesh of man
> And love niggers best, the Ku Klux Klan.
>
> We catch 'em alive and roast 'em whole
> And hand 'em around with a sharpened pole
> Whole Leagues have been eaten, not leaving a man
> And went away hungry, the Ku Klux Klan.

When terror tactics failed, the Klan did not hesitate to use violence against its enemies. Murder and mutilation literally drove blacks into hiding, espe-

A Demonstration of the Ku Klux Klan

This photograph was taken at a gathering of the Klan in Beckley, West Virginia, on August 9, 1924. (*Library of Congress*)

cially on election day. Although strong federal action finally crushed the Klan, its methods had succeeded in "redeeming" the South from Radical Reconstruction by 1877. The Klan became a legend. It was accepted as the savior of white civilization, the heroic defender of Southern rights.

The South was not the only section affected by the legend. In the 1890s it was Midwestern farmers who found their way of life threatened as a depression, the Panic of 1893, devastated the economy of the upper Mississippi Valley. The farmers promptly formed a secret organization.

The American Protective Association, founded in Clinton, Iowa, ascribed America's troubles, particularly the Panic, to papal plots. Led by the astute William J. Traynor, the APA capitalized on a surge of anti-Catholic sentiment and launched a massive membership drive. By 1896 the APA had enlisted 2,500,000 members, for whom it published an *APA Magazine* and some seventy weekly newspapers. The APA press opposed the growth of parochial schools, criticized federal grants to the Bureau of Catholic Indian Missions, and circulated anti-Catholic tales.

Political action, however, represented the great hope of the APA. In 1894 it promoted the election of Republican candidates in five states; in Michigan it sent one of its own, William S. Linton, to Congress.

Unhappily for the APA, its triumphs were illusory. Courageous denunciation of the organization by Protestant leaders and the return of prosperity in 1896 weakened its appeal. Above all, the election of President William McKinley, who had refused APA support, proved fatal.

The legacy of Klan and APA combined to produce a second Ku Klux Klan in the 1920s. Spawned by D. W. Griffith's sensational motion picture *The Birth of a Nation* and by the fraternal salesmanship of its founder, Colonel William J. Simmons, the new Klan was above all else an anti-Catholic organization. To be sure, it retained its anti-Negro bias and even added Jews, aliens, and communists to its enemies list. As Alabama's Grand Dragon put it, the Klan represented those who hated "niggerism, Catholicism, Judaism, and all the isms of the whole world."

But Catholicism ranked first among the hatreds of the Klan, which professed alarm over increasing immigration from Slavic and Mediterranean areas. Scottish Rite Masons, Orange Lodges, Baptists, Methodists, and Disciples of Christ were all mainstays of Klan membership, drawn by fear of the alien Catholic.

Only rarely did Klan spokesmen go so far publicly as did Oregon's Exalted Cyclops, who said that "the only way to cure a Catholic is to kill him." Formally, at least, the Klan campaigned for quasi-respectable legislation against Catholic education and marriage practices. It supported bills to close parochial schools and make public school attendance compulsory; it tried to gain control of local school boards; and it introduced legislation to forbid prenuptial pledges promising Catholic training for children born of mixed marriages.

Behind the Klan's public program lay a systematic propaganda effort against Catholicism, much of it scurrilous, all of it absurd.

In North Manchester, Indiana, an overwrought Klan speaker warned the populace that the Pope "may even be on the northbound train tomorrow! He may! He may! Be warned! Prepared! America is for Americans!" The next morning more than a thousand citizens met the train. A ladies' corset salesman, the only passenger who got off, had a hard time convincing the hostile crowd that he was not the Pope in disguise.

In Detroit, Wesley Hiram Evans, Simmons' successor as Imperial Wizard, warned the hooded faithful that the Pope had planned a St. Bartholomew's Day Massacre for the city. But, he assured them, they had nothing to fear. He would send trainloads of Klansmen to ensure that oceans of Catholic blood would run down Woodward Avenue.

In Colorado, Klan rallies usually featured a former nun, Sister Mary Angel. Her lectures, "for men only," told tales of convent sin, climaxed when she displayed little gingham bags made to order "to convey the fruits of priestly lust to the furnaces."

It was gospel among Klan believers that:

—Presidents Lincoln, Garfield, McKinley, and Harding were all assassinated by order of the Knights of Columbus.

—The Knights of Columbus oath required members to promise to "hang, burn, boil, flay, and bury alive" all non-Catholics.

—When a male child was born to a Catholic family, the father donated a rifle and ammunition to his local church.

—The Pope had purchased the militarily strategic points overlooking West Point and the District of Columbia.

—Ninety percent of the deserters in World War I were Catholics.

Such irrationality inspired numerous acts of Klan violence. It also brought profit and power. To a great extent, the Klan was run by its Imperial Kleagle, Edward Young Clarke, and his associate, Mrs. Elizabeth Tyler. They sent out an army of lesser kleagles to recruit new members, sell official Klan regalia, and peddle Klan publications. At ten dollars a head for each recruit, and a membership that approached three million by 1924, this was big business.

The power of the Klan was great but short-lived. It was wrecked by changing times and battered by scandals. Clarke and Mrs. Tyler were arrested in a house of ill fame. The Indiana Grand Dragon, the Klan's most powerful political figure, was convicted on a murder charge. Membership fell to 30,000 by 1930, and all later attempts to recoup Klan fortunes have failed.

RECOMMENDED READING: David M. Chalmers, *Hooded Americanism. The History of the Ku Klux Klan* (New York: Doubleday & Company, 1965; Chicago: Quadrangle Books, 1968). Donald L. Kinzer, *An Episode in Anti-Catholicism: The American Protective Association* (Seattle: University of Washington Press, 1964).

DR. MORRISON is professor of history at Mt. St. Mary's College in Emmitsburg, Maryland.

SAINT MARY'S FEMALE SCHOOL, VINCENNES, INDIANA

The Sisters of Charity from Emmitsburg, Maryland, opened a boarding and day school on a different site in Vincennes in 1838 under the name of Saint Mary's Female School. The Sisters of Providence of Saint Mary-of-the-Woods took charge of it in 1843, and the location was changed at the same time to the two-story yellow brick building with the smaller frame house adjoining shown in this drawing; the school remained here until 1848. (Drawing by Sister Georgiana from oral traditions, printed in *The History of the Sisters of Providence of Saint Mary-of-the-Woods* by Sister Mary Borromeo Brown [New York, 1949])

29

The Rise of Catholic Schools

HAROLD A. BUETOW

The marvel of the world, the unique contribution of a group to their country, and the very best of the American heritage are all represented in United States Catholic schools. The statement of the Massachusetts Code of 1648 that "the good education of children is of singular benefit to any Commonwealth" applies in ways beyond the $12 billion or so of current financial investment in Catholic schools, the 5 million students now enrolled, and the money contributed and young people schooled in the past.

Catholic schools have been of benefit, first of all, to their students— especially those whom the Bible called the *anawim*—minority groups, the poor, immigrants, and the handicapped. St. Mary's school, established at Philadelphia in 1781, possibly the first parochial school in the English colonies, represents in microcosm what has happened to much of Catholic urban education: Originally small, independent, and isolated, it is now an "inner city" school with most of its pupils the underprivileged who are bussed from surrounding areas.

Catholic schools, according to sociological studies, influence their students' behavior significantly in church attendance, religious knowledge, ethical attitudes, tolerance, and—in a society with strong temptations to despair— hopefulness. Our country will always need those "great-souled persons" of whom the Second Vatican Council spoke and whom Catholic schools try to form. And if the fundamental axiom is true that God's helping grace builds upon nature without contradicting it, good schooling must always add to such other important educational influences as home, peer group, and television.

The truth of Henry Adams' words that "a teacher affects eternity" was corroborated by the prestigious study of James S. Coleman in 1966, which asserted that one of the most needed teacher qualities is dedication. Catholic school teachers have had a unique measure of this quality. Their training has put them in a close seesawing race with their counterparts elsewhere. Many religious communities provided teacher training almost twenty years before the first public normal school opened; by their community life they also offered daily opportunities for growth through exchanges of experience and advice, and they often met demands for innovative techniques.

Laity were teaching in Catholic schools from earliest times. Even in the face of hostile legislation in colonial Maryland, complaints reached England that "popish" schoolmasters were teaching children. At St. Peter's Free School in New York the teachers were exclusively lay persons from the beginning to 1831. Lay teachers also staffed six of the first seven schools founded between 1800 and 1860 in Savannah, and schools in other widely separated places. Although most have remained anonymous, they demonstrated that it is not the number of religious that makes a school Catholic, but dedication to Catholic goals. Mid-nineteenth-century Catholic preference for religious over lay teachers for economic as well as apostolic reasons began to change with World War I, more rapidly after World War II, and with a quickened pace after the Second Vatican Council.

Catholic school teachers' sacrifices are noteworthy. Salary and other benefits almost never rewarded them equally with other schools. Most teaching sisters faced a shortage of vocations, traveled to Europe to recruit money and personnel, and sometimes tramped this country, two by two, begging. Often they took on such outside work for support as laundering and were prey to the personal problems brought on by overwork. Frequently they undertook long journeys that gave second thoughts even to strong men, and they unhesitatingly allowed their dedication to carry them into border warfare and to work among people sometimes described as backward, mean, and narrow-minded. They set up their schools, especially in the westward movement, in log cabins, church basements, sacristies, choir lofts, rectory and convent rooms, and abandoned buildings (including, in one instance at least, a still).

The teachers' contributions to the nation as well as to the Church were prodigious. First coming when this country was, on the whole, culturally deprived, they brought learning in many disciplines. Besides preventing religious illiteracy, they provided a cultural enrichment and quality of life most beneficial to society at large.

To the question "Why?" some answer that the whole purpose was to preserve the faith in a hostile atmosphere. But it was more positive than that. Always fulfilling the observation of Daniel Webster that "whatever makes men good Christians, makes them good citizens," Catholic schools tried to introduce youth to Jesus as a model for their lives. Some type of personal formation is a goal of all schools, as the 1951 statement of the National Education Association and the American Association of School Administrators admitted when it asserted that "the development of moral and spiritual values is basic to all other educational objectives." In the midst of ever increasing secularism Catholics have found their mode of formation to be singularly consonant with the Christian ideals that characterized colonial America, inspired the Declaration of Independence, and sustained the early Republic.

In "secular subjects," Catholic-school achievement has been at least on a par with, and sometimes superior to, others,. But the Catholic-school curriculum has made its greatest contribution in its inclusion of religious-based values. Thomas Paine's *Common Sense* observed as far back as 1776 that "when we are planning for posterity, we ought to remember that virtue is not hereditary." The Ordinance of 1787 pointed to its order of curriculum priorities when it remarked that "religion, morality and knowledge being necessary to good government and the happiness of mankind, schools and the means of education shall ever be encouraged." William James in 1890 spoke of "the hell we make for ourselves in this world by habitually fashioning our characters in the wrong way." With our rising crime rate at ever-decreasing age levels, our times substantiate the wisdom of the past.

There have been many instances from colonial times to the present in which state, society, and church have cooperated in schooling. These have included the "public-parochial" school—church schools which, through the amicable agreement of civil and ecclesiastical authorities, have been incorporated into local school districts; religious communities or local parishes own and run the schools, for which the civic community pays all costs. Their participants have found "singular benefit" for all: government, church, youth, parents, administrators, and teachers.

While no school is really "nonpublic" or "private"—all affecting the public weal—what are called "nonpublic" schools have provided not divisiveness but needed diversity. America's need of the school for "melting pot" homogenization, if ever present, has for a long time been superseded by modern means of communication and transportation which take people out of their isolated and isolating physical or mental valleys. And the addition of a nonpublic pattern has helped to avoid such dangers as lack of challenge, megalithic and monolithic structures, decreased experimentation and innovation, and creeping "Big-Brotherism." What the United States has contributed to the history of the world in religion (pluralism) and in business (anti-trust), it does not seem to have learned in education (anti-monopoly).

RECOMMENDED READING: Harold A. Buetow, *Of Singular Benefit: The Story of Catholic Education in the United States* (New York: Macmillan Company, 1970). *Catholic Education in America. A Documentary History*, edited by Neil G. McCluskey, S.J. (New York: Bureau of Publications, Teachers College, Columbia University, 1964).

FATHER BUETOW is a professor of education in the Catholic University of America and program director of Foundations of Education.

GEORGETOWN COLLEGE

This original building was first opened to students in 1791. The drawing is printed in *Memorial of the First Centenary of Georgetown College, D.C.,* by John Gilmary Shea (New York, 1891).

30

Catholic Education in the United States:

Starting at the Top

EDWARD J. POWER

Catholic education in the United States, following a trail blazed by colonial predecessors, started at the top—with colleges and seminaries—and
worked its way down the scholastic ladder.

When we look for the first signs of Catholic education we see mixed
schools: places that either were or wanted to be both colleges and seminaries. This mixed-school aspiration lived for decades and was abandoned
only after the inability of a school to blend secular college study with professional theological training became clear.

Young men entering an early Catholic college (for example: Georgetown,
St. Mary's of Baltimore, Spring Hill in Alabama, Mount St. Mary's in Emmitsburg, Saint Louis, Fordham, Villanova, Holy Cross, Notre Dame, and
St. Vincent) between 1786 and 1850 were mostly Catholics from families
of social and economic substance. With few exceptions, their motives for
study were broadly professional. Though they were similar in these respects,
they differed from one another principally in age and academic foundation. Some were just little boys barely able to read while others, in their
late teens, possessed a respectable background in schooling. All, however,
were classified as college students. The disciplinary code of the college—
and more often than not the curriculum, too—applied to everyone without
dispensation or exception.

The college movement started in the colonies with the founding of
Harvard (1636), and so the first Catholic college, Georgetown (1786), was
not sailing entirely uncharted waters. In company with colonial colleges
preceding them, Catholic colleges adopted the prevailing philosophy that

education should be religious in content and purpose. They were different, however, insofar as they only prepared students for the seminary, whereas Protestant colleges were really theological schools or seminaries.

A course of study believed to be best suited to seminary preparation and entirely compatible with the current educational practice was classical. To master the Latin and Greek languages and their ancient literatures required considerable time and effort, and so the conventional college course was seven years.

In these seven years, with few vacations and only limited distractions for leisure, sport, and fun, students followed what today amounts to a high school and a college course of study. The curricular model was inspired by the Jesuit philosophy and practice of education even when the college was not under Jesuit control because in Europe Jesuits enjoyed a two-century reputation for scholastic excellence.

These early college students were unfamiliar with the class nomenclature of today's schools. Instead of freshman, sophomore, junior, and senior, there were year-long classes in first, second, and third grammar, first and second humanities, poetry, rhetoric, and sometimes (if grammar took only two years) philosophy. Besides, students in Jesuit colleges had only one teacher —the class teacher—for their entire college course. This teacher took a beginning class of boys and stayed as its master for seven years. Upon completing the academic cycle the teacher took another class of first grammarians and the process began anew.

The educational commitment was to discipline of the mind, a theory carrying with it an assurance that a properly formed mind was capable of wrestling with the burning questions of the day. Specialization was paid no heed, and, despite the colleges' allegiance to Mother Church, special courses in religion were absent from the curriculum. The college teacher was confident of his ability to exploit the classical course, drawing from it all important religious and theological lessons, without setting religion apart for separate instruction. The only early-college departure from this practice occurred in the case of young students who needed basic catechetical training.

As long as colleges were classical schools the seven-year program remained in force, but with the erosion of the classical course shortly after the Civil War Catholic colleges began to adopt patterns of school organization they found all around them: the separate high school and the four-year college.

Along with variations in the classical curriculum—such as the addition of commercial courses and English—Catholic colleges saw the need for and began to develop separate studies in religion. It was admittedly hard to extract from non-classical studies (say, bookkeeping) a religious perspective, so for the first time religion began to be required for all students and eventually was adopted as the central and distinctive feature of the Catholic college in the United States. The assumption that separate religious instruction is a perennial characteristic of Catholic higher education is mainly historical myth.

Catholic colleges experienced some difficulty in divorcing themselves both from secondary-school studies, on the one hand, and from seminary and theological studies, on the other. Keeping seminaries and colleges close together had a practical advantage that bishops and religious superiors wanted to retain, that is, seminary students could be used as college teachers. As long as the classical course enjoyed pride of place this practice could be justified, but when the colleges began to turn away from classical tributaries to enter the mainstream of a pragmatic, fermenting society in response to their students' demands, up-to-date, practical curricula required faculty specialists, and laymen began to appear as college teachers.

In the beginning, the status of lay professors was uncertain and sometimes unenviable. Even when welcomed by clerical colleagues, laymen were often regarded as intruders by Catholic parents. The image of a Catholic school was clear and unambiguous: it was a school kept by men in Holy Orders or religious vows. These attitudes, however, did not stop the calendar: the colleges went on to broaden their programs of study and to diversify their faculties. Yet in doing so they created another problem for themselves—cost.

In the old college—Georgetown, for example, in 1820 or so—room, board, and tuition amounted to about ten dollars a year. But larger faculties —many laymen—needed to teach an expanded curriculum along with more costly materials of instruction in, say, science, with buildings to accommodate the newer features of college study, made financial costs mount. By 1850 the typical fees for room, board, and tuition were raised to about $200 a year.

Throughout most of its first century in the United States the Catholic college was a school for men; women were excluded. Catholic colleges for women and coeducation were a long way over the horizon.

Catholic colleges were affected by the example of higher schools around them and these schools were now emphasizing three new areas of study: English, science, and commerce. Catholic colleges began abandoning the principal elements of the classical course, adopting the four-year curriculum already common in other American colleges, introducing more practical courses of study, and thinking seriously about establishing programs in graduate education.

The age of the college was about to be transformed into the age of the university as a new model for Catholic higher learning was introduced with the founding of the Catholic University of America in 1884.

Recommended reading: Edward J. Power, *Catholic Higher Education in America* (New York: Appleton-Century-Crofts, 1972).

Dr. Power is professor of educational history in Boston College, Chestnut Hill, Massachusetts.

The Notre Dame Memorial Library

Catholic Higher Education:
Crisis in the Twentieth Century

PHILIP GLEASON

Catholic colleges and universities passed through a spiritual crisis in the 1960s and many of them face an economic crisis now. Although the outlook for the future is uncertain, a glance at the past may give some reason for encouragement. Catholic colleges were in serious straits when the century opened, but they came through that crisis and enjoyed a long period of relative stability and growth. About twenty years ago new strains began to show up, bringing on the new identity crisis that is still not resolved.

The first period extended from 1900 to about 1925. At that time, the difficulties were primarily organizational. Catholic colleges were badly out of step with prevailing American patterns. They had to get into line or face extinction. And a good many did go under.

Catholic collegiate education for women was just beginning and most of the men's colleges were very small. Of the eighty-four colleges for men existing in 1916, only eleven had 200 or more undergraduate students. More than a third of them had fewer than fifty collegians! Although they called themselves colleges, these places were really high schools since they depended on their preparatory departments to keep them going.

Such marginal Catholic colleges were especially weak in scientific and technical studies. Unable to compete with the growing state universities or leading private institutions, they began to lose their clientele. Increasing numbers of Catholic students turned to non-Catholic universities for higher education.

The growth of public (and Catholic) high schools and the development of accrediting associations brought the problem to a head. As the accrediting bodies developed strict standards for different levels of education, Catholic institutions had to make up their minds which they were going to be, high schools or colleges.

A number of the "colleges" did drop down to secondary level, but the stronger schools gradually eliminated their prep departments and concentrated on meeting the standards for accredited college work. The Catholic Educational Association, formed in 1904, helped mightily in this effort by bringing Catholic college people into closer contact with what was going on in the world of American higher education.

The end of World War I witnessed a rush of students into colleges and universities, a phenomenon that would recur on a larger scale after World War II. The boom in students facilitated the dropping of prep departments. As enrollments increased, Catholic colleges also had to improve their administrative machinery and modernize their curricular offerings. More systematic appeals to the alumni, often aided by success in athletic competition, helped finance these improvements.

With these developments, the period of organizational crisis shaded off into a second era, stretching roughly from 1925 to 1955. It was marked by tremendous growth—a fourteen-fold increase in enrollment between 1920 and 1950—and by a high level of self-confidence on the part of Catholic educators. Growth itself bolstered morale, but Catholics were also convinced that they had had a distinctive intellectual position which happened to be the correct one. The contemporary Catholic literary revival in Europe, and especially the revival of Scholastic philosophy represented by such men as Jacques Maritain, supported this view. These movements enhanced the intellectual prestige of Catholicism at the very time that totalitarianism and war were undermining secular liberal optimism and paving the way for a religious revival in the 1940s.

In the third era this Catholic confidence waned. Paradoxically, growth contributed now to the weakening of confidence. A Catholic university with several thousand students and a predominantly lay faculty, mostly trained in secular graduate schools, differed radically from the small liberal arts college of old. It had a different and far more skeptical spirit.

Sharp criticism of Catholic intellectual life in the mid-1950s marked the first important symptom of the coming identity crisis. Soon colleges were included with parochial schools among the "ghetto" institutions whose continued existence was challenged. As Catholic educators more and more accepted Harvard or Berkeley for models, it became increasingly difficult to specify what was distinctively Catholic about a Catholic college. When academic freedom problems erupted in the early 1960s, Catholic professors were heard to say that the expression "Catholic university" was a contradiction in terms!

The Second Vatican Council and its aftermath intensified the identity crisis. According to some of their own professors and students, Catholic institutions of higher education were outmoded structures of the past which should be abandoned. Many of their religious faculty members—priests and nuns—did leave. The confidence of those who remained, and of concerned lay professors, was badly shaken. Indeed, the old self-assurance of the past was so completely lost that it was embarrassing even to be reminded that it had ever existed. It smacked too much of triumphalism.

All this took place against a larger national background of turmoil—racial strife, war, militant protest, campus riots. Not only the Catholic university, but higher education itself was called into question.

By 1970 a semblance of calm returned, but almost immediately new difficulties arose in the area of finances. A combination of skyrocketing costs, recession, and fewer jobs for their graduates threatened to push private colleges over the brink. Indeed, the country's Official Catholic Directory recorded a decline from 292 Catholic colleges in 1970 to 245 in 1976.

The Catholic institutions of higher education that survive in 1976 have a challenging task before them. They must assimilate the teachings of the Council, the reflections of scholars in various fields, and the lived experience of recent years in order to reformulate the meaning of faith. This is a more difficult assignment than the one that confronted Catholic educators in 1900. But their courage and success should give confidence to their intellectual and spiritual descendants of the present day.

RECOMMENDED READING: *The Shape of Catholic Higher Education*, edited by Robert Hassenger (Chicago: University of Chicago Press, 1967).

DR. GLEASON is a professor of history in the University of Notre Dame.

United States
CATHOLIC MISCELLANY.

Congress shall make no law respecting an establishment of religion, or prohibiting the free exercise thereof.—Art. I. Amend. Con. United States.

VOL. I.]   CHARLESTON, WEDNESDAY, JUNE 26, 1822.   **[No. 4.**

THE FIRST CATHOLIC NEWSPAPER IN THE UNITED STATES

The first issue of the *United States Catholic Miscellany*, founded and edited by Bishop John England of Charleston, appeared on June 5, 1822. (*Buckler Studios of Charleston*)

32

The Early Years of the Catholic Press

SISTER MARY LONAN REILLY, O.S.F.

The beginnings of the Catholic press in the United States were feeble and uncertain, and the press underwent extended periods of infancy and adolescence before finally reaching maturity. This was not due to lack of dedication by those Catholics who were concerned with the printed word, but to conditions within the country.

Although America was supposedly a land of religious freedom, during the Colonial period and far into the nineteenth century intense anti-Catholic prejudices remained. Inherited from the Reformation era, they were heightened by the influx of thousands of poor German and Irish immigrants, who were seen as not only a religious threat but also a political and economic one. Leading Catholics realized some way must be found to remove the prejudices held by American Protestants and to stop this circulation of misrepresentations and calumnies of the Catholic Church. Some attempts were made to utilize public newspapers to explain Catholic doctrine and practices. These secular papers, however, felt no obligation to promote the Catholic cause—or even to treat Catholic matters justly and objectively.

The Irish, for centuries accustomed to persecution in their homeland, were among the first to arrive at a solution. In the early 1800s several papers appeared which focused attention on Catholicism and Ireland. More political than religious in content, they carried such nationalistic names as *Shamrock*, *Erin*, and the *Globe and Emerald*.

Other Catholic immigrants, especially the French and Germans in this era, also founded journals. Coming from a background different from that of the Irish, they were not so quick to use the press for the defense of their civil and religious liberties, but concentrated on news from the homeland and other items of interest to their national groups.

There was no real Catholic press as we know it today, therefore, when

Bishop John England arrived in Charleston, South Carolina, in 1820 as the first bishop of that diocese. Young, able, full of energy and vision, Bishop England had edited a paper in his native Ireland. He was distressed to find that American Protestants understood little of the Catholic faith, and at first he attempted to instruct them through the secular press. He realized very soon that this was not sufficient and decided that an independent organ was a necessity.

Although Catholics were still an insignificant minority, about one-fortieth of the population, Bishop England launched his own paper. He was confident that he could reach Americans not only in Charleston but throughout the entire country. Since no other distinctively Catholic weekly existed, it would seem that Catholics, at least, should have hurried to the support of the *United States Catholic Miscellany* when the first issue appeared on June 5, 1822.

Instead, the paper suffered financial losses and had to be suspended temporarily more than once. It probably would have been extinct within a few months had it not been for the bishop's talented sister, Johanna, who had come with him from Ireland. Not only did she spend her small fortune on the *Miscellany* and other diocesan needs, but Johanna also had much influence on the contents of the paper itself until her death in 1827.

Most of the other bishops before the Civil War did not publish their own papers but welcomed independent ones that began to emerge especially in the 1830s and 1840s to defend Catholicism as nativists added acts of violence to their customary oral and printed assaults.

By the outbreak of the Civil War more than twenty Catholic periodicals were being published. Most of them were also nationalist, serving a particular immigrant group and often more interested in news of the old country than in events in the United States. A few were edited by clergymen, but many were directed by lay editors who ran them according to their own insights and interests. There was no news service in this period, and each paper carried the distinct stamp of its editor's personality. Occasionally, these editors carried on protracted controversies with one another, and editorials often lacked discretion.

Meeting in the Second Plenary Council of Baltimore in 1866, the bishops in a pastoral letter designated lack of finances as the major cause of the shortcomings in existing Catholic journals, and they urged the faithful to support those publications. Nonetheless, they made it clear that the contents of such papers did not necessarily have the sanction of the local bishop or present his personal views.

In the last third of the nineteenth century, the Irish and Germans who had made up most of earlier Catholic immigration were joined by thousands from eastern and southern Europe. When the Third Plenary Council met in Baltimore in 1884, there were more than seven million Catholics in the country, about one-seventh of the total population. The bishops' pastoral that year recommended that each Catholic home receive at least one Catholic periodical of good repute. The reminder was timely, for numerous "Catholic" journals were being published by that date, but without ecclesiastical supervision. Sometimes when two or more papers were competing for subscribers within the same area, controversies arose between the rival editors.

By the late 1880s a new wave of nativist bigotry was sweeping the country, and Catholic lay journalists themselves began to realize that lack of cooperation in the Catholic press dissipated its energies and even weakened the entire American Catholic community at a time when it was essential that the Church be united.

When a Catholic lay congress met in Baltimore in 1889, therefore, editors and business managers from twenty-six publications met informally and selected a date for a convention of Catholic press representatives to be held the following May. An organization was formed, but it soon disappeared as did two later such groups. It was not until August of 1911 that organizational efforts were successful, and a viable Catholic Press Association was born. The purposes of the CPA as set forth in the new constitution were "the gathering and dissemination of correct information throughout the world; the spread of Catholic truth; the promotion of Catholic literature; and to further the interests of all Catholic publications."

To many Catholic journalists this gave new hope and promise for the future. Indeed there was reason to be encouraged, though not exactly in the way they thought. As a result of changing conditions, independent Catholic papers all but disappeared from the American scene shortly after World War I. The bishops supported a nationwide Catholic news service, and the official diocesan newspaper grew up. Personal journalism gave way to the American Catholic press we know today, one that is more professional and efficient, but also more uniform and less colorful.

RECOMMENDED READING: Paul J. Foik, C.S.C., *Pioneer Catholic Journalism* (New York: United States Catholic Historical Society, 1930). *The Religious Press in America*, edited by Martin E. Marty (New York: Holt, Rinehart and Winston, 1963). Sister Mary Lonan Reilly, O.S.F., *A History of the Catholic Press Association, 1911–1968* (Metuchen, New Jersey: Scarecrow Press, 1971).

SISTER MARY LONAN teaches the social, cultural, and intellectual history of the United States at the College of St. Teresa in Winona, Minnesota.

NEWMAN HALL AND SAINT BEDE'S CHAPEL AT THE UNIVERSITY
OF PENNSYLVANIA, PHILADELPHIA

The first Newman Club established in the United States was housed in these
buildings which are shown as they looked shortly after the founding in 1893.
(*Courtesy of the* Catholic Standard and Times *of Philadelphia*)

33

The Origins and Growth

of the Newman Apostolate

JOHN WHITNEY EVANS

Perhaps the best way to understand the Newman Apostolate is to start with the fact that it no longer exists. Instead, "Catholic campus ministry" flourishes in hundreds of places. Most intriguing of all, this situation represents a return to forms of pastoral care and religious education that Catholic bishops initiated in public colleges and universities in the first decade of this century.

Thus, the story of the Newman movement unfolds in three stages. The first was characterized by strong episcopal leadership aiding professors, students, and priests who organized "the chaplain movement" in state universities. Even skeptics termed this diocesan-based innovation a "new link" in the evolution of American Catholic life. It promised dynamic involvement with the emerging American university.

The second phase witnessed the rise of student associations after 1910. These sought to regain lost episcopal leadership in a period dominated by a twofold apologetic: Newman Clubs trying to defend members against sometimes hostile teachings while also trying to validate their own existence for sometimes unsympathetic churchmen. This latter effort culminated in the formation of the National Newman Apostolate in 1962.

The present stage, Catholic campus ministry, once again enjoys strong diocesan leadership. Diocesan directors, women religious, and lay persons assume increasingly important roles along with ordained chaplains. This signals a return to the dynamic pastoral engagement of the first phase and substitutes positive principles of evangelization for the defensive mood of the second.

The Newman movement had its origins at the University of Wisconsin in

1883 when Catholics, seeking social and intellectual companionship, formed the Melvin Club. Ten years later one of its members, Timothy L. Harrington, a medical student at the University of Pennsylvania, used this club as a model for the first Newman Club, which became the inspiration for the Catholic student movement that flowered after 1915.

Meanwhile, Pope Pius X in 1905 issued an encyclical letter on religious education, *Acerbo Nimis*, in which he commanded that "schools of religion" be founded in every center of higher learning that did not teach about God. The first American bishop to obey the Pope was Archbishop Sebastian G. Messmer of Milwaukee. In 1906 he appointed Father Henry C. Hengell to the University of Wisconsin as full-time chaplain and authorized the erection of a chapel and educational hall to be known as The Catholic College.

Other bishops followed his example. By 1910, seventeen dioceses had announced full-time chaplaincies that included chapels, club houses, or educational buildings. Foremost was the canonically erected campus parish at the University of Texas. Here Paulist Fathers set up accredited religion courses, and Dominican Sisters opened a women's dormitory. But soon this enthusiastic initial development ended. Members of the Catholic Educational Association claimed that the chaplain movement would destroy church colleges, undermine the Catholic University of America, and even endanger parish schools.

The bishops did not fully agree. Confronted with the issue in 1907, they refused to excommunicate parents whose children attended non-Catholic colleges. Nevertheless, the spirit of the time and questions of canon law inhibited more wholehearted involvement with Catholics in secular institutions.

For example, in the 1920s charges of "modernism" were hurled at Father John A. O'Brien's successful efforts to provide accredited religion courses for Catholics at the University of Illinois. As late as 1948 the Youth Department of the National Catholic Welfare Conference recognized the Newman Club Federation only on condition of protecting "the prior right" of Catholic colleges to offer religious education and to receive pastoral attention.

So, after 1908, when they formed the Catholic Student Association of America, Catholics in non-sectarian colleges were largely on their own. This association was a war casualty in 1918, but by then the Newman Club Federation, originally named the Federation of College Catholic Clubs, was three years old.

Foremost in this effort was Father John W. Keogh. In 1913 he became chaplain of the first Newman Club (at the University of Pennsylvania). In 1915 he became chaplain general of the new national federation, a position he held until 1937. Ceaselessly citing *Acerbo Nimis* to bishops and Cardinal Newman's example of intellectual honesty to students, Father Keogh organized more than 600 clubs and brought dozens of priests into the cause. In the 1930s he helped the Confraternity of Christian Doctrine to develop special programs for college students.

By 1950 Newman Clubs enrolled 80,000 of the 310,000 Catholics in non-Catholic colleges; Catholic institutions registered 293,000 students that year. Realizing that this statistical gap would widen and that the need for spiritual leadership would heighten, campus priests organized the National New-man Chaplains' Association. Led chiefly by Father Paul Hallinan of Cleve-land, the association joined the student federation to develop sound liturgical and educational programs.

Some officials still argued that canon law forbade bishops to finance New-man Centers because this would encourage Catholics to attend non-Catholic institutions. But Newman leaders meanwhile developed their movement so effectively that eventually former critics began to advocate its full accep-tance as a strong arm of the Church in higher education, and in 1962 the bishops mandated the National Newman Apostolate as "the work of the Catholic Church in the secular campus community."

But the years following the Second Vatican Council led the Newman movement back to its earlier inspiration. Council teachings on the Church in the modern world, collegiality, liturgy, ecumenism, and the apostolate of the laity confirmed central aims of the Newman Movement, and swept aside canonical doubts.

The rapid increase of Catholics enrolled in state universities and commu-nity colleges, the emergence of religious studies in formerly secular schools, and cooperative programs between these and Catholic colleges underlined the usefulness of Catholic campus ministry for each diocese.

Finally, decentralization of the hierarchy provided impetus for the return to original approaches. This was dramatized in 1969 when the National Newman Apostolate dissolved itself in favor of primarily diocesan-oriented effort.

Today, more than 200 diocesan directors coordinate the ministry of about 2,000 sisters, priests, and lay persons serving more than two million Catholics on the 2,500 campuses of the nation. Emphasis on liturgy, counselling, Bible study, prayer groups, retreats, and social justice sets the pattern in most places.

But now higher education is far more complex than even ten years ago. For Catholic campus ministers the harvest is great; the laborers are still too few; their financial support in many places is still inadequate. Having re-turned to its origins, the pastoral and educational mission of the Church in American post-secondary education, in a sense, is just beginning.

FATHER EVANS, who is chaplain and associate professor of history and religious studies at the College of St. Scholastica, Duluth, Minnesota, is preparing a history of the Newman movement for publication.

ARCHBISHOP EDWIN V. O'HARA

In 1923 Father O'Hara organized the first National Catholic Rural Life Conference at Saint Louis. He is shown here aboard ship in 1951 (when he was Bishop of Kansas City) returning from the first International Catholic Rural Life Conference (held in Rome), which he had helped to create and which elected him its president. (*Religious News Service Photo*)

34

The National Catholic Rural Life Conference

VINCENT A. YZERMANS

I am writing about "country boys" in American Catholic history. This is not a plea for compassion or understanding. They need none. They knew what they had in mind and were "restless pilgrims" long before the term was coined.

I refer especially to two brilliant young men who were discussing the idea of an encyclical on rural and population problems during a train ride between Fargo, North Dakota, and Spokane, Washington. The year was 1939. It was twenty years before that idea bore fruit in the great encyclical by Pope John XXIII, *Mater at Magistra*. But the important fact is that their ideas did come forth, and both of these then young men had more to do with the composition of that encyclical than they would ever admit. One was then the youngest member of the American hierarchy, Bishop Aloisius J. Muench of Fargo, and the other was pastor of a small country parish in Granger, Iowa, Monsignor Luigi G. Ligutti.

Bishop (later Cardinal) Muench and Monsignor Ligutti were only two of a long stream of "country boys" who built Catholicism in our nation. That tradition started with one of the greatest country gentlmen in American history, John Carroll of Maryland, the first bishop of the United States. Among others in this century, one needs to recall only a few of the most noteworthy names: Bishop Edwin Vincent O'Hara of Great Falls, Montana, and later of Kansas City-St. Joseph, Missouri, a product of southern Minnesota; Monsignor John A. Ryan from central Minnesota, a major pioneer in Catholic social thought; and from southern Maryland the Jesuit Father John LaFarge, a pioneer in race relations.

Such men had a common trait that made them great, their closeness to the land and the people. And it was out of this spirit that the National Catholic Rural Life Conference (NCRLC) received its impetus and became a major force in American Catholic history.

In 1920 Father Edwin Vincent O'Hara, a pastor in Eugene, Oregon, who had been studying the problems of Catholic farming families, was appointed director of the new Rural Life Bureau of the National Catholic Welfare Conference. A year later, after making a religious survey of his own county, he published a report of his findings, along with suggestions of what the Church could do, as "A Program of Rural Catholic Action." This publication became the foundation stone of the National Catholic Rural Life Movement in the United States. By 1923 he had developed the Rural Life Bureau, which was really a clearinghouse of information, to the point where it needed auxiliary organization in all parts of the country. With this purpose in mind he invited Catholic rural leaders to a meeting in St. Louis, and about eighty persons—bishops, priests, brothers, and lay men and women—heeded the call. They created the National Catholic Rural Life Conference, and Father O'Hara served as its executive secretary until he was appointed bishop of Great Falls in 1930. The fledgling organization had to contend with the indifference and scoffing of many who did not appreciate the seriousness of the problems with which it dealt or the urgency of solving them. These pioneers, nevertheless, continued to hold annual meetings for the purpose of study and discussion and of formulating and issuing statements of policy. Gradually they demonstrated to all the importance and value of their work.

The wisdom of NCRLC leaders is beginning to receive a renewed appreciation even in urban America with the concern for ecology. One dictum expressed frequently by Bishop O'Hara was simply stated: "One foot in the soil and the other foot in industry." Another dictum, popularized by Monsignor Ligutti, was: "The land to the people and the people to Christ." A former president of the NCRLC, Bishop Peter W. Bartholomé of St. Cloud, Minnesota, was fond of quoting the railroad magnate James J. Hill: "Land without people is a waste, and people without land is a mob."

No good historian of the Catholic rural life movement, however, could overlook the three most dominant contributions that the NCRLC made to our national and world culture. As a city boy who has spent most of his priesthood in rural areas, I am confident that I can register the objections many of my city cousins might raise against the NCRLC, not because of indifference but rather because of ignorance. For this reason, these three principal contributions should be recorded: the establishment of the Confraternity of Christian Doctrine (CCD), the development of the International Catholic Migration Commission, and the development of international awareness in our agricultural heartland.

I am convinced that there would be no such institutions as summer schools of religious instruction or CCD classes if the young Father Edwin O'Hara had not introduced them into his far-flung parish of Eugene, Oregon, and later, as bishop of Great Falls, Montana, throughout his diocese. The first national Confraternity Day was a part of the 1934 meeting of the NCRLC, and it was the NCRLC that urged the bishops to establish a national bishops' committee to foster CCD work. It can be readily documented that the CCD would not have the prominence it has today in the United States if it were not for the efforts of the NCRLC.

The second great contribution made by the NCRLC came under the leadership of the late Cardinal Muench. He was one of three North Dakotans who exerted, perhaps, the most vital intellectual leadership upon the conference. The other two were Bishop Vincent Ryan of Bismarck and Bishop William Mulloy, a native of the state who became bishop of Covington, Kentucky. These three, with the assistance of such men as Frank Bruce of Milwaukee, Benedictine Father Virgil Michel of St. John's Abbey in Collegeville, Minnesota, and the executive secretary of the NCRLC, Monsignor James Byrnes, in 1939 published the "Manifesto on Rural life," which is still a classic in its field. It was the leadership of Cardinal Muench and Bishops Mulloy and Ryan that held the NCRLC together in the stormy years of the 1930s.

As apostolic visitator and later nuncio to Germany, Cardinal Muench marshalled the forces of the NCRLC to aid the suffering and dying people of Germany after World War II. Knowing that the prostrate nation needed food, clothing, and money, he turned to his friends in the NCRLC and they responded. He knew, too, that the millions expelled or fleeing from the Eastern nations could not all be absorbed by a desperatey shattered West Germany. He appealed to Monsignor Ligutti, than executive director of the NCRLC, for support. Monsignor Ligutti, in turn, called upon James Norris of the Catholic Relief Services (CRS), then Monsignor Edward Swanstrom, CRS director, and Dr. Johannes Schauff, a German refugee living in Brazil. Out of this association grew the International Catholic Migration Commission, officially established by Pope Pius XII in 1951, which has performed a service for the Church and its people that eludes the confines of this article.

The third great influence of the NCRLC really centers around Monsignor Ligutti. He almost single-handedly brought the conservative heartland of the United States into the mainstream of international life. Through his work as executive director of the NCRLC from 1939 to 1960 he brought an awareness to the leaders and members of the organization that there is a Third World, a world of poverty and need where two-thirds of the people "go to bed hungry at night." Through his labors and boundless energy he instilled in seminarians, clergy conferences, and lay organizations a commitment on the part of the Church in the United States to accept responsibility for the needs of suffering mankind throughout the world.

There is one touching episode that should be related at this point. Several years ago I asked the monsignor (who now lives in Rome) where he planned to be buried. His reply was simple and direct, as are all his speeches and writings: "That's all taken care of. I plan to be buried in Granger, Iowa. On my headstone I want engraved only these few words, 'Home at last with the people I love.' "

In the bicentennial of our American Revolution, perhaps the work of the NCRLC will help us to rediscover a reverence for God's good earth. Perhaps a sense of that intimate relationship of the earthly trinity of soil, soul, and body, which is such a central part of the NCRLC's spirit, will be reawakened in American society.

RECOMMENDED READING: Raymond Philip Witte, *Twenty-Five Years of Crusading: A History of the National Catholic Rural Life Conference* (Des Moines, Iowa: The National Catholic Rural Life Conference, 1948). J. G. Shaw, *Edwin Vincent O'Hara. American Prelate* (New York: Farrar, Straus and Cudahy, 1957). Vincent A. Yzermans, *The People I Love. A Biography of Luigi G. Ligutti* (Collegeville, Minnesota: Liturgical Press, 1976).

MONSIGNOR YZERMANS, a priest of the Diocese of St. Cloud, a long-term editor in the Catholic press, and author of religious articles and books, is director of Church-related Affairs in the College of St. Thomas, St. Paul.

35

The Confraternity of Christian Doctrine

SISTER MARY CHARLES BRYCE, O.S.B.

The twentieth century may some day be referred to as the alphabet era, as the daily papers are constantly filled with stories about the FBI, IRS, NEA, AIM, NCC, and innumerable other initialed organizations. The sixteenth-century founders of the Confraternity of Christian Doctrine may not have seen any need to use an acronym, but when the Confraternity came into its own in this country nearly four centuries later—about the same time as the NRA, the SEC, and the CCC appeared—it became known as the CCD. The brevity of its initials, however, is not the measure of its influence on Roman Catholics in this country.

The CCD began in Italy in the years immediately following the Council of Trent, and it was strongly promoted by Pope Pius X at the beginning of this century. But it gained official recognition in the United States only in 1934, when the National Catholic Rural Life Conference (NCRLC) featured a "Confraternity Day" as part of the program at its annual meeting. The event had been suggested by Archbishop John Gregory Murray of St. Paul, who was the host of the meeting. He was not the first to promote the CCD, however, for by then diocesan and parochial units existed in nineteen dioceses, and for several years their leaders had been seeking recognition and coordination of efforts.

The NCRLC, which was in its heyday in the 1930s, had long recognized the particular need for religious education in rural America. Unlike their urban coreligionists, Catholics in many areas of the agricultural heartland were separated from one another by distance and served by few parochial schools. They deeply felt the need for some kind of formal instruction. The NCRLC understood what the CCD was trying to do and supported it wholeheartedly. In 1934 the time seemed ripe for bringing the fragmented efforts into a vibrant, unified movement with its own identity.

A Religious Vacation School

This class was sponsored by the parish unit of the Confraternity of Christian Doctrine of Saint Martin's Church in Washington, D.C., in 1959 and was conducted by a Sister of Charity. (*Courtesy of the Department of Archives and Manuscripts of the Catholic University of America*)

The 1934 Confraternity Day ended by addressing a formal petition to the national hierarchy requesting an episcopal committee which would have the express task of fostering and promulgating the work of the CCD in the United States. Later that same month, at the annual meeting of the National Catholic Welfare Conference, the bishops approved the plan, naming Bishop Edwin V. O'Hara of Great Falls, Montana, the committee's first chairman. About the same time Pope Pius XI directed the hierarchies in all countries to establish diocesan and national offices to promote, support, and coordinate the work of the CCD.

Thus one of the first actions of the episcopal committee was to give official recognition to a National Center for Religious Education—CCD. The center was first headed by Benedictine Father Francis A. Walsh (1934–1938). Among its other early heads were Father Stephen A. Leven, later to become bishop of San Angelo, Texas, and Sulpician Father Joseph B. Collins, who served from 1941 to 1967.

The success in organizing a national CCD office was the culmination of thirty-two years of sporadic and widely scattered efforts by dedicated Catholics. Besides the NCRLC, other groups and individuals made important contributions to this movement.

In 1902 the parish of Our Lady of Good Counsel in New York City organized this country's first CCD unit, an inter-parochial chapter. Like many subsequent units, it owed its origin to a small number of lay persons who were concerned about the low level of Christian knowledge prevalent among adults and children, especially pupils in public schools. Charter members had participated in a training program for catechists held during the winter of 1901–1902 at a Catholic settlement house in the metropolitan area. Interest and zeal grew apace. An annual training program sponsored by the settlement house prepared catechists and helped to increase the number of able teachers. In 1909 a diocesan CCD congress furthered the cause.

By 1913 the movement that had started at Good Counsel reached beyond the few neighboring parishes and created a vigorous foundation, the Theta Pi Alpha. This organization was formed by a small number of Catholic principals and teachers in public schools to provide after-school-hours religious instruction for Catholic children attending public schools. Cardinal John Farley approved and encouraged the new society, and it grew in numbers and activities. By 1929 Theta Pi Alpha counted more than 3,000 teachers among its members.

The beginnings of the CCD are also rooted in the ministry to immigrants. In 1908 three lay teachers began providing Christian instruction for the mostly foreign-born Catholics in the mining districts around Pittsburgh. Their ministry mushroomed, and by 1919, 500 teachers were involved in 153 schools of religion in the area. More than 13,000 children and adolescents were enrolled in their classes.

Inspired by the work of the CCD in Pittsburgh, in 1922 Miss Verona Spellmire, a public school teacher and a volunteer in the Los Angeles Catholic Charities office, initiated a similar project for Spanish-speaking inhabitants of her city. The idea caught on. By the end of 1923, 150 teachers were involved and Bishop John J. Cantwell's hearty approval and blessing encouraged the movement.

From 1921 to 1930 parish and diocesan CCD units sprang up across the nation. Councils were established in the dioceses of Brooklyn, Monterey-Fresno (California), Santa Fe, Boise (Idaho), Leavenworth (Kansas), Great Falls, and Sioux City (Iowa).

Early in the 1920s another arm of the CCD that would soon become a vigorous apostolate began to reach out cautiously. Father Edwin V. O'Hara, then pastor of St. Mary's Church in Eugene, Oregon, sensitive to the catechetical needs of large numbers of children in school-less parishes, organized the first parish summer vacation school in 1921. The practice spread rapidly. Within five years the NCRLC reported that vacation schools "were conducted in twenty dioceses with a total registration of 15,000 pupils."

From that point on, the natural leadership of Father O'Hara brought the Confraternity movement steadily into the foreground. Indeed, to narrate the historical growth of the CCD in this country is to write the biography of that priest and bishop. Within a year after he was appointed bishop of Great Falls in 1930, he canonically established the CCD in every parish in his diocese. Four years later, as chairman of the newly formed Episcopal Committee for the Confraternity of Christian Doctrine, he was able to co-ordinate the three major CCD outreaches: the existing parochial and diocesan units, the missionary chapters, and the vacation school movement. Furthermore, he was in a position to expand the scope of the CCD through the newly established National Center in Washington.

With the activities of the center and national episcopal backing, the CCD assumed new life. National CCD Congresses convened annually from 1935 through 1941 and periodically thereafter to share ideas and experiences. At its height the National CCD Center fostered such widely diversified programs as adult discussion groups, parent educator programs, correspondence courses, radio programs, catechetical publications, Inter-American Relations, and street preaching.

An especially notable contribution of the Confraternity to the Church in this country was its sponsorship of a new translation of the Scriptures. Catechists had long found the Douay-Rheims version difficult to use in religious instructions because of its archaic words and constructions. In January, 1936, Bishop O'Hara organized a committee of Scripture scholars and theologians to consider the possibility of a new translation of the Latin Vulgate. It was out of this group that the Catholic Biblical Association of

America was formed. In the 1940s revisions of the Douay-Rheims version began to appear, until in 1970 an entirely new translation based on the original languages was published as the *New American Bible*. It is copyrighted by the Confraternity of Christian Doctrine.

For all its long history and diverse activities, some associate the CCD exclusively with the religious education of children in public schools. Those who know only this aspect of the Confraternity are willing to abandon it in favor of some new, as yet unspecified organization or program.

A delegate at the last national CCD congress, in Miami in 1971, proposed saving the initials but changing their meaning to read, "Continuing Christian Development." Given the purpose of the Confraternity, its list of achievements, and its continuing vitality, one might argue that this is what CCD has stood for all along.

RECOMMENDED READINGS: Joseph B. Collins, *Religious Education Through the Confraternity of Christian Doctrine* (Washington: Catholic University of America Press, 1960); *The Confraternity Comes of Age*, edited by Joseph B. Collins (Paterson, New Jersey: Confraternity Publications, 1956).

SISTER BRYCE is a professor in the Department of Religion and Religious Education at the Catholic University of America, Washington, D.C.

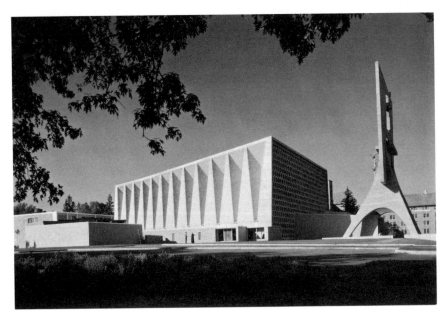

THE CHURCH OF SAINT JOHN'S ABBEY AND UNIVERSITY,
COLLEGEVILLE, MINNESOTA

Designed by Marcel Breuer and consecrated in 1961, this was the first modern church to approach the scale and majesty of the nineteenth-century
neo-Gothic cathedrals. With its form determined strictly by liturgical needs,
it was an architectural expression of the leadership that these Benedictines
had given to the liturgical movement in the United States. (*Bill Hedrich,
Hedrich-Blessing, Chicago*)

36

American Liturgical Pioneers

FREDERICK R. McMANUS

The movement for liturgical change is generally thought of as a twentieth-century phenomenon, culminating in the major reforms of Catholic
worship during the 1960s. Its pioneers and promoters are chiefly people of
this century, but the contemporary development has a kind of prehistory
in the United States during the late eighteenth century. This remote beginning is represented by the person of John Carroll (1735–1815), first
Bishop of Baltimore.

The liturgical concern of John Carroll was with what later came to be
the most striking sign of change, the use of English and other vernaculars
in the Roman liturgy. In correspondence during 1787 and 1788, Carroll,
who was then prefect apostolic, expressed views as forceful as any vernac-
ularist of later generations.

Judging it preposterous that small Eastern territories should have their
own vernacular worship while North America, Great Britain, and Ireland
had to use the unknown Latin tongue, he argued: ". . . The great part of
our congregations must be utterly ignorant of the meaning and sense of the
public offices of the Church. It may have been prudent, for aught I know,
to refuse a compliance with the insulting and reproachful demands of the
first reformers [the sixteenth-century Protestants who insisted on vernacular
liturgies]; but to continue the practice of the Latin liturgy in the present
state of things must be owing either to chimerical fears of innovation or to
indolence and inattention in the first pastors of the national Churches in not
joining to solicit or indeed ordain this necessary alteration."

Little came of these strong views of the first American bishop. It did
become the practice to read an English translation of the readings at Sunday Mass, but only after the official Latin. The effective pioneer work had
to wait for the twentieth century.

The first and perhaps greatest of the pioneers was Father Virgil Michel (1890–1938), a monk of St. John's Abbey, Collegeville, Minnesota. His principal achievement was the founding of the journal *Orate, Fratres*, now called *Worship* and now in its fiftieth year as the major liturgical publication in the English-speaking world. A priest of intense and creative energy, Father Michel set up the still flourishing Liturgical Press, edited textbooks with fresh catechetical and liturgical dimensions, and organized the first National Liturgical Day (1929)—forerunner of the Liturgical Weeks first held in 1940.

Dependent on the European roots of the liturgical movement, Virgil Michel moved far beyond its monastic and aesthetic concerns. Like his Belgian predecessor and counterpart, Dom Lambert Beaudoin, Father Michel saw the social and ecclesial implications of the liturgy. In innumerable ways but chiefly through *Worship*, he charted the course of the American liturgical apostolate. Always less a movement of reform than of growth and understanding, it had and has a twofold scope: "If the first purpose of the liturgical movement is to lead the faithful into more intimate participation in the liturgy of the Church, then the further objective must also be that of getting the liturgical spirit to radiate forth from the altar of Christ into every aspect of the daily life of the Christian" (1936).

The work of Father Michel was continued and enlarged by his successor, Father Godfrey Diekmann, another monk of Collegeville, who joined the staff of *Orate, Fratres*, in 1933 and is still its editor in chief. Diekmann, a publicist and retreat master as well as a scholar and teacher, became a prime mover in the North American Liturgical Conference during the 1940s and 1950s and an expert of the Second Vatican Council in the 1960s. For a decade, he has played a leading role in the translation of liturgical texts for the International Commission on English in the Liturgy. More than anyone else, he bridges the pastoral concerns and the spiritual, theological goals of liturgical change.

Other magazines—and other centers of scholars such as the University of Notre Dame and the Catholic University of America—had great contributions to make, but another of *Worship's* many writers deserves mention. This is the altogether unique H. A. Reinhold (1897–1968), a diocesan priest who came to the United States in 1936 as a refugee from Germany. A man of mild, gentle, generous spirit, he wrote with caustic fervor about the need for reform. Like Father Michel, his concerns were never limited to sanctuary liturgy: mysticism, the needs of society, politics, the arts, church architecture, all were integrated into the "Timely Tracts,' which appeared in *Worship* for a generation. Articles and books spelled out, for those then prepared to listen, specific reforms needed for the liturgy.

No one should minimize the dependence of these leaders upon the German and French liturgical movements, nor should anyone exaggerate the impact of their writings. Until the Constitution on the Liturgy (1963), neither papal encyclicals nor Roman directives had any wide impact upon the liturgy in America; much less did the writings and efforts of the pioneers stir up a mass movement. One whose influence was widespread, however, was Father Gerald Ellard, S.J. (1894–1963). With a background in scientific liturgical studies, Ellard became a textbook author and his book, *Christian Life and Worship*, influenced thousands of Catholic college students after its publication in 1941. He was a reformer, too, and his *Mass of the Future* (1948), like Reinhold's *Bringing the Mass to the People* (1960), helped to enlarge the numbers who appreciated the depth and breadth of the liturgical apostolate, as it was then called.

For a movement which had strong beginnings in liturgical music, the major pioneers in this facet of the field were fewer, perhaps because there is a dichotomy between professional music and popular liturgy as well as a necessary integration of the two. But in putting the arts and architecture at the service of worship, one name stands out, Maurice Lavanoux (1894–1974). For the forty years of its existence, he edited the quarterly, *Liturgical Arts* (1931–1972), a magazine the equal of any of its kind throughout the world. At times more appreciated by non-Catholics than by his fellow Catholics, Lavanoux was persevering and untiring in his commitment to the arts. Like the other pioneers, he was open to growth and change; in his last years he was as ebullient and as deeply dedicated as ever.

If the liturgical movement was not a universally popular success, no listing of pioneers would be complete without reference to the very many parish priests and lay leaders who translated pastoral theories into practice. One who may stand for all the others is Msgr. Martin Hellriegel of St. Louis, now pastor emeritus of Holy Cross parish in that city. A towering and impressive figure of great faith and enthusiasm, Hellriegel has been known less for his writings than for his pastoral sense and ingenuity. With strong folk piety from his native Germany, he approached every parish celebration with warmth. His influence spread through his major role at the Liturgical Weeks, his translations of German hymns, his example of parish liturgy—even in the unreformed Latin—at its best.

With the exception of Diekmann and Hellriegel, these pioneers are dead, some only recently. One of their number was Archbishop Paul Hallinan of Atlanta (1911–1968). A diocesan priest of Cleveland, engaged in the specialized work of campus ministry, Archbishop Hallinan had the same breadth of Christian commitment as Virgil Michel. In 1962, almost by accident, he was thrust forward as the only American bishop-member of the conciliar commission on the liturgy.

Archbishop Hallinan became a champion of the liturgical reform, integrating it with his strong ecclesial and social concerns. As a preacher and publicist, he was called upon to support and defend all manner of progressive causes. The liturgy was his most effective cause, and he brought to it a simple piety and deep faith. He was a cofounder of the International Commission on English in the Liturgy, and he succeeded Archbishop John Dearden of Detroit as chairman of the Bishops' Committee on the Liturgy, which had been established through the efforts of Archbishop Karl J. Alter of Cincinnati in 1958.

Paul Hallinan died too soon, his last efforts spent in resisting compromises in the post-conciliar liturgical reform. He was one of the pioneers, younger than the others selected for this sketch, but as vigorous and purposeful as any of them. To go beyond him would be to list only a long series of names, but he stands for the best because to the day of his death he never feared the future of liturgical growth and never deserted the needs of the praying people of God.

RECOMMENDED READING: Paul Marx, O.S.B., *Virgil Michel and the Liturgical Movement* (Collegeville, Minnesota: Liturgical Press, 1957).

FATHER McMANUS, for many years director of the secretariat of the National Conference of Catholic Bishops' Committee on the Liturgy, is professor of canon law and vice-provost and dean of graduate studies in the Catholic University of America and a member of the International Commission on English in the Liturgy.

37

Conversions in American Catholic History

JOHN TRACY ELLIS

The twice Pulitzer Prize winning playwright, Tennessee Williams, a convert to Catholicism? "Impossible" may well have been the reaction of more than the fans of *A Streetcar Named Desire* when they heard the news in 1969.

For some that event may have become more credible on the score of what the financial expert, John Moody, himself a convert, once remarked: "The general public . . . finds it difficult to understand converts, unless the latter are authors." Authorship may, indeed, lend a certain plausibility, but with the general decline of religious interests since the 1960s, even an author's conversion may present a puzzle to those who stop to think about it at all. It would not, however, puzzle Clare Boothe Luce, a convert in 1946, who declared in an interview in June, 1974: "No man can live and no society can survive for very long without a religion and a faith of some sort that explains man's nature and the meaning of his life and death."

The revolution through which of late the world has been passing has taken its toll in virtually every aspect and category of human affairs, and, except for fundamentalist groups, all organized religious bodies in the Western world—except in Africa—have seen a drop in conversions at least equal to that recorded for the Catholic Church of the United States. Here the 1959 total of 146,212 converts had by 1972 been cut almost in half, to 73,925, though the number for 1975 rose again to 80,035.

It seems generally agreed that the advance of secularism, plus the ecumenical movement of the last decade, account in part for this decline. Among the good effects of the Second Vatican Council has been the inducement for many Catholics to take a more mature attitude toward their faith, reconciling them to the fact that to many of life's ultimate questions there is no answer this side of eternity. In a word, it has helped them to learn to live

LEVI SILLIMAN IVES

He is shown here vested as the Protestant Episcopal Bishop of North Carolina. After holding that office from 1831 to 1852, he journeyed to Rome and
made a formal submission to Pope Pius IX. (*Library of Congress*)

with mystery. If they rightly conclude that the Church still has more answers to ultimate questions than any living institution, their once naive belief that she had all the answers is no longer operative.

From the dawn of European settlement on the soil of what became the United States men and women have sought answers to ultimately unfathomable questions, and in their search many have found a haven from their doubts within the Church of Rome. Their number is known to God alone, but among the earliest would have been those native Indians, relatively few in number, who responded to missionary efforts. In the course of time they were followed by the small group of New England Protestants taken to Canada as captives during the Anglo-French wars of the seventeenth and eighteenth centuries, where some remained and adopted the prevailing religious beliefs and practices of that French colony.

Nor should it be forgotten that Maryland, founded in part as a refuge for persecuted English Catholics, owed its origin to a convert, Sir George Calvert, who in becoming a Catholic about 1625 had jeopardized every material interest. Moreover, the continuance of Catholic life in Maryland, after the Puritans and later the Anglicans had seized control, depended not only on those who had been Catholics from birth but, too, on stalwart families like the Brookes and Taneys, ancestors of the Chief Justice of the United States, Roger Brooke Taney, who, once converted, remained true to their conscience despite complete civil ostracism.

Only with the Revolutionary generation, however, did distinct personalities in any number emerge among converts to Catholicism. These men and women often belonged to families of means and social prominence such as Elizabeth Bayley Seton, the first native of the future United States canonized by the Church, John Thayer of stout New England Protestant background who became a priest, and Thomas Sim Lee, governor of Maryland during the Revolution, who embraced the faith about 1800.

The previous relationship of such converts to the Church presented no set pattern. If Lee's acquaintance came originally from his devout Catholic wife, there were others who enjoyed no such gentle introduction, people whose experience was more like that of the greatest English-speaking convert of the century, John Henry Newman, who less than a year before his reception stated: "I have no existing sympathies with Roman Catholics; I hardly ever, even abroad, was at one of their services; I know none of them, I do not like what I hear of them." If some Catholics failed to edify their Protestant neighbors in the United States too or even scandalized them, there were many others who gave them inspiration and moral support. The motivation of most converts remained a matter between God, themselves, and their directors, for few have written spiritual autobiographies such as *The Trials of a Mind in Its Progress to Catholicism: A Letter to His Old Friends* (1854) by Levi Silliman Ives, formerly the Protestant Episcopal

Bishop of North Carolina, *The Path Which Led a Protestant Lawyer to the Catholic Church* (1860) by Peter H. Burnett, the first governor of California and later a member of the Supreme Court of that state, *Salve Mater* (1920) by Frederick J. Kinsman, formerly the Protestant Episcopal Bishop of Delaware, *Rebuilding a Lost Faith* (1921) by John L. Stoddard, a public lecturer, and *The Seven Storey Mountain* (1948) by Thomas Merton, the famous Trappist monk.

Limitation of space precludes anything more than a sampling here of conversions to Catholicism in the United States. For example, among the converts were fifteen members of the hierarchy—five archbishops and ten bishops. The first of these, Samuel Eccleston, was received in 1809 and died as fifth archbishop of Baltimore in 1851, and the last, Duane G. Hunt, was bishop of Salt Lake City for more than twenty-two years before his death in 1960. The most distinguished name among these prelates, however, was that of James Roosevelt Bayley, nephew of St. Elizabeth Seton, member of the family of the two Roosevelts who were Presidents, and eighth archbishop of Baltimore at his death in 1877.

A rather marked increase of conversions from around 1830 up to the Civil War prompted some to hope that the American Church might duplicate the Oxford Movement then at its height in England. The English experience was not repeated here, but it was in this same period that Isaac T. Hecker and his convert priest companions founded the Paulist Fathers, and the nationally known philosopher, Orestes Brownson, entered the Church. Somewhat akin to these writers were a number of journalists such as Jedediah V. Huntington of the *Metropolitan Magazine* and the Saint Louis *Leader*, John R. G. Hassard of the New York *Tribune*, and James A. McMaster of the *New York Freeman's Journal*, a group to which there were added in the 1930s the names of William Hard and Heywood Broun. In support of the belief that literary pursuits have often proved a ready route to Rome, there has been a relatively large representation among historians; for example, among the first twenty-five presidents of the American Catholic Historical Association (founded in 1919) nine were converts.

Now and then the conversion of an individual has led, in turn, to that of his or her family. The best-known instance is probably that of the Barbers of New Hampshire, who all followed the father, Daniel, a Protestant minister, after his conversion in 1818; one of his sons, Virgil, even became a Jesuit priest. In the next generation, and far distant from the more sophisticated settlements along the Atlantic Coast, there were conversions of a very different kind. Two men of prominence found their way into the Church amid the rough and tumultuous political life of the Oregon and California frontier. Dr. John McLoughlin, fur trader and leading official of the Hudson's Bay Company, and Peter H. Burnett (mentioned above) converted in the early 1840s with hardly any influence of the Oxford Movement, which was at its peak at that time. The same was true of the foremost convert of the period among the military, William S. Rosecrans, who entered the Church while he was a student at West Point and went on to gain fame as a general in the Civil War. In the world of sports Knute Rockne's conversion in 1925 added another honored name to the list.

Certain bishops and priests of the American Church have held a special attraction for men and women interested in the Catholic faith. Such was the case with Philadelphia's Bishop Francis Patrick Kenrick during the 1830s and 1840s, as it has been true now for almost a half-century with Archbishop Fulton J. Sheen. While Bishop Kenrick was making converts in Philadelphia, the reception of two distinguished persons in the same years in the Archdiocese of Cincinnati had notable consequences for the Church in the Middle West. Catholic life in Ohio was immeasurably strengthened by the conversion in 1842 of Reuben R. Springer, a civic leader and philanthropist, and of Sarah Worthington King Peter, daughter of an early governor of that state and United States senator, who made her profession of faith at Rome in 1854.

The listing of men and women who became Catholics in the United States presents no difficulty for the historian. It is quite another matter, however, to analyze deeper matters such as the reasons that lay behind their move, the sharp drop in conversions during the past fifteen years, and the psychological development that subsequently led some to depart Catholicism again for another communion or to lapse into unbelief. Who but God and the men in question could, for example, explain the fact that in 1849 two New York Episcopalian clergymen, John Murray Forbes and Thomas Scott Preston, entered the Catholic Church together and were ordained to the priesthood, only to have the former return ten years later to the communion of his birth, while the latter remained a Catholic priest until his death forty-two years later and even became vicar general of the Archdiocese of New York?

"The spirit blows wherever it pleases," said Jesus to Nicodemus during that night conversation long ago, and it has been blowing in the same free manner ever since. Historians can often establish some of the results in human lives, even if the deeper traces elude them.

RECOMMENDED READING: John O'Grady, *Levi Silliman Ives. Pioneer Leader in Catholic Charities* (New York: J. P. Kenedy & Sons, 1933). Sister Mary Augustine Kwitchin, O.S.F., *James Alphonsus McMaster. A Study in American Thought* (Washington, D.C.: Catholic Universty of America Press, 1949). Anna Shannon McAllister, *In Winter We Flourish: Life and Letters of Sarah Worthington King Peter, 1800–1877* (New York: Longmans, Green & Company, 1939).

MONSIGNOR ELLIS is a noted author and lecturer on the history of American Catholicism.

GENEVIEVE GARVAN BRADY MACAULEY

Born at Hartford, Connecticut, in 1884, and graduated from Manhattan-
ville College of the Sacred Heart, she married Nicholas F. Brady, a financier
and business leader, in 1906. Together they supported many charitable undertakings over the years. When her husband died in 1930, he left her
$12,000,000 with which she continued the benefactions to Catholic organiza-
tions. She founded the Carroll Club in New York as a social, recreational,
and cultural center for young business women and served as its director and
president. Prominent in civic as well as religious circles, Mrs. Brady was
chairman of the Board of the Girl Scouts of America and president of the
World Council of Girl Scouts. She organized the National Women's Committee of the Welfare and Relief Mobilization to alleviate the distress of the
poor and unemployed during the worst winter (1932–1933) of the Great
Depression. She was decorated by the Belgian and French governments for
her relief work during World War I, and she was made a papal duchess by
the Holy See as well as a Dame of Malta and a Dame of the Holy Sepul-
chre; she also received *Pro Ecclesia et Pontifice* medals from Popes Pius X
and Pius XI. In 1937 she married William J. Babington Macauley, the Irish
Minister to the Holy See, and thereafter lived in Rome, where she died the
following year. Catholic institutions were the main beneficiaries of her
estate. (*Courtesy of the Novitiate of Saint Isaac Jogues, Wernersville,
Pennsylvania*)

38

Catholic Philanthropy:

Building the New American Church

JOHN TRACY ELLIS

"He was the most adroit, suave and noiseless man that American finance has ever known." Such was the description of Thomas Fortune Ryan (d. 1928), a Catholic philanthropist, by an associate who had every reason to know, William C. Whitney, transit entrepreneur and scion of a family famous in the financial annals of the United States. If the acquisition of personal fortunes by most American millionaires has not, typically, been "noiseless," sizable donations to charitable causes by many Catholic philanthropists have frequently been of that pattern. John W. Mackay (d. 1902), Dublin-born member of San Francisco's Irish Big Four who made their millions in the Comstock Lode, was such a man. No true estimate of his benefactions—and he was by far the most generous of the four—will probably ever be known because, as a recent writer said of him, "When he gave to a charity that interested him, he nearly always insisted on absolute anonymity." Mackay's best-known benefaction, incidentally, was Saint Mary's in the Mountains, the parish church of Virginia City, Nevada, a town known around the world in the 1860s and 1870s for the amazing strikes of gold and silver in its environs.

A "noiseless" pattern in giving cannot be improved upon, for as Jesus told the crowds on the hillside centuries ago, "When you give alms, do not have it trumpeted before you. . . . Your almsgiving must be secret, and your Father who sees all that is done in secret will reward you." That the works of philanthropy should be "done in secret" is as it should be, even if that method deprives the historian of many of the data from which to tell their story. What follows here is a general sketch. Because of space limitations many generous benefactors must remain unnamed. Moreover, any one at all familiar with American Catholic history must be conscious that from the beginning in this country the Church's good works were supported in the main by the constancy in giving of the "little people" to whom Catholicism is indebted in a way that can never be fully estimated nor adequately acknowledged.

Throughout the area that ultimately became the United States, Catholic philanthropy appeared with the first European settlements. Among the Spaniards, for example, Gonzalo Méndez de Canzo, governor of Florida, in 1598 erected the first hospital on American soil at Saint Augustine, and when the next year it was given over as a residence for the Franciscan friars, the governor, at his own expense, built a new hospital which he dedicated to Santa Bárbara. Far to the west at New Orleans, during the Spanish regime, Don Andrés Almonester y Roxas rebuilt Charity Hospital after the hurricane of 1779, donated a new convent for the Ursulines, and furnished the funds for a new parish church which before he died in 1793 became Saint Louis Cathedral. In the case of France, wealthy and aristocratic patrons, both at home and in the new world, in the words of one historian, "lavished their bounty" on the American missions, and in so doing revealed mixed motivations which prompted the same writer to state:

> Some donors simply hoped to save heathen from a perpetual life in outer darkness. But many more anticipated a personal reward as well: the religious, expiation of past sins; the worldly, profits; still others, the pleasure of helping to extend French culture and empire.

It was hardly "profits" that motivated the best-known Catholic philanthropist of the revolutionary generation, Charles Carroll of Carrollton, although "expiation of past sins" probably had something to do with it. Carroll was reputed the richest man in the young republic, and his name headed the list of donors to many charitable causes. Among them Carroll's favorite, perhaps, were orphans, a fact attested by his regular checks of $50 sent to the Archbishop of Baltimore for their care. Yet his love of money impeded his doing anything really handsome, and in his old age he seemed to experience a certain disquiet because of it. "Too much of my time and attention," he told a friend, "have been misapplied on matters to which an impartial Judge . . . before whom I shall soon appear, will ascribe [no] merit deserving recompense." It was on God's mercy that he relied for salvation, he said, for though he had performed good works out of obedience to divine precept, he feared that even these "a mixture of alloy will render unavailing, and cause to be rejected." The old statesman—he was then eighty-eight—apparently had in mind the Master's words, "it will be hard for a rich man to enter the kingdom of heaven." But Carroll could take consolation in Jesus' answer when His disciples asked who, then, could gain eternal life.

"For men," He told them, "this is impossible; for God everything is possible."

The sources for the wealth of those of a philanthropic turn of mind varied with each individual. Charles Carroll's fortune, derived in part by inheritance from the lucrative tobacco plantations of his native Maryland, was notably increased by his personal shrewdness and business acumen. Two other outstanding instances of Catholic philanthropy before the Civil War, both Irish immigrants, shared in Carroll's keen business sense, although they had little or nothing of his substantial family inheritance. The first was John Mullanphy of Saint Louis who made his money on trade in cotton and real estate and who was responsible for the first hospital west of the Mississippi River, which opened in 1828 in the charge of Elizabeth Seton's Sisters of Charity from Emmitsburg. Speaking of Mullanphy's death in August, 1833, an historian of the Archdiocese of Saint Louis remarked, "With him died the noblest Catholic layman St. Louis has ever known. . . ." The second was Andrew Carney (d. 1864) who came out to Boston in 1816 at the age of twenty-two, hired out at first as a simple tailor, and soon owned a clothing firm. Carney invested successfully in real estate and ultimately reached the pinnacle of Boston's business community as a director of the John Hancock Insurance Company. Of this wealthiest Catholic in New England a Boston historian said, "Whatever he touched—real estate, insurance, banking, or industrial securities—seemed to turn to gold." Andrew Carney had a deep sense of obligation to those less favored than himself, however, as the responsible people at Boston College, Saint Vincent's Orphan Asylum, and Carney Hospital—to name only three of his many beneficiaries —would attest. In all he left over $200,000 to Catholic causes of one kind or another, a handsome sum for that time.

Saint Thomas More once declared, "If God should give the goods of this world only to evil folk, then would men believe that God were not the Lord thereof. If God would give the goods only to good men, then would folk take occasion to serve Him but for them." In the second century of this nation's history, one who had much of the "goods of this world" and who would have understood what More meant was a convert philanthropist, Reuben R. Springer (d. 1884), whose fortune was made in steamboating and in the well-known grocery firm of Taylor and Company. This Cincinnati civic leader's gift of the city's Music Hall and College of Music could not remain hidden, but more frequently than not his repeated donations to the Church were veiled from the public gaze. These Catholic benefactions were thought by close associates to have averaged at least $75 a day, a generous outpouring that was especially helpful in 1876 when a grave financial crisis overtook the Archdiocese of Cincinnati. It was Springer's gift of $100,000, for example, that enabled Mount Saint Mary's Seminary of the

West to reopen in 1887 after having been closed for nine years as a result of the disaster.

During that time two other fortunes were building up from which Catholic good works were to benefit abundantly. The Irish-born Myles P. O'Connor (d. 1909) crossed the border into California in August, 1849, at the age of twenty-six, in the midst of the gold rush. Through a lucrative law practice and lucky mining investments O'Connor accumulated a fortune from which he was to aid numerous Catholic institutions. In his own state they included the hospital at San Jose that now bears his name, Notre Dame Institute, Saint Patrick's Seminary at Menlo Park, and the University of Santa Clara. In Washington, D.C., Trinity College was the recipient of Mrs. O'Connor's generosity, and perhaps the largest single O'Connor bene-faction, $500,000, went to the Catholic University of America as an endow-ment for chairs of canon law and philosophy. In the meantime the "rags to riches" story of Thomas Fortune Ryan, orphaned at fourteen, was unfold-ing first at Baltimore and then at New York. From messenger of a Wall Street brokerage firm he rose to be one of the commanding figures of American finance with a fortune estimated at over $200,000,000. In all Ryan and his first wife gave about $20,000,000 to Catholic charities, the most con-spicuous being Saint Jean Baptiste Church in New York and the Cathedral of the Sacred Heart in Richmond, Virginia.

If the history of American philanthropy, Catholic and non-Catholic alike, is told mainly in masculine terms, behind a number of these men stood equally generous women, wives who often inspired and shared in their hus-bands' giving. This was especially true of Mrs. Myles O'Connor and the first Mrs. Thomas Fortune Ryan. Moreover, philanthropy takes other forms besides monetary gifts, as was the case with Sarah Worthington King Peter (d. 1877), a convert who enriched Catholic life beyond measure in the Archdiocese of Cincinnati. On her repeated trips to Europe she recruited several congregations of women religious for various kinds of social service in and about Cincinnati and assisted them with funds from her relatively modest income. Throughout the nation's history there were women, such as Saint Elizabeth Seton, who gave all they had to the Church without it being recorded as philanthropy.

Two outstanding examples in the present century were women whose lives were spent in strikingly different ways. One was Genevieve Garvan Brady Macauley (d. 1938), to whom, among others, American Jesuits were be-holden as their seventeenth-century confreres had been beholden to the bountiful Marquise de Guercheville. Mrs. Brady likewise shared in the charitable bequests of her first husband, Nicholas F. Brady (d. 1930), public utilities magnate, among which was the Jesuit Novitiate of Saint Isaac Jogues at Wernersville, Pennsylvania, where they are buried, and the family's Long Island estate, Inisfada, which was willed to the Jesuits.

The second of these women was Mother Katharine Drexel (d. 1955), foundress of the Sisters of the Blessed Sacrament (1891) for missions to the blacks and Indians. She was the daughter of the Philadelphia multi-millionaire, Francis A. Drexel, the income from whose $14,000,000 trust fund went entirely to Mother Drexel after the death of her two sisters. Mother Drexel was another who gave all for philanthropic purposes, with the result that there is scarcely a section of this country where the Church was untouched by her generosity. The most noted instance is the first American Catholic institution of higher learning intended primarily for blacks, Xavier University in New Orleans.

In 1888, James Bryce, British ambassador to this country wrote, "In works of active beneficence, no country has surpassed, perhaps none has equalled, the United States." A striking instance in recent years was John J. Raskob (d. 1950) whose immense fortune, earned from his connections with the E. I. du Pont and General Motors enterprises, was willed in the main at his death to the Raskob Foundation for Catholic Activities, from which innumerable Catholic institutions and individuals have benefited. Another recent benefactor was Ignatius A. O'Shaughnessy (d. 1973) who shared large amounts of his income from the Globe Oil and Refining Company with Catholic institutions, especially the College of Saint Thomas in his home city of Saint Paul, the University of Notre Dame, and the Ecumenical Institute for Advanced Theological Studies at Tantur between Jerusalem and Bethlehem.

The particular rationale that lies behind one's giving, or not giving, is known only to God and to the individual, and whether in the changed mood of many American Catholics their record for philanthropy will be sustained, only time will tell. In terms of the general Catholic community, the gigantic operation known as Catholic Relief Services, official arm of the American Church for charitable causes abroad, was, in terms of budget, in 1958 the largest American voluntary overseas agency. To the leading historian of American philanthropy, Merle Curti of the University of Wisconsin, this was a reflection of the training Catholics had received in their own schools. Whether today the situation is that seen by this non-Catholic scholar nearly two decades ago, it is impossible to say. In any case, for the sake of the world's millions who stand in need of assistance, one can only hope that his anticipation may be as valid in 1976 as he viewed it when he stated:

"Thanks to the sustained program of teaching in parochial schools the Christian obligation of charity, the rising generation of Catholics promised to be well grounded in the sense of responsibility for the unfortunate wherever they might be."

MONSIGNOR ELLIS is a noted author and lecturer on the history of American Catholicism.

MOTHER MARIANNE COPE

Mother Marianne was the first sister of an American religious foundation to
initiate and direct missionary activities for the lepers of the Hawaiian Islands.

Mother Marianne of Molokai

SISTER MARY LAURENCE HANLEY, O.S.F.

"I am hungry for the work . . . I am not afraid of any disease.
It will be my greatest delight to minister to the abandoned 'leper.' "

In her lifetime she was decorated by the king of the Hawaiian Islands with the pendant cross of the Royal Order of Kapiolani for her acts of benevolence to his suffering people; she was celebrated in poetry and letters by Robert Louis Stevenson for her comforting presence in a place of "infinite pity"; and she was the subject of a musical composition by Professor Henri Berger, the longtime leader of the Royal Hawaiian Band, for her role in the "protection of womanhood and the uplifting of the races."

The recipient of these testimonials and many others was Mother Marianne Cope, the second mother provincial of the Sisters of St. Francis of Syracuse, New York, who sacrificed position, security, and the companionship of cherished friends and relatives to respond to an immediate need in the care of leper patients in the Hawaiian Islands. By doing so, she became the first sister of a religious community founded in the United States to initiate and lead mission work in a foreign land.

In 1883, when America was a mission field itself and the Sandwich Islands a faraway monarchy in the Pacific, the Hawaiian government was near desperation in its attempts to find assistance in caring for its citizens stricken by leprosy, the disease that King Kalakaua termed a "national affliction." The beneficent leaders believed that good nursing care and improved sanitary conditions would help alleviate the lepers' sufferings and help check the spread of the disease that had cast an ugly shadow over the beautiful islands.

A place demanding attention was Branch Hospital or Kakaako Receiving Station for suspected cases of leprosy on the islands. Located on the Honolulu waterfront, it served as a point of departure for confirmed "cases" to a more permanent location on Molokai. The wisdom of sending patients immediately to Molokai was being debated, and so the station was serving mainly as a hospital. About 200 men, women, and children were huddled together with the services of only a visiting doctor who merely prescribed medicines and a superintendent who was antagonistic to the patients. No other personnel could be found regardless of remuneration offered.

The question was, "Who had the devotion of spirit to give the needed care?"

Although the royal family was Protestant, the Hawaiian government asked Bishop Herman Koeckemann, Vicar Apostolic of the Sandwich Islands, to use his influence to obtain help through "the blessed sisterhoods of charity." Father Leonor Fouesnel, emissary of the Hawaiian government through the auspices of the vicar apostolic, appealed to more than fifty religious communities in the United States and Canada before he received an affirmative answer at the Franciscan convent in Syracuse. Mother Cope recognized the call as "one coming from God," despite the other pressing needs of her community. Six sisters were selected from among the many volunteers. They set out for the faraway land with Mother Cope whose intention was to establish the missions and to return to Syracuse. The small community she directed had charge of several large schools and two expanding hospitals which required her attention in the United States.

In a brief time, however, the qualifications and capabilities of this re-markable sister caused the government and church authorities alike in Hawaii to declare her presence necessary for a while to the success of the mission. During her extended "brief stay" of five years at Honolulu, she managed the hospital as a home for the patients and truly was a mother to all. Whenever there was a need she tried to meet it, and she created a new atmosphere at the hospital: spiritually, physically, and morally. In 1885 her attention was called to the plight of the daughters of lepers on Molokai, who were devoid of opportunity and exposed to the disease and the law-less environment at the settlement. She soon opened Kapiolani Home for them on the hospital grounds in Honolulu. At the request of the govern-ment, she also set up the first general hospital on the island of Maui and opened a school for girls.

"We cheerfully will undertake the work" was her response to a govern-ment request to open a home for "unprotected women and girls" at Molokai in 1888. Finally it had been decided to remove the receiving station from the Honolulu harbor and to transfer hospital cases to the leper colony. Her acceptance of the mission and her subsequent departure with some of the women patients and two volunteer sister companions was particularly sig-nificant and heroic because it was apparent that she might never be able to return to Syracuse.

Again, as in 1883, the government stated a need for self-sacrificing personnel, and this time it said the duties were of such a nature that it could not urge any woman to devote herself to the work. It is little wonder, however, that the good mother who had such great faith in God and who was so devoted to her charges at Honolulu was protected from marauders at the "settlement without law." Soon after Father Damien DeVeuster succumbed to leprosy in 1889, she, with her limitless charity, took charge of the home he had initiated for homeless men and boys. Her opinion on all matters of consequence was sought constantly by authorities and was given humbly and without fanfare. Later, in 1894, she suggested quietly that brothers be invited to teach the boys farming and carpentry, and it was done.

Her role as a missionary was well described in the Honolulu *Advertiser* at the time of her death in 1918 by Mrs. John F. Bowler:

"Sister Marianne was a martyr, a heroine.... Seldom has the opportunity come to a woman to devote every hour of 30 years to the mothering of people isolated by law from the rest of the world. She risked her own life in all that time, faced everything with unflinching courage and smiled sweetly through it all. She came to Honolulu ready to do whatever was required of her. Without blare of trumpets, she entered upon her duties (at Molokai) through 30 long, wearisome years, living apart from the world and its comfort, she labored in the cause of a stricken people. Sister Marianne was a heroine in life; she was a martyr in death."

As foundress of the Franciscan missions in Hawaii, she left a legacy of uncounted numbers who never contracted leprosy or whose children were saved because of the improvements she fostered. She also left a spiritual legacy in the Sisters who still carry on her work at Molokai and the numerous vocations drawn to her order, inspired by her and her successors. And she left to the world her saintly example of the true meaning of love in her daily concern for those in need: "I was sick and you visited me."

Accolades for her heroic charity and accomplishments have continued since her death, and in 1974 the preliminary research for the cause of the beatification of Mother Marianne Cope was initiated in Rome. Perhaps Dr. T. Wood Clarke indeed spoke prophetically in 1938 while reading a paper before the Oneida County Historical Society, of which he was president: "By her self-imposed exile, by her sacrifice, by her endurance, and by her enthusiasm, Mother Marianne ... has taken her place as one of the world's greatest women. ... This woman ... will undoubtedly some day be canonized by the Catholic Church and enrolled among the greatest of its saints."

RECOMMENDED READING: L. V. Jacks, *Mother Marianne of Molokai* (New York: Macmillan and Co., 1935).

SISTER MARY LAURENCE, of Maria Regina College in Syracuse, is the secretary to the Postulator in Rome for the beatification cause of Mother Marianne.

THE FIRST FOUR MARYKNOLL MISSIONERS SENT TO THE FAR EAST

These priests, shown before their departure for China in 1918, are (seated, from left to right) James E. Walsh, Thomas F. Price (cofounder of the society and superior of this group), Francis X. Ford, and (standing) Bernard F. Meyer. After Father Price died a year later in Hong Kong, Father Walsh became superior and, in 1924, prefect apostolic of the first canonically organized American mission in China. (*NC Photos*)

40

American Catholic Missions in the Far East

WILLIAM J. COLEMAN, M.M.

The year was 1918. The end of World War I was in sight and with it, the end of American isolationism which had been national policy since the founding of the country. The first organized American Catholic foreign mission group was on the way to China, and American Catholic presence in the Far East had become a fact after a dozen years of preparation.

It had all begun at a meeting in the Boston office of the Society of the Propagation of the Faith, the worldwide agency for the support of Catholic missions. Four mission-minded priests—Fathers James F. Stanton, John I. Lane, Joseph Bruneau, S.S., and the director of the office, James A. Walsh—had come together "to organize a literary propaganda to deepen and widen the mission spirit in the United States and ultimately to establish a Foreign Mission Seminary." They began their publication, *The Field Afar*, in 1907. In issue after issue it brought to the attention of American Catholics the great need of American men and money for the missionary world, in particular, for China.

Before World War I a limited American Catholic presence had begun in the Far East in 1903 when Pope Leo XIII appointed Bishop (later Cardinal) Dennis Dougherty to head the Segovia diocese in the Philippines. With the American occupation of the Philippines the Vatican looked to the Church in America to aid the Filipino Church in its hour of crisis. To the small number of diocesan priests from Philadelphia were added several Christian Brothers in 1916 to staff Catholic schools.

But the departure for China in September, 1918, of three young Maryknoll priests—Fathers Francis X. Ford, Bernard F. Meyer, and James E. Walsh—and of Thomas F. Price, the cofounder of Maryknoll and an experienced home missionary from North Carolina, marks the first foreign mission representation of American Catholics in the Far East. This first missionary effort of the American Catholic Church was to continue to grow and prosper without interruption for the next thirty years until communist domination of all of China.

Various factors help to explain the late entry of American Catholics into the foreign mission field of the Orient. Until shortly after the turn of the century (1908) the Church in America was itself officially classified as missionary in status. Though it entered the twentieth century with some 12,000,000 Catholics, a large percentage were immigrants whose spiritual care depended on large numbers of European priests and religious. For a century the American Church had received, rather than sent, missionaries as well as financial aid. The very largeness of the country made for many dispersed Catholic populations especially in the South and West so that the cause of home missions seemed much more urgent than that of foreign missions.

Meanwhile, voices were heard lamenting the fact that it was past time for American Catholics to assume some share of the universal missionary obligation of the Church. This, it was pointed out, was only missionary justice after they had received so much help from abroad. It was argued that only the United States could furnish an adequate English-speaking Catholic presence in the foreign mission field where many Protestant denominations from both Great Britain and the United States dominated the English-speaking foreign mission field.

As it was for all things American, World War I and its aftermath was a turning point for American Catholics and the foreign missions. Various orders like the Jesuits, the Franciscans, and the Brothers of Mary spoke out in favor of filling the vacuum in Catholic foreign missions created by the loss of many European missioners due to four years of war.

In 1909 the Society of the Divine Word had opened a mission house in Techny, Illinois, and in 1912 the Catholic Foreign Mission Seminary called Maryknoll was opened at Ossining, New York. The Maryknoll Society had been founded the previous year with the approval of the American bishops. The "literary propaganda" begun by Father Walsh in 1907 began to bear fruit for the foreign mission cause, aided by other societies who began missions in China. The American Franciscans arrived in 1920, the Vincentians, Passionists, and Jesuits in 1921, and the Dominicans in 1923. The Benedictines opened the University of Peking in 1925 but transferred it to the Society of the Divine Word in 1933. American Jesuits helped their colleagues at the University of Auroa in Shanghai.

By the eve of Pearl Harbor, or a quarter of a century after the arrival of the first American group of four priests, there were 315 priests and brothers in fourteen China missions representing some fifty different religious orders. These were aided by 290 sisters from thirteen different congregations, the first of which, the Maryknoll Sisters, arrived in 1921. This total personnel of approximately 600 represented seventy percent of all the American Catholic foreign missionaries throughout the world. Outside of China there were other American Catholic missioners in the Philippines, Japan, Korea, and Manchuria. Small in comparison with the total Catholic missionary force in the Far East, which exceeded 5,000 priests, brothers, and sisters, it represented, nevertheless, a generation of effective American effort. The Church in the United States had assumed its missionary role and had only to enlarge it in the decades ahead.

This quarter-century of mission work brought much good to the Chinese people, not only spiritual but also social. Each mission engaged in the traditional works of charity as a means of preaching the Gospel by example. Orphanages and homes for the aged were opened as well as dispensaries and hospitals. With the mission church was often connected an elementary school. American Catholics at home contributed generously to the building and maintenance of these hundreds of mission institutions. The prospect for the future seemed bright, especially since mission seminaries and novitiates increased the number of Chinese priests, brothers, and sisters.

But this was not to be. With the coming of World War II and its aftermath, a generation of American missionary work came to a sudden halt. Conditions under which foreign missioners worked in China had never been stable and now out of the chaos of war emerged an aggressive communist state (1949) bent on the systematic destruction of the Church.

The communist campaign focused principally on the foreign missioner who, whatever his nationality, was pictured as a "running dog" of Western imperialism. The 600 American Catholic missionaries became the special object of this outright persecution thanks to the United States Government's support of the Nationalist Chinese cause against the communists. A familiar pattern of harassment began which included frequent interrogations, then public accusations "as enemies of the People," and finally a "People's Trial" with a jail sentence followed later by expulsion from the country.

Meanwhile, mission property was confiscated and turned over to communist use or otherwise disposed of without any legal proceedings. As the communist takeover spread from North China year by year the three million Chinese Catholics saw their Church disappear before their eyes. From a total of 5,380 Catholic missionary priests, brothers, and sisters in 1950 there remained only 267 in 1954, a third of whom were in jail. These were gradually expelled in the following few years after serving jail sentences.

The final and classic example of communist persecution was the arrest of Bishop James E. Walsh in 1958 and his sentencing to twenty years' imprisonment for alleged spying. He had arrived in 1918 with the first group of Americans to come to China and forty years later began a prison term that was to last twelve years before he was released.

The loss of the Church in China as a mission field when viewed in the perspective of nineteen centuries of missionary work, is only a momentary setback. The very missioners expelled from China went elsewhere to carry on similar work. Meanwhile, the mission challenge received more and more response from American Catholics as evidenced in the latest statistics. Today there is a total of nearly 7,500 priests, brothers, sisters, and lay people throughout the missionary world with still the largest number (1,875) in the Far East in spite of the total exclusion from China. Sixty-nine mission-sending groups of priests and brothers furnish more than 3,800 of their members for mission work, while no less than 160 communities of sisters send more than 2,900. The American Catholic Church has thus taken on its share of mission service in the twentieth century.

RECOMMENDED READING: John C. Murrett, *Tar Heel Apostle: Thomas Frederick Price, Cofounder of Maryknoll* (New York: Longmans, Green & Company, 1944). Daniel Sargent, *All the Day Long* [a popular life of Bishop James A. Walsh, co-founder of Maryknoll] (New York: Longmans, Green & Company, 1941). Raymond A. Lane, *The Early Days of Maryknoll* (New York: David McKay Company, 1951). Albert J. Nevins, *The Meaning of Maryknoll* (New York: McMullen Books, 1954). Glenn D. Kittler, *The Maryknoll Fathers* (Cleveland: World Publishing Company, 1961).

FATHER COLEMAN is archivist of the Maryknoll Missioners.

41

Architect of Christian Unity:

Father Paul Wattson of Graymoor

CHARLES LA FONTAINE, S.A.

One warm spring day in 1902, a crowd of Wall Street stockbrokers, some tourists, and a few pigeons gathered on the steps of New York's City Hall to listen to a brown-robed Episcopal priest tell them exactly what many of them did not want to hear. Though he was banned from preaching in any pulpit of the Episcopal Church, Father Paul Wattson of Graymoor, an Episcopal monastery in the beautiful Hudson River Highlands, was nonetheless taking his controversial message to the people of countless villages and towns throughout America by preaching in the streets. A Franciscan friar, Father Wattson was both a religious curiosity to his fellow Episcopalians and an affront to the doctrinal sensibilities of most Protestants.

After all, how could any committed priest of the Episcopal Church seriously advocate not only the corporate reunion of Anglicans and Protestants with the Roman Catholic Church, but also the necessary primacy of the Pope within the Christian Church as a whole? How could such a clergyman honestly remain in his own church and still proclaim a belief in the Immaculate Conception of St. Mary and the urgency of saying the Rosary? Father Wattson must have delighted some Catholics with his pro-Roman positions in those pre-ecumenical days. But in 1902 he had absolutely no intention or desire to become a Roman Catholic, as many of his friends and all his enemies suggested he should.

But seven years later, in 1909, Father Wattson became a Catholic. He never suspected that but fifty years afterward Pope John XXIII would inaugurate the Second Vatican Council which would provide the incentive to reexamine questions like corporate reunion and papal primacy, matters

FATHER PAUL WATTSON OF GRAYMOOR

that Roman Catholics thought had long been definitely settled. The extraordinary life story of Father Paul Wattson provides a useful paradigm of thought and action for ecumenical Christians of succeeding generations.

Born January 16, 1863, Lewis Thomas Wattson was the third son of Joseph and Mary Electa Wattson of Millington, Maryland. An Episcopal priest himself, Joseph Wattson was of Anglo-Catholic or "High Church" persuasion, both theologically and liturgically. Near the end of his studies at General Theological Seminary in New York, he had been forced to leave school under a cloud of suspicion of being a "Jesuit in disguise." He spent his whole ministry in small rural parishes because of the reputation he gained from that incident.

Influenced by his father's love for the Episcopal Church in spite of grave difficulties, Lewis Wattson in turn entered General Theological Seminary in 1882 to study for the Episcopal ministry. By that time, conditions in the Episcopal Church were far less adverse to a "High Church" position than in Joseph Wattson's day, and so Lewis Wattson managed to graduate at the top of his class with a promising future ahead. First as rector at Kingston, New York, and later as head of the Associate Mission, an Episcopal community of preachers in Omaha, Nebraska, Father Wattson gradually revealed his pro-Roman views in his writing and preaching. No less than his father, he faced opposition and condemnation from most Episcopalians.

Becoming more and more confirmed in his pro-Roman positions, Father Wattson kept thinking back to an early childhood inspiration, a "voice" he called it, which had told him that he would one day "found a preaching order like the Paulists." Early in July, 1893, in imitation of St. Francis, Father Wattson opened his King James version of the Bible three times to seek divine guidance about his future religious community. The second time he did so, his eyes fell on the text of Romans 5:11: "And not only so, but we also joy in God, through our Lord Jesus Christ, by whom we have now received the atonement." There it was—the word "atonement." The new community which he believed God was calling him to found would thus be named the Society of the Atonement.

Possessing only the name of his society, Father Wattson waited for three more years before he took another step. In 1896 he began communicating with an Episcopal sister from Albany, New York, Lurana Mary White, who shared many of his aspirations and was searching for an Episcopal community of religious which was vowed to corporate poverty. After much correspondence and negotiation Father Wattson and Sister Lurana met at Warwick, New York, early in October, 1898, to make a covenant together, agreeing to proceed with their plans to found the Society of Atonement in the near future.

Across the Hudson River, near Garrison, New York, at a place called Graymoor, there might be the perfect spot for just such a foundation, Sister

Lurana suggested. With Father Wattson's approval, she arrived that year in the dead of winter at Graymoor where she took up residence in an abandoned farmhouse. The next year Father Wattson followed her and lived at first in a run-down paint shack which he dubbed "The Palace of Lady Poverty."

Now that their community had been initiated and had acquired a permanent home, Father Paul (his new name in religion) could concentrate on propagating his ideas about corporate reunion and papal primacy among Anglicans and anyone else who would listen. Many did, but few were convinced. Amid enormous pressures to cease activities which must have seemed ridiculous, even dangerous, to most Anglicans and Protestants, Father Paul continued to spread his message through a monthly magazine, *The Lamp*, since all pulpits were by then closed to him.

Insisting that Christian unity is a gift from God for which Christians must pray, Father Paul in 1908 began the Church Unity Octave, an eight-day period of prayer for the unity of Christians. At first strongly papal and Roman in its orientation, the Church Unity Octave gradually evolved into what is known today as the Week of Prayer for Christian Unity.

As the opposition to him mounted, Father Paul became less and less sure that he should remain in the Episcopal Church. After much agonizing, Father Paul, Mother Lurana, and fifteen associates entered the Roman Church on October 30, 1909, at the hands of Monsignor Joseph Conroy, Vicar General of the Diocese of Ogdensburg and later its third bishop. Thus for the first time since the Reformation, an entire community of religious women and men was received corporately, not individually, into the Roman Church.

Although Father Paul and his Society had thus solved the problem of their ecclesiastical commitment, they still had to face the very real difficulty of identifying the Society's specific role in the Catholic Church. How was their vision of the ultimate reunion of the Christian churches to be realized within the Roman Church? Because of the "fortress mentality" prevailing among the churches during the early twentieth century, Father Paul was frequently hampered in his efforts to disseminate the ecumenical message. By many Protestants and Anglicans he was considered a traitor, while some Catholics viewed him as still too "Protestant."

Yet, Father Paul and his friars were able to make some headway against anti-ecumenical attitudes by publishing *The Lamp* and *The Antidote*, through propagating the annual observance of the Church Unity Octave, by fostering social works like St. Christopher's Inn for homeless men of every or no religion, by beginning the Union That Nothing Be Lost, a fund-raising organization for overseas and home missions, and through pastoral activity among blacks and Chicanos. Many were the works but one was the aim: "That all be one that the world may believe."

When Father Paul died in early 1940, the Society of the Atonement had been firmly established as an ecumenical consciousness-raiser for Roman Catholics at least. Themes such as "return to Rome" and the supremacy of the Pope, however, made most cooperation with other Christians, even in prayer, quite impossible for many years.

Then came the Second Vatican Council. If some Roman Catholics were hardly surprised by the principles enunciated in the council's Decree on Ecumenism, particularly its stress on the need to pray for Christian unity, this was no doubt due in large measure to the influence of Father Paul Wattson and his society. A stubborn faith in the correctness and necessity of Christian unity, a persistent determination to work for the realization of that end despite almost overwhelming odds, a strong sense of Christian mission to an unbelieving, unwilling world, and a profound conviction that the ultimate unity of mankind would be achieved by the cooperation of men and women in God's own will and work for the world—all these qualities have won Father Paul the lasting admiration of Christians disturbed by the continuing division and inhumanity on this earth.

RECOMMENDED READING: Charles Angell and Charles LaFontaine, *Prophet of Reunion: The Life of Paul of Graymoor* (New York: Seabury Press, 1975). Sister Mary Celine [Fleming], S.A., *A Woman of Unity* (Graymoor, Garrison, New York: Franciscan Sisters of the Atonement, 1956).

FATHER LaFONTAINE, an Atonement Friar, is associate director of the Graymoor Ecumenical Institute and assistant editor of *Ecumenical Trends*.

42

The Development of

Catholic Lay Organizations

SISTER M. ADELE FRANCIS GORMAN, O.S.F.

Lay activity in the Catholic Church has come almost full circle from the lay trustees of the early nineteenth century to the contemporary parish council. In between, lay participation in the Church was mainly through societies, sodalities, and other pious groups, unions, congresses, and the great American Federation of Catholic Societies.

One of the earliest societies was the St. Patrick's Funeral Benefit Society, imported from Ireland in 1836, and incorporated in New York as the Ancient Order of Hibernians. Concurrently, the German mutual benefit societies were forming because, like the Irish, German immigrants needed help in time of illness or for funeral expenses. In 1855 about a third of the German societies formed the German Roman Catholic Central Society, known as the Central Verein.

During the nineteenth century Catholics were harassed first by the American Protestant Society, then by the Supreme Order of the Star Spangled Banner (Know-Nothings), and finally by the American Protective Association (APA). Often Catholics refused to identify themselves as such for fear of revealing their religion to the enemy. Relief came only with the Civil War when all had to unite in a common cause. But after the Reconstruction, a recrudescence of bigotry appeared in the APA.

Shortly after the Civil War, Catholics became aware of the strength to be found in unity and of the need for something larger than the society. Pope Pius IX made his first public appearance after his voluntary imprisonment in the Vatican in 1871 to a delegation of the Belgian Catholic Union, urging the formation of similar unions in other countries.

A New York lawyer, Richard Clarke, was moved by this exhortation and with others wrote a constitution for a union to be comprised of societies and of individuals. Although Clarke wrote to every bishop in the United States asking that circles of unions be formed, only Buffalo, Boston, and New Jersey created unions. Until 1878 news items about union activities appeared frequently, but after that little was heard on the topic. The idea appears to have been forgotten by 1917.

Even as the union movement died out, a new thrust in lay activity through organizations took shape. As early as 1868 a writer in the *Catholic World* pointed out the need for Catholics to assemble to discuss their problems (including the press and education). But no assembly took place until 1889 when William J. Onahan, a prominent Chicago layman, and Henry Brownson, son of the convert-publicist Orestes Brownson, asked Cardinal James Gibbons of Baltimore for permission to call a Catholic congress that was to bring together well-known laymen and clergy as well as representatives of the Catholic societies.

Although Cardinal Gibbons had some misgivings about allowing a large assembly of Catholics when the APA was gathering strength, he was finally persuaded by his friend Archbishop John Ireland of St. Paul and other bishops to give his permission. So successful was the first congress at Baltimore that participants created a Committee for a Permanent Congress which was to meet regularly. However, only one more congress was held. It brought together for the first time delegates of a number of Catholic societies in Chicago in 1893 at the time of the Columbian Exposition commemorating the fourth centenary of the discovery of America. For many reasons the second congress was not so successful as its predecessor.

Even while the congresses were being planned, a new type of lay leadership through organizations was germinating. The *Pittsburgh Catholic* announced on February 1, 1890, that most of the societies in the diocese were taking steps to form a federation, noting that Pope Leo XIII had urged Catholics to unite in an encyclical on the duties of Christians as citizens, *Sapientiae Christianae.*

Winning episcopal approval, gaining the confidence of societies, especially the ethnic groups, writing an acceptable constitution, and many other matters delayed federation for a decade. However, on December 10, 1901, the first national convention of the American Federation of Catholic Societies (AFCS) met in Cincinnati, elected officers, approved a constitution, and made plans for annual meetings. A giant organization whose members were societies, the AFCS did meet annually except in 1905 (because of an epidemic in the designated city). Through constituent societies, the AFCS claimed about three million members by 1913 and took credit for a number of achievements.

Alone, or with assistance, the AFCS announced that it had aided the

Catholic Press Association to become viable after a number of false starts. It began what appears to have been the first organized effort to raise moral standards for plays, silent movies, and postcards. It fostered the study of the encyclicals, promoted Catholic education, formed a Social Service Commission to encourage the spread of Christian justice, and attacked the enemies of the Church. It assisted in the formation of a rural life organization, the Catholic Drama Society, the Extension Society, Catholic youth organizations, and other associations that still exist.

Because of internal dissension and the formation of the National Catholic War Council during World War I, the AFCS gradually faded out after 1917. When the bishops formed the National Catholic Welfare Council (later Conference) on the foundation of the War Council, the National Councils of Catholic Men and Women directed organized lay activity within the NCWC. Other lay organizations already operative, such as the Knights of Columbus, and beneficial societies, such as the Catholic Knights of America, remained strong, and new ones such as the Catholic Youth Organization and the Serra Club rose as needed.

Since the Second Vatican Council, lay activity in the Church in the United States has expanded both through organizations and by individuals.

The fears of lay control of the Church, so strong as a result of the activities of the earlier lay trustees, have been put to rest, and strength has been found in the parish councils as well as in organizations. Consequently, lay activity in the Church has come full circle but to a richer participation of the laity in the life of the Church.

SISTER MARY ADELE FRANCIS is a professor of history in Our Lady of Angels College, Aston, Pennsylvania.

AN EMPLOYMENT BUREAU OPERATED BY THE KNIGHTS OF COLUMBUS
AFTER WORLD WAR I

During the demobilization period the Knights employed 27,250 volunteers
to help the discharged servicemen to find jobs; they also opened evening
schools and conducted correspondence courses to make the men better
qualified. In this photograph servicemen considering opportunities for work
surround a Knights of Columbus secretary in front of the Longacre Hut on
Broadway in New York. (*NC Photos*)

43

Knights of Columbus:

Service in Peace and War

ELMER VON FELDT

The Knights of Columbus, who were founded in 1882 by Father Michael J. McGivney with six members in New Haven, Connecticut, have grown into a society of 1.2 million Catholic men gathered in about 6,000 councils, in the United States, Canada, Mexico, the Philippines, Puerto Rico, Guatemala, Panama, Cuba, Guam, and the Virgin Islands.

The Knights were founded in an era of social and economic tension. Catholic immigrants were flooding into the United States and the massive inflow had a depressing impact on the job market, making unemployment common. Unstable working conditions led to the formation of labor societies which adopted oath-bound secrecy to increase their effectiveness in dealing with management. Many societies also used a quasi-religious ritual with the result that Catholics who joined them frequently became alienated from the Church. Bishops faced the dilemma of allowing Catholics to join such organizations for economic and social advancement or of promoting similar Catholic-oriented groups. Father McGivney strongly favored the latter course.

He and his lay collaborators first tried to organize a local chapter of the Massachusetts Catholic Order of Foresters. That attempt failed when the Foresters refused to accept them as insurance risks. The group then decided to form a new organization with the suggested name of "Sons of Columbus." However this was quickly changed to the "Connecticut Knights of Columbus" and finally to the "Knights of Columbus."

As Father McGivney explained to the first six members, he had several purposes in calling them together: to help the men and their families to remain steadfast in their Catholic faith through mutual encouragement; to promote closer ties of fraternity among the men; to set up an elementary system of insurance so that the widows and children of any in the group who might die would not find themselves in dire financial straits. These original objectives were to be amplified in ever broader forms of service to Church and country.

In keeping with the tenor of the times three degrees of membership were devised and a ritual was prepared for each degree. The rites dramatized to new members the values of charity, unity, and fraternity. Later a new degree was instituted to dramatize the lesson of patriotism. The new organization differed from other secret societies because its members took no oath of secrecy and its ritual was prepared in consultation with Church officials.

The society spread very slowly the first few years but it had a distinct advantage over other Catholic-oriented fraternal groups, most of which were based on ethnic or linguistic grounds. The Knights of Columbus accepted all male Catholics between the ages of eighteen and forty-five. Those over forty-five were rejected initially because every member automatically became an insurance member and men over forty-five were considered too high an insurance risk.

Early in their history Knights concentrated on translating their Catholic idealism into action and exerting religious influence on society. Thus they became engaged in "Catholic Action" more than three decades before Pope Pius XI popularized the term in his 1931 encyclical, *Non Abbiamo Bisogno*.

The Knights gained national attention almost by accident. During the Mexican campaign under General John Pershing it was discovered that very few Catholic chaplains served the armed forces and no recreational facilities were conducted for the troops under Catholic auspices. Responding to the pleas both of councils in the affected areas and of concerned parents, the Knights established a network of nineteen centers from Brownsville to El Paso where auxiliary chaplains offered Mass and where recreational facilities were provided for the troops.

The program received such acclaim that the society offered to carry on a similar effort when the nation entered World War I. It put up a million-dollar fund to assure the army that it could back up its proposal to provide "buildings for social purposes" and the offer was accepted.

The original one million dollars were raised by assessment and another fifteen million were garnered by solicitation.

Breaking with the tradition observed by other service groups, the Knights operated recreational facilities under the slogan: "Everybody welcome. Everything free." This was a source of irritation to other voluntary groups at first but eventually became the norm.

Because of this success, Knights were allotted for their work among the troops $25 million of a $170 million United War Fund drive. When the Catholic bishops formed the National Catholic War Council (NCWC) to coordinate services to Catholics in the armed forces, the Knights turned this fund over to the bishops but immediately were designated as agents of the NCWC for war welfare work.

With nearly $8 million still available at the end of World War I the Knights set up free employment bureaus, evening schools, and correspondence courses to help returning servicemen fit into peacetime life. Almost 500,000 veterans received free academic, commercial, or technical training in the various evening schools and correspondence courses set up by the order.

Among other pioneer activities, a council in Brooklyn originated the Catholic Hour on radio which later was taken over by the National Council of Catholic Men but continued to be supported by the Knights of Columbus.

In 1922, when voters in Oregon passed a law making it a misdemeanor punishable by fine and imprisonment for any parent to send his child to a nonpublic school, the Knights mobilized support to have the law declared unconstitutional. The Supreme Court in 1925 agreed with the Knights.

These initial programs translating the society's deep concern for the welfare of the community and the advancement of the Catholic faith laid the groundwork for most of the later projects that were adopted with increasing speed and variety by councils throughout the United States and in other parts of the world.

At present the fraternal society spends about $3 million a year in support of various educational programs, $9 million for charitable and beneficient causes, more than $1 million for promotion of the Catholic faith, and almost $3 million for the care of the sick and needy. At the same time it donates millions of man-hours to various beneficent activities.

This record of service prompted Pope Paul VI to tell the order's board of directors in 1973 that "the glory of the Knights of Columbus is not based on humanitarian works alone. Even more admirable has been your insistence upon the supremacy of God and your fidelity to the vicar of Christ."

Former news editor of National Catholic News Service, Mr. Von Feldt is editor of *Columbia* magazine and director of information for the Supreme Council of the Knights of Columbus.

THE INTERIOR OF THE SAINT PAUL CHAPEL

This railroad chapel car was furnished by the Catholic Church Extension Society and was used in countless places where no permanent house of worship existed. (*Courtesy of* Extension Magazine)

44

The Catholic Church Extension Society

JAMES P. GAFFEY

The Catholic Church Extension Society represents a rare combination of a man's vaulting imagination and the soundest practicality. America's home missionary society began with the dream of a young Canadian-born priest who was serving as pastor of a small Michigan town. A man of supreme energy and charm, Father Francis Clement Kelley perceived the desperate need to reach the numberless remote places where there was no presence of or even contact with the Church. His own parish was not self-supporting, and this condition led him to spend several years giving lectures and touring the country.

The young priest "saw America," he recalled, "not the America of the great cities but the real America which feeds and sustains the other—the America of the small towns, villages, and countryside." Encounters with neglected rural communities, especially in the Middle West, persuaded Father Kelley that the urban Church must not become blinded to the grim realities beyond the city limits; rather, it must take on the responsibility of evangelizing the countryside.

It was no easy task to get others to share this dream. No major Eastern diocese was willing to commit its resources. In time, a benefactor with sufficient means did emerge, the Archbishop of Chicago. On October 18, 1905, nineteen men—bishops, priests, and laymen—founded the Catholic Church Extension Society in the home of Archbishop James Quigley, who accepted the post of chancellor. Thus began a movement designed to introduce and preserve the Church in the scattered, sparsely settled, poverty-ridden areas of the United States.

From the start, the society was remarkably inventive in coping with rural problems. It developed the "chapel car," inspired by the historic train in which Pope Pius IX had traveled through the Papal States before 1870.

Protestants had first experimented with the idea in America, and its missionary potential appealed to Extension. Railroads pulled such cars free. They cost little to maintain. They provided living accommodations for a priest and a chapel for the congregation. Their novelty drew the curious, and their practicality awakened the interest of wealthy Catholics. The first was a wooden Pullman dedicated to St. Anthony, and this was followed by two steel-framed ones. Together, they were perhaps the greatest single factor in the society's early success.

Extension did not win unanimous approval. To many of the Eastern clergy, who did not understand its goals, it appeared a needless duplication of apostolic societies. Distinguished members of the hierarchy accused it of extravagance. Archbishop John J. Keane of Dubuque, Iowa, mistook its well furnished and carpeted office in Chicago as the ostentatious display of a prosperous bank. Even the apostolic delegate, Archbishop Diomede Falconio, joined the chorus of criticism. A former Franciscan missioner, he was opposed to the use of the "chapel car" as too luxurious a vehicle for this work. Only a special intervention of Archbishop Quigley quieted the doubts of authorities in Rome.

"Little by little," acknowledged Father Kelley, its first president, "The East became friendly." Perhaps what prompted this trend was the gradual approval of the Holy See. Extension had begun under the direction of Americans, but its protector, Archbishop Quigley, wanted Rome's endorsement. In 1907 Pius X blessed the work and in 1910 elevated the society to pontifical status.

Parallel to these developments in Europe were the American Missionary Congresses sponsored by Extension. The first, held in Chicago in 1908, attempted to dispel doubts and to clarify the vision guiding the movement— to make each Catholic in America a home missionary. By 1914 the East had genuinely warmed to this idea, and so the second congress was held in Boston in that year and was attended by prominent bishops. Thus the two congresses awakened national interest in home missions.

An interest in communication characterized the spirit of Extension. To keep its work constantly before its benefactors, the society exploited the advantages of photo-journalism. The earliest format of *Extension Magazine* was ambitious—a colorful pictorial monthly describing with compelling vividness the work of missioners in the American field. But it was not limited to this one topic; the magazine soon included fiction, some of it distinguished.

Its original press runs reflected the optimism invested in the enterprise. For the first two years, 50,000 copies circulated, an incredible figure for a starting magazine that was based on the hope that each priest in the United States, who would receive a sample, would subscribe. The response was at first less than expected, but the magazine was eventually able to meet its expenses.

As worthy as missionary efforts in the American countryside might be, they had to be founded on solid sources of income. The society evolved a variety of ways to meet this practical need. Aside from burses, wills, and other traditional sources, it offered a Charitable Gift Annuity Plan. In a lump sum a gift-investment was made in return for a guaranteed annual income for life. This plan combined saving and missionary charity—a combination that was particularly attractive to low-income and middle-income Catholics. Over the years the society has succeeded in providing returns at the highest rate compatible with a conservative investment policy.

Another popular source of revenue has been the multi-color Catholic Art Calendar. Parishes continue to purchase millions of these to distribute to Catholic homes.

An early experiment was the "Dollar Club." If Extension was to answer the appeals of priests in the field, it would have to look to new methods that would touch small donors. Father Kelley hit upon a direct-mail plan. Carefully wording his request, he asked thousands to trust him with one dollar. This was no loan, he explained: "I am asking you to trust me to spend one dollar for you" in behalf of American missioners at home. In six months the revenues of the "Dollar Club" grew from a net of $35 on the first day to a daily receipt which averaged $500. This extraordinary response, he judged, was evoked only because people were genuinely interested in evangelization and were moved by a clear presentation of the need.

With such success from the start, the society released audits of its work. An early report noted that between 1909 and 1919 Extension—after only fourteen years of existence—had accounted for more than half of the new church building by Catholics in the United States. A recent study showed that the society has helped to build more than 7,000 churches. Such regular disclosures confirmed the confidence of benefactors that their contributions were effectively used in mission work.

Extension is a singular American success. Though it has engaged in relief work in such countries as Mexico and Austria, it has been a movement independently supported by Americans and designed to serve Americans at home and abroad. It destroyed the myth that the Church had grown as rapidly in the countryside as in the cities at the turn of the twentieth century.

It represented an early effort to divert American Catholics from a smothering provincialism that confined their interests within diocesan or parochial boundaries, and to awaken a national bond among them. It required the closest collaboration between cleric and layperson, a collaboration which extended from the policy-making board of governors to the daily operations of the society. From the beginning, its spirit of evangelism was carefully secured to the most modern of business practices and communications techniques.

The fulfillment of this dream was noted by Bishop Kelley in 1924 when he left Chicago to become bishop of Oklahoma. "The society itself was well founded," he later recalled, "and had assumed its permanent form. Its growing pains were over. No one was criticizing any more." For half a century and more since he expressed these thoughts, Extension has continued in the "Kelley style," communicating the message of home-missionary needs to America's Catholics and funding a variety of projects in remote places. In a letter to the Archbishop of Chicago in 1960 Pope John XXIII again blessed the "genuine missionary spirit" and "proud achievements of the past."

RECOMMENDED READING: Francis C. Kelley, *The Story of Extension* (Chicago: Extension Press, 1922); Francis Clement Kelley, *The Bishop Jots it Down: An Autobiography* (New York: Harper & Brothers, 1939).

MONSIGNOR GAFFEY, superintendent of schools and a priest of the Diocese of Santa Rosa, California, is writing a biography of Bishop Kelley.

45

The Origins of the National

Catholic Welfare Conference

ELIZABETH McKEOWN

World War I was a turning point for Catholic Americans. In the outburst of national energy that followed the declaration of war in April, 1917, the old public animosities toward Catholics were temporarily forgotten. Catholics formed a substantial portion of the American population, and public officials were quick to realize the importance of Catholic support in the war effort. Members of the Catholic hierarchy found themselves courted by a steady stream of war leaders asking their help in the mobilization effort.

Because many Catholic immigrants had strong ties to the Central powers, or in the case of the Irish, harbored a deep-seated animosity toward Great Britain, war leaders were openly anxious that the Catholic clergy should encourage their followers to put aside older claims and demonstrate their patriotism in the Allied cause.

The Catholic bishops responded vigorously to this invitation to civic leadership. In pastoral letters, speeches and actions, the bishops signaled their support for the American war effort and encouraged American Catholic participation. But while the enthusiasm of Catholic leaders was genuine and their support unstinting, there was a strong element of self-interest present in their response. Non-Catholic Americans continued to suspect that Catholicism was antithetical, if not inimical, to American principles and institutions. Church leaders saw in the mobilization effort an opportunity to dispel questions about the ability of Catholics to perform their duties as American citizens.

It was this combination of patriotism and interest in advancing the Catholic cause in the United States that formed the climate in which the national organization of Catholic bishops had its origins. The original idea

FATHER JOHN J. BURKE

Father Burke was the first general secretary of the National Catholic Welfare Conference. (*NC Photos*)

for a national Catholic organization belonged to Father John Burke. A Paulist and editor of the *Catholic World*, Father Burke had had ambitions for a national organization of American Catholics which predated the war by at least a decade. He had long recognized the growing pluralism of American culture and its increasing indifference to ecclesiastical distinctions. His concern was to ensure internal cohesion among American Catholics and to maintain the integrity of the traditional faith in the midst of contrary forces in the American environment.

At the same time, Father Burke fully believed that the survival of American institutions and values in the twentieth century depended in large measure upon the ability of Catholic leaders to infuse American public life with Catholic leadership. World War I provided him with the kind of leverage that eventually resulted in episcopal support for a national Catholic organization, the National Catholic War Council.

The War Council was formed by Father Burke and others with the consistent backing of Cardinal James Gibbons of Baltimore, who gained approval for it from other American bishops. In addition to the obvious wartime needs which Catholics were called upon to meet and which demanded organized and concerted Catholic effort, Cardinal Gibbons voiced to bishops the deeper rationale for national organization. He emphasized the urgent necessity of protecting Catholic interests in national affairs and pending legislation. He was in effect requesting the Catholic hierarchy to create a national voice for Catholic affairs, and was exhibiting a new kind of political sophistication in recognizing that Catholics could muster organizational strength to act as a special-interest group in national politics.

Officially, the War Council was composed of the fourteen archbishops of the country, who designated a committee of bishops to act in their name in attending to the national wartime concerns of the Church. The actual day-to-day business of the council was conducted by Father Burke and his staff in Washington. In addition to monitoring national legislation of interest to Catholics and promoting Catholic participation in the war, the work of the council included the preparation and provisioning of chaplains, religious and recreational work in the war camps, and the many facets of postwar reconstruction. In all these activities the War Council leaders gained a new degree of prominence for the Catholic Church in national affairs and provided a focus for a national Catholic outlook.

This wartime experience gave advocates of national organization for the American Church strong support for their views, and they were anxious to transform the War Council into a permanent body, composed of all members of the hierarchy, whose purpose would be mutual consultation and direction for the entire American Church. The diverse elements of American Catholicism seemed to those leaders to demand some trans-diocesan source of leadership and identity.

American Catholics were finding new kinds of political, regional, and class affiliations apart from the Church. Their identities as Catholics were becoming more strictly a matter of sacramental observance, less comprehensive of their lives as a whole. Catholics tended to remain faithful to their ecclesiastical obligations, but Catholic leaders were increasingly aware that the problem of American Catholic identity and the weight of Catholic impact on American life demanded action outside the sanctuary and the confessional. These conditions favored the creation of the National Catholic Welfare Council, an organization devoted to the national welfare of the Church under the formal leadership of the entire American hierarchy—one of the earliest efforts of national bodies of bishops in the world.

The initial steps in the formation of the Welfare Council were taken in February, 1919, at the golden episcopal jubilee celebration of Cardinal Gibbons. There the remarks of the Pope's representative, Archbishop Bonaventura Cerretti, recommending to the American hierarchy unity and action in regard to social and educational problems, provided episcopal advocates of national organization with the occasion to propose plans for such an organization. Those plans included an annual meeting of the entire American hierarchy to deal with matters of common concern, and a standing committee of leaders delegated by the hierarchy to act in their name in the interests of Catholic welfare in the interim.

The episcopal organizers, led by Bishop Peter Muldoon of Rockford, Illinois, and Bishop Joseph Schrembs of Toledo, Ohio, with the backing of Cardinal Gibbons, encountered immediate and sustained opposition to their organizational efforts from other bishops. Certain bishops felt that the existence of the council threatened episcopal autonomy within the dioceses, challenged traditional channels of authority, and hinted of Gallicanism in its conciliar tone and national outlook.

The criticisms of these prelates resulted in an effort on the part of the Vatican's Consistorial Congregation to suppress the council early in 1922. An immediate and sustained objection to such action was registered by the bishops of the administrative committee of the council, with the result that the decree of suppression was revoked. The congregation gave its approval to the American organization, declaring only that the decisions of the council could not be legislative in nature or binding upon the membership, and that the name of the organization should henceforth be the National Catholic Welfare Conference.

RECOMMENDED READING: John B. Sheerin, C.S.P., *Never Look Back: The Career and Concerns of John J. Burke* (New York: Paulist Press, 1975).

DR. McKEOWN is an assistant professor of theology in Georgetown University, Washington, D.C.

46

Orestes Brownson:

The Role of Catholics in America

HUGH MARSHALL, S.T.

Splashed across the pages of nineteenth-century American history is the bold, erratic figure of Orestes Augustus Brownson.

Born on the Vermont frontier of 1803, he grew to a strong, vigorous manhood in the hurly-burly of the development of the young American republic. Though self-educated and rough-hewn, he became a teacher, a Universalist minister, and the editor of a religious magazine by the age of twenty-five.

When twenty-three years old he had married Sally Healy, who was to be a loving and devoted wife for the next forty-five years. She was to be the only one in Brownson's life who could allay, at least somewhat, the bitter loneliness of his savage speculations.

In 1836 Brownson, then a Unitarian minister, moved his family to Boston. Besides his preaching he founded his own quarterly review, full—till 1875—of his strong opinions on politics, religion, the American and world scene. He was an active member of the Transcendentalist movement of William Ellery Channing and Ralph Waldo Emerson. He approved of the principles of Brook Farm, was a frequent visitor there, and sent his eldest son to live there. Church reform was a main concern of this group of Boston ministers in the 1830s, and Brownson soon developed in sermons and published articles his own ideal church: the Church of the Future. The more he struggled to establish this imaginary church, the more firmly he was drawn to the historical reality of the Catholic Church.

After a long, reluctant passage he became a Catholic in 1844 along with his whole family, which by then included seven children. His quarterly re-

ORESTES A. BROWNSON

(Courtesy of the Department of Archives and Manuscripts of the Catholic University of America)

view quickly became a vehicle for the ardent expression of his Catholic thought on most subjects. Often in controversy with ecclesiastical and civil officials because of his outspokenness and independent manner, he managed to run counter to the prevailing thinking of virtually every group of Americans. Despite his lack of tact, his forceful, logical articles were read by friend and foe alike.

Brownson was as ardent a patriot as he was a Catholic, and equally as controversial. He plumbed with unwavering logic the true meaning of the American nation and found the Constitution the highest political form ever reached by mankind. In its unique federal nature—dividing powers of government between constituent state governments and a general government in Washington—tyranny on either level could be effectively prevented, he believed, and liberty and justice ensured for the citizen.

Thoroughly convinced that this Constitution had developed organically out of many centuries of Catholic history and thought, he believed that God had guided even the details of its development in His loving concern for the good of mankind. The written Constitution was a faithful expression of this long-developing organic constitution, not a doctrinaire, purely philosophical expression of bodiless ideals.

The God-given mission of America was to be the freedom-giving political model for all nations. The Americans were a "providential people" with a duty to preserve their historical Constitution intact and live up to the highest ideals of their divine calling. They could do this, Brownson was convinced, only by becoming Catholics. Only then could they gain the virtue that would preserve the Constitution against the Protestant extreme of self-seeking mobocracy rocking the nation.

During the Civil War Brownson thought the American people showed an amazing and unselfish determination to preserve their God-given union. He was convinced that these "awakened" people would soon embrace the Catholic faith and thus be able to carry out their duty to mankind as well as to God. Hoping for a quick return of the seceded states and the forward movement of a united, dedicated, and Catholic nation, after the war Brownson became disgusted with the political revenge being taken on the prostrate South and the selfish, corrupt politics prevailing everywhere during the Grant Administration.

In desperation he decided by 1870 that the American people were too corrupt and selfish to become virtuous Catholics and that the Constitution could not survive in their hands. Had they not supinely accepted the Fourteenth and Fifteenth Amendments to the Constitution which destroyed completely the fine balance between general and state governments?

The last years were difficult for Browson. Three of his sons were killed by the end of the Civil War, his favorite dying in battle. His health, which had been so rugged in his youth and middle age, declined dramatically. He became corpulent and suffered from very painful gout of hands, feet, and even eyes. His hair, long and usually unkept, turned completely gray. His temperament worsened, and he became very demanding with his family, eccentric and domineering with others. He completely alienated the few friends he had made through the years. After the death of his gentle wife in 1872, two children took care of their ailing father—first his only daughter Sarah, then Henry. Both had inherited his gruff, unsympathetic disposition, and life was not easy when any two of them were together.

Brownson's interests now centered solely on his Church and its theology as his health ebbed away. He received the last rites of the Catholic Church on Easter, 1876, and died the next morning.

Brownson's monumental efforts to convert the whole nation to the Catholic faith were not the apocalyptic failure they seemed to him in his last years. An ardent disciple, Isaac Hecker, had followed Brownson through Transcendentalism into the Catholic Church. He became, at Brownson's prompting, a priest and the founder of a community of priests—the Paulists —to convert America to the Catholic Church.

Though Hecker and the Paulists failed in their goal of converting all Americans, they did popularize Brownson's love of American political institutions as something God-given and took this to the common Catholic through the many retreats they gave throughout the country. The great mass of immigrant Catholics pouring into the country were—thanks to this influence—converted to American democracy, ensuring the vibrant (and quite American) Catholic Church of twentieth-century America. Thanks to Brownson's earlier efforts, Catholics became an integral part of American politics and life, not a frustrated minority in opposition as often happened in European countries.

RECOMMENDED READING: Hugh Marshall, *Orestes Brownson and the American Republic: An Historical Perspective* (Washington, D.C.: Catholic University of America Press, 1971). Theodore Maynard, *Orestes Brownson. Yankee, Radical, Catholic* (New York: Macmillan Company, 1943). Americo D. Lapati, *Orestes A. Brownson* (New York: Twayne Publishers, 1965). Per Sveino, *Orestes A. Brownson's Road to Catholicism* (New York: Humanities Press, 1970). Leonard Gilhooley, *Contradiction and Dilemma. Orestes Brownson and the American Idea* (New York: Fordham University Press, 1972).

FATHER MARSHALL, a priest of the Congregation of the Missionary Servants of the Most Holy Trinity, received his doctorate in history from the Catholic University of America in 1962 and is currently pastor of St. Patrick's Church in Perry, Georgia.

47

Lay Apostle: Anthony Matre

SISTER M. ADELE FRANCIS GORMAN, O.S.F.

Among the giant lay leaders in the Catholic Church in the late nineteenth and early twentieth centuries was a man whose work was little known and recognized until relatively recently: Anthony Matre. Less colorful than some of his contemporaries, Matre probably played more roles in the Church and demonstrated greater qualities of leadership than most of his peers.

Born in Cincinnati on December 16, 1866, to Joseph and Magdalena Seubert Matreux (later changed to Matre), Anthony was the youngest of six children. When his parents died within a week of each other, his older sister Rose tried to hold the family together. But with Anthony only six and the oldest children already married, she was not successful. Anthony went to live with his godparents, the Anthony Hartmanns.

Thinking himself a candidate for the priesthood, he entered St. Francis Seraphic Seminary where, after four years, his confessor advised him to transfer to Pio Nono College in Milwaukee to be trained as a teacher and choirmaster and in business subjects. After graduation, he became principal and boys' teacher at St. Philomena School in Cincinnati, where he met and married Catherine Godar and began to rear their four sons.

Although photographs hint that Anthony Matre was a stern, unbending person, accounts of his family life indicate differently. The boys, one of whom is still living, always revered and respected him, calling him "father." It might be said that he was an early practitioner of child psychology because he kept his very normal sons well in hand without corporal punishment, while at the same time instilling in them principles of the ideal Christian family. An example of his devotion comes out of the incident in which one son injured another in a fit of temper. Neither would tell what had happened, but the injured boy became quite ill. Anthony knew who was guilty, but he wanted him to reveal himself. Consequently at family night

ANTHONY MATRE

(*NC Photos courtesy of Richard Matre*)

prayers he included a petition that the sick boy would not lose his leg as a result of the injury. This brought out a wail from the culprit who told the whole story and learned an important lesson.

Besides teaching, Matre wrote plays, directed and often acted in them. He produced alone or with his sister-in-law, Rose Godar, more than 70,000 copies of comedies, tragedies, and religious plays. The last royalties were paid to his heirs in 1951. In addition, with F. H. Loeffler, he published the bilingual (German-English) *Teacher and Organist*, which by 1905 had changed its name and become the official organ of the Catholic Teachers' Society of the United States.

Matre was also an ardent organization man, belonging to and holding office in the Holy Name Society, Catholic Knights of America, Third Order of St. Francis, and Knights of Columbus, in which he reached the fourth degree.

Very likely his most impressive contribution to lay activity in the Church was as the only secretary of an organization that he helped to form, the American Federation of Catholic Societies (AFCS), which existed from 1901 until 1919. As secretary he carried on all interim work between national annual conventions, helped to write and edit the organization's bulletin, raised funds, and performed whatever other tasks demanded immediate attention. At one time the federation claimed a total of more than three million individuals represented by officers of member societies.

The federation was made up of societies, not individuals, although it accepted individuals as associates. As the single full-time officer, Matre made efforts to establish an international federation of Catholic societies and made contacts with Catholic leaders in England and other countries of Europe and as far away as Australia.

He used the American federation to create a climate of Christian idealism by denouncing in the bulletin immorality wherever it existed and urging Catholics to assist their fellow believers to live better lives. At times he seemed to be working alone, but he used every instrument available to spread what he considered major federation principles.

After 1916 the federation began to decline for many reasons: the outbreak of World War I, the formation of the National Catholic War Council, the growing desire of the bishops to control the work of the federation more directly, and in particular the tensions between Matre and Father Peter E. Dietz, secretary of the federation's Social Service Commission. The conservative Matre and the more liberal Father Dietz clashed philosophically over many matters. Ultimately, Father Dietz was asked to leave the commission because of apparent indiscretions, and Matre was left to carry the burden of the federation alone. After the war the bishops formed the National Catholic Welfare Council (later Conference) on the foundation of the War Council but made no provision for either Matre or Father Dietz in the new structure.

As the federation went to a practically unmourned grave in 1919, Matre did not become inactive. He moved to Chicago and helped organize the Marquette Fire Insurance Company of which he became president. Using Chicago as a hub, Matre lectured about a hundred times a year, participated in arranging the first national congress of the Third Order of St. Francis, served on a committee to prepare and carry out the work of the first International Eucharistic Congress in the United States in 1926, and assisted one of his sons to open a religious articles store.

In 1930, Matre decided to retire, but after spending some time with each of his sons, he leaped at an invitation to teach at the Divine Word Seminary in Techny, Illinois. He also continued his lectures, play direction, and organization activities. Having become very interested in Father Damien, the leper priest, and his colorful confrere, Brother Dutton, he promoted the cause of the Damien-Dutton Clubs. In January, 1934, he was on his way to speak at the reception of a member into the Third Order of St. Francis when a hit-and-run driver turned his car over. Matre lingered for several days and died on January 17.

In 1926 he had had a premonition of death and had written to his son Frank precise stipulations about matters relating to his death and burial. Matre had been made a Knight of St. Gregory by Pope St. Pius X as a result of federation achievements and was a member of the papal household. At his request, he was buried as a knight in a quiet ceremony attended by many bishops, priests, and laymen.

RECOMMENDED READING: Mary Harrita Fox, *Peter E. Dietz, Labor Priest* (Notre Dame, Indiana: University of Notre Dame Press, 1953).

SISTER MARY ADELE FRANCIS is a professor of history in Our Lady of Angels College, Aston, Pennsylvania; she has completed a book-length biography of Matre which is awaiting publication.

48

Jane Hoey and Agnes Regan,
Women in Washington

DOROTHY A. MOHLER

Most people think of women, particularly Catholic women, as new-comers to social activism. This may be so if one defines an activist in terms of today's confrontation, demonstration, and protest. But there are other ways to be involved in action, as the lives of Jane Hoey and Agnes Regan show.

Almost a generation apart in age, they had much in common. Both were remarkably gifted women, deeply committed to the service of others. Their commitment was based on a strong Catholic faith. Both were daughters of Irish immigrants; both came from families of nine children; both were Westerners by birth.

Jane Hoey was born in 1892 in the pioneer community of Greeley County, Nebraska. Agnes Regan was born in 1869 in San Francisco to parents who had lived for a time in Chile—a circumstance that influenced her lifelong empathy with Latin Americans. Both were educated in Catholic schools. Miss Hoey was a graduate of Washington's Trinity College; Miss Regan completed grade and high school studies at St. Rose Academy, San Francisco.

Both came under the influence of Monsignors William J. Kerby and John A. Ryan of the Catholic University of America, influential advocates of social reform. For Jane Hoey they were mentors who stimulated her choice of a career in social work and whose writings she cited in her own speeches and papers. For Agnes Regan they were colleagues with whom she shared heavy responsibilities at the National Catholic School of Social Service and the National Catholic Welfare Conference.

JANE HOEY

This portrait, painted by C. Boswell Chambers, now belongs to Trinity College, Washington, D.C.

Both moved quickly into distinguished careers. Following graduate study at Columbia University and the affiliated New York School of Social Work, Miss Hoey held staff positions in several New York social agencies and was a member of state commissions on crime and corrections. Through a brother who had served in the state legislature she came to know such prominent Democrats as Al Smith, Robert Wagner, and Franklin Roosevelt.

For more than thirty years Agnes Regan served in the San Francisco school system as teacher, principal, and member of the Board of Education and its Playground Commission. She worked with the governor of California, Hiram Johnson, to secure enactment of the first teachers' pension law in the state. Ironically, she never profited fully from the benefits of the new legislation because she left California to begin a new career.

With solid experience at the local and state levels behind them, both were called to national service.

In 1936 Jane Hoey was appointed the first director of the Bureau of Public Assistance, Social Security Board, a post she held for seventeen years. She was one of the tiny group of women who filled one percent of the key executive positions at the federal level. She began her work in Franklin Roosevelt's first term, during the early years of the Depression. She was charged with major responsibility for administering the relief programs of the new Social Security Act. When individual effort could not provide the essentials of living she believed ultimate responsibility must be assumed by government. She was an early advocate of guaranteed annual income, which she regarded as an essential support for strong family life.

Advocacy of human rights is far more popular today, but Jane Hoey spoke out early on behalf of migrants, American Indians, working women, and other minorities whom "we fear, dislike, or distrust," and she anchored her defense in religion. In her presidential address to the National Conference of Social Work in 1941, she noted how hard it is to minimize racial, national, and personal differences and went on to say: "History and our own experience indicate only one source of strength and inspiration that can be depended upon to impel men in this direction—and that strength is spiritual and based on religious concepts."

Agnes Regan came to national prominence by way of Church-related work. Chosen to represent the Archdiocese of San Francisco at the organizational meeting of the National Council of Catholic Women (NCCW) in 1920, she soon became its executive secretary, a position she held for the next twenty years.

It was a crucial time for the Church in the United States. Partly as a result of World War I, American Catholics had been pushed from local and parochial concerns to a new awareness of the need for organization and action at the national level. The American bishops established the National Catholic War Council, later the National Catholic Welfare Conference.

The NCCW was a constituent part of the NCWC and Miss Regan traveled throughout the country interpreting the role of the NCCW as a federation of women's organizations and a body coordinating their work with that of the hierarchy. It was pioneering effort and she had to contend with objections, misunderstandings, and apathy. She stimulated the development of leadership in members of the NCCW and urged them to study and support legislation for housing, hours and wages, and racial problems. She testified before congressional committees in support of subsidies for maternal and child health care and on behalf of the ill-fated child labor amendment, but she opposed the "equal rights" amendment. In 1927 the NCCW, under her leadership, joined a coalition of other women's groups (the YWCA, the National Council of Jewish Women, and the Women's Industrial League) in support of a change in restrictive immigration laws.

Both women were closely identified with the social work profession— Agnes Regan as an educator, Jane Hoey as a practitioner. The American bishops had asked the NCCW to take over a training school for women social workers that had been established during World War I. Miss Regan, in addition to her duties with the NCCW, became assistant director of the National Catholic School of Social Service and its most loved and respected figure. In her view professional competence was important not as an end in itself but as an instrument of service for God's people. The link between religion and social work was a fact of life.

Writing to students and alumnae shortly after the passage of the Social Security Act, she said: "Here in the United States, we are making a great experiment—seeking to establish social security through federal and state enactments. If this experiment is to succeed it will be because it is based on Christian principles of social justice and because Christian principles are applied in putting the program into effect."

Jane Hoey pressed hard for professional training for social workers because she saw it as essential for a high quality of service. Her conviction about the professional character of social work was illustrated in the stand she took in 1953 when, in the new Eisenhower Administration, the post of director of the Bureau of Public Assistance lost its civil service status and became subject to political appointment. Miss Hoey refused to resign or to apply for retirement and was dismissed.

Recognition came in various ways to Jane Hoey and Agnes Regan. Both received the Siena medal of the Theta Phi Alpha fraternity given annually to an outstanding Catholic woman. The papal decoration, *Pro Ecclesia et Pontifice*, and an honorary academic degree were among Miss Regan's honors. When a new residence hall for women social work students was erected on the Catholic University campus it was named for her. Miss Hoey was president of the National Conference of Social Work, the Council on Social Work Education, and the William J. Kerby Foundation. She served as

United States delegate to the United Nations Social Commission. She received two awards from the New York School of Social Work, and honorary degrees were conferred on her by three universities.

Agnes Regan died on September 30, 1943, Jane Hoey on October 6, 1968.

DR. MOHLER is associate professor at the National Catholic School of Social Service in the Catholic University of America.

PETER MAURIN

This drawing by Fritz Eichenberg captures the character of the philosopher
of the Catholic Worker movement. (Courtesy of the *Catholic Worker*)

49

Peter Maurin, Teacher

WILLIAM D. MILLER

It would have been difficult to distinguish him from other speakers on their soapbox rostrums at New York City's Union Square in the early 1930s telling the world what its troubles were and what it had to do to cure them. Like the rest, he was shabbily dressed and, like the rest, he directed his message to whoever would listen. He was like the others, too, in that his concern was with a new social order.

But when it came to describing how this social order was to be achieved and what its character would be, the similarities ended. Most of the speakers thought in terms of capitalizing on the mass unrest of the Depression era to bring about revolutionary change in government. This man talked of revolution, too, but it was one of changing the minds and spirits of persons, of bringing the kingdom of God on earth.

The man was Peter Aristide Maurin, the cofounder with Dorothy Day of the Catholic Worker movement. He was born on May 8, 1877, on a small farm in southern France. The family was large, well ordered, and secure in a tradition that came from fifteen centuries of Maurin ownership of the land on which they lived. Years later, Maurin would exclaim proudly, "I am neither a bourgeois nor a proletarian. I am a peasant. I have roots!"

As a young man he was sent to a Christian Brothers boarding school near Paris and in 1893 he entered the order as a novice. But the life did not suit him and on January 1, 1903, at the expiration of his annual religious vows, he left the order.

A new interest, a Catholic youth movement called Le Sillon, whose aim was to support the rise of democratic forces in Europe, enlisted his ardor. For a while he attended its meetings and sold its newspaper on the streets of Paris. But after several years his Sillonist enthusiasm cooled. He got a little tired, it seems, of Le Sillon's parades and oratory, believing that liberalism by itself was not enough, that a more analytical and thoughtful approach to the social problem was needed.

In 1909 Maurin emigrated to Canada, lured there, probably, by the prospect of free land and freedom from forced military service. For nearly two years he and a partner worked hard at homesteading, but when his partner was accidentally killed, Maurin left Canada for the United States. For six years he wandered about the country as an itinerant laborer.

In 1925 the character of his life changed. In an episode which he never fully explained, he seemed to have reached a kind of revelatory insight into the spiritual source of the social problem. In a phrase he used so much in his teaching years with the Catholic Worker movement, he had had a profound "clarification" after years of reading and thinking on the subject. It was a vision so compelling that thereafter nothing mattered to him except that he should teach people the outlines of his synthesis.

Integral to his new sense of the meaning of things was his attitude toward the Catholic Church, which during his American years had apparently become casual. He now saw it as the one, divine, and indispensable means of infusing the substance of life with the spirit of the Gospels. When he was with the Catholic Worker he used to write down his thoughts in a simplified free-verse style which he thought would help him get his ideas across to working men and women. One poem was called "Blowing the Dynamite," and these are some of its lines:

> To blow the dynamite
> of a message
> is the only way
> to make the message dynamic.
> If the Catholic Church
> is not today
> the dominant social force,
> it is because Catholic scholars
> have failed to blow the dynamite
> of the Church.
> Catholic scholars
> have taken the dynamite
> of the Church,
> have wrapped it up
> in nice phraseology,
> placed it in a hermetic container
> and sat on the lid.
> It is about time
> to blow the lid off. . . .

In December, 1932, Maurin met Dorothy Day, journalist, radical, and recent Catholic convert. At the time she was seeking to relate her social concern to her new faith and she found Maurin, as she would say many times later, an answer to a prayer. For three months he came almost daily to the small apartment which she and her little daughter, Tamar, shared with her brother and sister-in-law. Maurin wrote digests of books for her to study—Church histories, social philosophies, and especially those by religious thinkers of the time, Emmanuel Mounier, Jacques Maritain, and Nicolas Berdyaev.

What Maurin aimed at was a restoration of the communal aspects of Christianity. He wanted the ethic of cooperation, suffused with a spirit of the charity of Christ, to supplant the values of a bourgeois culture that emphasized the acquisition of things as the ultimate mark of a person's worth.

He favored a cooperative world society based on a free association of persons in integrated economic, social, and intellectual endeavors. He believed that society could be made good, but it could not be manipulated into this state by social engineering. Meaningful social betterment could come finally from changed persons—those who in a crucial exercise of freedom would turn away from the world of bourgeois values and forms and develop their own communitarian ventures.

From the time of the founding of the Catholic Worker movement on May 1, 1933, until his death on May 15, 1949, Maurin spent his time working and teaching at Catholic Worker farms or houses of hospitality. And in his persistent hammering away at his ideas and clarifications he did not live apart from the spirit of what he taught. He became truly the poor man —poor of goods and poor of spirit, so that no need of his own ego could intrude its abrasive edge between him and what he wanted to communicate to anyone who would listen.

What had Maurin accomplished as a teacher? Dorothy Day gave her answer at the time of his death: "He taught us what it meant to be sons of God, and restored us to our sense of responsibility in a chaotic world. Yes, he was . . . holier than anyone we ever knew."

RECOMMENDED READING: William D. Miller, *A Harsh and Dreadful Love: Dorothy Day and the Catholic Worker Movement* (New York: Liveright, 1973).

DR. MILLER is professor of history in Marquette University, Milwaukee, Wisconsin.

ARCHBISHOP MARTIN JOHN SPALDING

A native of Kentucky, Martin John Spalding was a distinguished writer,
speaker, and bishop first in Louisville and then, from 1864 to his death in
1872, in Baltimore. At the First Vatican Council he was the leader of the
American prelates who favored a moderate definition of papal infallibility.
(*Kentucky Collection of Francis P. Clark*)

50

Americans at Vatican Council I

JAMES HENNESEY, S.J.

Forty-eight bishops and an abbot represented the United States at the First Vatican Council of 1869–1870. It was a predominantly European meeting called to face European problems. Topics ranged from German philosophy and the relationship between faith and reason to the spiritual life of priests and a proposed worldwide elementary catechism. But the council's most significant event was on July 18, 1870, when, after two months of debate, Pope Pius IX solemnly proclaimed the dogmas of papal primacy and infallibility.

Bishop Bernard J. McQuaid of Rochester wrote home that he had to push his way through the crowd to get into St. Peter's Basilica on opening day. His difficult entry was symbolic for the first Americans ever to attend an ecumenical council.

A succession of nineteenth-century popes had fought the political, intellectual, and social forces shaping Europe. The council was planned to reinforce their stance. An added complication was that the existence of the independent Papal State was the chief barrier to Italian national unity.

The Church in the United States had other problems. Reconstruction after the Civil War; pastoral care for the freed blacks; Northern industrialization and the growth of cities, their slums packed with immigrants; financial panics and depressions in a dog-eat-dog economy; the scandals of the Grant Administration. Pioneers pushed westward. Church structures were needed to replace exotic jurisdictions like that of Bishop John B. Miege, S.J., apostolic vicar of the Indian Territory east of the Rocky Mountains, headquartered at Leavenworth, Kansas. American and European needs were very different.

Father James A. Corcoran of Charleston worked on the council's preparatory theological commission. He reported "a mania for defining a great

219

mass of propositions, and on every subject," and objected to proposals endorsing church-state union and defining the pope's infallibility. Father Corcoran echoed the American scene, where theologians and national councils at Baltimore consistently supported constitutional principles of religious freedom and non-entanglement of church and state.

Definition of the pope's infallibility, thought by many in Europe necessary to safeguard papal authority, was not a burning issue in the United States. It was known to be a theological opinion that papal teachings, under certain circumstances, were infallible, but bishops and catechisms taught that Catholics might accept this or not. Archbishop John McCloskey of New York and Archbishop Martin John Spalding of Baltimore spoke the mind of many when they declared that the ultimate teaching authority of the Church in matters of faith rested with the bishops of the world in union with their chief bishop, the pope, either gathered in an ecumenical council or dispersed throughout the world. Only recently had a campaign for definition of papal infallibility begun, promoted by James A. McMaster, a convert and the editor of the *New York Freeman's Journal*, and by Father Francis X. Weninger, a Jesuit missionary, whose book, *On the Apostolical and Infallible Authority of the Pope*, appeared in 1868.

In the first American intervention at the council, Archbishop Peter Richard Kenrick of St. Louis protested that committee elections were scheduled before the council fathers knew the candidates. He was overruled, as were other petitions with American signatures. Bishops from the United States objected to closed committee meetings and poor acoustics which made it hard to hear speeches, and urged press briefings for accurate reporting of events. They were pragmatic with a pragmatism that came from a pastoral sense of responsibility to the Church.

The first major division in the council grew out of the choice of members for the "deputation on faith," the committee which processed theological proposals. Two informal caucuses presented candidates. Bishop Michael Heiss of LaCrosse, Wisconsin, was a part of the group which prepared a list of those expected to favor a definition of papal infallibility. While the topic was not yet formally on the agenda, it proved to be the key to the way the council developed.

Archbishop Kenrick and other Americans joined those opposed to the definition. The infallibilists were successful, electing all their candidates, who included Archbishop Spalding and Archbishop Joseph Alemany of San Francisco, both of whom now sought compromise on the infallibility question. Other American members of commissions were Bishop Heiss and Archbishop McCloskey (for Church Discipline), Bishop Stephen V. Ryan, C.M., of Buffalo (for Religious Orders), and Bishop Louis de Goesbriand of Burlington, Vermont (for Eastern Churches and Missions).

Americans showed greater vigor in written interventions than in floor speeches. Their input reflected sensitivity to the pluralistic and democratic society in which they lived. Recurring themes were the demand for careful attention to Scripture and dropping of passages offensive to Protestants and secular governments. They argued against the idea that the Church was a separate society parallel and hostile to civil society, and they wanted elimination of claims to coercive powers of punishment. Condemnations they thought ineffective. Bishop Richard Whelan of Wheeling, West Virginia, urged that the treatise on the Church begin—as the Second Vatican Council's Constitution on the Church was to begin nearly a century later —with scriptural images, and that the overriding emphasis be on the Church's function of leading mankind to eternal salvation through faith and charity.

Veterans of successive Councils of Baltimore, the Americans boasted the strongest collegial tradition in nineteenth-century Western Catholicism. They were acutely sensitive to the role of bishops as a body. This made them protest procedural irregularities which prevented free discussion. It also caused many to hesitate about exclusive emphasis on the pope's teaching authority. They had definite opinions on the relationship of Church to State. Archbishop John Baptist Purcell of Cincinnati summed it up when he said that "the perfect liberty to all" granted by the American Constitution was better than kingly patronage. His thesis was that "truth is mighty and will prevail," that all the Church should ask was to be permitted to function freely in a free society.

Infallibility divided the Americans. A dozen, mostly Franco-Americans, but including Bishop Heiss and Bishop William Henry Elder of Natchez, Mississippi, strongly favored a definition. Archbishops Kenrick and Purcell and others were opposed. Their difficulty was not merely that a definition was politically inexpedient (the "inopportunist" position). They also had problems with scriptural and historical evidence and because of their understanding of the collegial nature of Church authority. Most Americans were in between. James Gibbons, then the youngest bishop in the country and later a cardinal, wrote afterwards that a majority were intially inopportunists.

Twenty-one Americans petitioned in January that infallibility not come to the floor. Some later sided with Archbishop Spalding in proposing a compromise which would avoid the word "infallibility" but preserve its substance.

The most frequent American speaker was Bishop Augustin Verot of Savannah and later of St. Augustine. His sense of humor repeatedly provoked rebukes from the council presidents, but his ideas were good as he called for recognition of values in modern science, breviary reform, improvement in the spiritual life of priests, and attention to real problems, such as the racist theories he daily confronted in his diocese. In the debate on primacy and infallibility, he and Archbishop Purcell spoke in opposition. Bishop Whelan gave a nuanced speech, pleading that the "whole salvation and strength of the Church does not depend on the pope." Bishop Michael Domenec of Pittsburgh outlined adverse reactions that a definition could produce in the United States. Archbishops Spalding and Alemany spoke in favor of definition, while Archbishop Kenrick wrote two long pamphlets against it.

A preliminary vote on the document declaring papal primacy and infallibility was taken on July 13. Twenty-eight Americans voted. Many had gone home. Eighteen voted yes, seven no, and three asked further revisions. The final vote of approval came at the solemn session in Pope Pius IX's presence on July 18. Sixty-one opponents had addressed protests to the Pope and then left Rome. Among them were Archbishop Kenrick and Bishops Verot and Domenec. Two American opponents attended the July 18 session. Bishop William McCloskey of Louisville joined twenty-four Americans in voting yes; Bishop Edward Fitzgerald of Little Rock, Arkansas, was one of two council fathers to vote no. Four hundred and thirty-three voted yes. Once they had been made, all the bishops of the world accepted the definitions of primacy and infallibility.

The First Vatican Council was a unique experience for its American participants. Several of them, on either side of the central issue of infallibility played significant roles. More importantly, they introduced into the proceedings something of the peculiar genius and ideas of their own country, a nation born of a revolution and a constitutional development different from that of the older countries whose bishops dominated the council.

RECOMMENDED READING: James Hennesey, S.J., *The First Council of the Vatican: The American Experience* (New York: Herder and Herder, 1963).

FATHER HENNESEY is professor of modern and American religious history at the Jesuit School of Theology in Chicago, of which he is president.

51

Americans in the Service of the Vatican

ROBERT F. McNAMARA

"**A**mericans rarely make a career of the Vatican." So said a "Vatican insider" to the writer of a recent news article on the popes and their officialdom.

"Rarely," yes. Yet a count of the American Catholic clergymen whom the Holy See has engaged over fourteen decades in administrative or diplomatic service makes a surprisingly long list of names.

Admittedly, most of the assignments have been temporary. John England, Bishop of Charleston, South Carolina, from 1820 to 1842, was the first American sent on a temporary papal mission. In 1833 Pope Gregory XVI requested him to go to Haiti and work out an agreement between Haiti and the Holy See. Gregory XVI did not take kindly to the proposal which the bishop came back with, but time vindicated its wisdom. Another American, Bishop Joseph Rosati of St. Louis, was sent to Haiti by the same Pope in 1842 to make a second try. This time the Pope and the Haitian president approved a concordat based on Bishop England's earlier recommendations.

Half a century later, Pope Leo XIII entrusted to Archbishop John Ireland of St. Paul two less formal errands. In 1892 he asked him to go to France (where the archbishop had studied and was well known) to win over Catholic leaders to a friendlier view of the Third French Republic. Six years afterward, Pope Leo, with still greater urgency, entreated Archbishop Ireland to persuade his friend, President William McKinley, to ward off the impending Spanish-American war. The archbishop may have had some slight success on his first mission. He had none on the second.

Two popes have sent American bishops as official visitors to Japan. In 1905 St. Pius X requested Bishop William H. O'Connell of Portland, Maine, to undertake a diplomatic, missionary, and educational tour of a Japanese

Bishop Joseph P. Hurley of Saint Augustine, regent of the Apostolic Nunciature in Yugoslavia (shown on the left wearing a skullcap), rises and bows as the Archbishop of Zagreb is led into the courtroom in which he was to be tried by the Communists on trumped-up charges of having collaborated with the Nazis and Fascists in World War II and was to be convicted and sentenced to sixteen years' imprisonment. (*Wide World Photos*)

Empire that had just conquered Russia. Bishop O'Connell did well. He was later named archbishop of Boston and a cardinal. In 1946, after World War II, Pius XII deputed two American bishops to make a comparable survey of the vanquished Japan. They were Bishop John F. O'Hara of Buffalo, New York, and Bishop Michael J. Ready of Columbus, Ohio.

In 1928–1929 the Vatican used two prominent American priests as intermediaries in the establishment of a modus vivendi with Mexico: Paulist Father John J. Burke, general secretary of the National Catholic Welfare Conference, and Jesuit Father Edmund A. Walsh of Georgetown University. Father Walsh, who had headed the Papal Relief Mission to Moscow in 1922, was also sent as papal emissary on an educational errand to Iraq in 1931.

Popes often designate cardinals as their personal legates to special Church celebrations. Pope John XXIII sent Boston's Cardinal Richard Cushing as his representative to the national Eucharistic Congresses of Peru (1960) and Bolivia (1961). Pius XI chose Cardinal Dennis Dougherty of Philadelphia (who had been a bishop in the Philippines) to be his stand-in at the International Eucharistic Congress of Manila (1936); and Pope Paul VI appointed Cardinal Lawrence Shehan of Baltimore to a similar post at the International Eucharistic Congress of 1973 in Melbourne, Australia.

More important than temporary commissions are stable appointments, like those of apostolic nuncio or delegate. One reason why few Americans are named to these positions is that in many nations American citizens are looked upon with resentment or suspicion. On the other hand, their very Americanism can at times be diplomatically advantageous to the Holy See.

The first two Americans named papal delegates were chosen in part because of their fluency in English. Diomede Falconio, Italian-born but a naturalized citizen of the United States, was papal delegate to Canada (1892–1902) and then to the United States (1902–1911). Pius XI, in 1926, named a native American as apostolic delegate to India, Father Edward Mooney of Cleveland. In 1931, he transferred Archbishop—later Cardinal—Mooney to the apostolic delegation in Japan.

But it was during and after World War II that the Holy See found Americans especially valuable aides. In the course of the war, Monsignor Walter S. Carroll was an important liaison person between the Vatican and the Allied armies. After the war, Pius XII named Bishop Joseph P. Hurley of St. Augustine, Florida, regent of the papal nunciature in Yugoslavia (1945); and Bishop Gerald P. O'Hara to the corresponding position in Rumania (1946). Also, in 1946, he appointed Bishop Aloisius Muench of Fargo, North Dakota, apostolic visitator to West Germany. In 1947, Pius XII chose a Maryknoll missionary, Father Patrick J. Byrne, to be visitator in Korea, and in 1949 named him apostolic delegate there. The three men deputed to Communist countries had no happy lot. Archbishop Hurley withdrew; Archbishop O'Hara was expelled; Father Byrne died in prison. Bishop—later Cardinal—Muench alone continued in his German assignment, becoming nuncio to West Germany, 1951–1959. Archbishop O'Hara, returning to Rome, was also retained in diplomatic service, first as nuncio to Ireland (1951–1954) and after that as apostolic delegate in Great Britain (1954–1963).

Since World War II, four other Americans have held high diplomatic offices: Archbishop Celestine Damiano, delegate to South Africa; Archbishop Joseph P. McGeough, internuncio to Ethiopia, then delegate to South Africa, and finally nuncio to Ireland; Archbishop Martin J. O'Connor, pioneer papal nuncio to Malta; and Archbishop Raymond Etteldorf, internuncio to New Zealand and then to Ethiopia.

One reason for this development has been the gradual increase of American personnel in the Roman Curia. The first American curialist was Father —later Cardinal—Francis J. Spellman, who was an attaché of the papal secretariat of state from 1925 to 1932. Since then nearly two dozen other Americans have held Vatican posts. Furthermore, since 1940 there has always been at least one American judge on the Vatican high court, the Roman Rota. The first American judge, Father Francis J. Brennan, became senior Rota judge or dean in 1959, and in 1967 was created a cardinal. Two Americans have also been president of the permanent Pontifical Commission for Social Communications: Archbishops O'Connor and Edward L. Heston, C.S.C. And the current president of the Vatican bank is a Chicagoan, Bishop Paul C. Marcinkus.

Recent popes have also appointed Americans as official observers at international agencies. Monsignor Luigi Ligutti, for example, served as the Holy See's permanent observer to the Food and Agriculture Organization (FAO) of the United Nations from 1948 to 1971. Father Theodore Hesburgh, C.S.C., and Mr. Frank M. Folsom have represented the Holy See at the International Agency for Atomic Energy.

The top Vatican officials are cardinals who head congregations. The first American to reach this level was Cardinal Diomede Falconio, prefect of the Congregation of Religious, 1916–1917. Cardinal Samuel Stritch of Chicago was named acting head (pro-prefect) of the Congregation for the Propagation of the Faith in 1958; but he died soon after reaching Rome. Cardinal Francis Brennan was briefly chief of the Congregation on Sacraments (1967–1968). Cardinal John Wright, former bishop of Pittsburgh, was in 1974 appointed to his second five-year term as prefect of the Congregation for the Clergy.

Many other Americans have served the Vatican in lesser posts. Among them are four nuns attached at present to the Congregation for Religious. So although the United States has not contributed greatly to the adminis-

BISHOP ALOISIUS MUENCH OF FARGO AS APOSTOLIC VISITATOR TO GERMANY

Bishop Muench accompanied Pope Pius XII to the Vatican warehouse on February 18, 1947, to inspect supplies sent from the United States and ready for shipment to Germany. Also shown in this photograph are (on the left) the Reverend Andrew P. Landi of the Rome office of the War Relief Services of the National Catholic Welfare Conference and (on the right) the Reverend Thomas F. Markham, chaplain of the United States Army. (*Courtesy of the Cardinal Muench Museum, Fargo, North Dakota*)

trative personnel of the Holy See, the American presence has helped to make that personnel truly international.

RECOMMENDED READING: Peter Guilday, *The Life and Times of John England, First Bishop of Charleston (1786–1842)* (2 vols.; New York: America Press, 1927). Frederick J. Easterly, C.M., *The Life of the Rt. Rev. Joseph Rosati, First Bishop of St. Louis, 1789–1843* (Washington, D.C.: Catholic University of America Press, 1942). Robert I. Gannon, S.J., *The Cardinal Spellman Story* (Garden City, New York: Doubleday & Company, 1962). Colman J. Barry, O.S.B., *American Nuncio: Cardinal Aloisius Muench* (Collegeville, Minnesota: Saint John's University Press, 1969).

FATHER McNAMARA is professor of church history, St. Bernard's Seminary, Rochester, New York.

TERENCE V. POWDERLY

As the first Catholic head of the first great national union, Powderly (shown here in 1886, when he had already been Grand Master Workman for seven years) succeeded in eliminating the requirements of secrecy that had rendered the Knights of Labor suspect to the Church, and he secured the support of a majority of the American bishops led by Cardinal James Gibbons of Baltimore. (*Department of Archives and Manuscripts of the Catholic University of America*)

52

Catholicism and Trade Unionism:

From the Knights of Labor to the CIO

NEIL BETTEN

In the last three decades of the nineteenth century major American religious denominations reacted to the industrial depressions and labor violence
by developing a deeper concern for working-class needs and problems. For
the major Protestant churches this "social gospel movement" meant changing
their theological focus in regard to the poor, establishing church-related
social-welfare institutions, and taking a more positive stand toward organized
labor.

Roman Catholic leaders, in contrast, did not have to significantly alter their
perspective in responding to the problems of the working class because
Catholic theology had never equated poverty with evidence of sin (as had
much of Protestant thought). Moreover, working-class conditions traditionally concerned the American Catholic leadership. Not only were Catholic parishioners commonly workers, but most priests, even bishops, were
usually the sons of workers.

On the labor question—the support of unions or of just strikes—the
Church led the way for Christian institutions in America. There were, however, differences among Catholics on various labor issues. In the nineteenth
century, some German-American Catholic spokesmen rejected unions. Like
much of the middle class they viewed strikes as overly militant. After the
mid-1880's Catholic social reformers supported compulsory arbitration—
where a neutral third party would settle labor disputes concerning wages
and working conditions.

Although conservative publications, such as the New York *Catholic Review*, advocated arbitration to prevent revolution-spawning strikes, most

Catholic leaders supported arbitration as a way of strengthening weak unions and fostering workers' needs. Catholic spokesmen in the labor movement, however, supported strikes as the only realistic alternative in response to employer attitudes.

Working-class Catholics emerged as influential forces in both major nineteenth-century labor federations. Although the Catholic influence in the Knights of Labor has never been fully examined, the Knights partially abolished their principle of secrecy to respond to demands of Catholic members and to increase the union's appeal to potential Catholic members. The organization elected Terence V. Powderly, in 1879, as its head partly because as an active Catholic layman Powderly had a good relationship with American prelates. When Archbishop Elzear Alexandre Taschereau of Quebec obtained a papal condemnation of the Knights in Canada, many of the American bishops sprang to the organization's defense and supported Cardinal James Gibbons who successfully defended the Knights in Rome. The condemnation was lifted.

The American Federation of Labor (AFL), founded in 1886, had a clear Catholic orientation in several ways. As historian Marc Karson has shown, more than fifty presidents of AFL-affiliated unions were Roman Catholics. Of the eight vice-presidents of the AFL executive board from 1900 to 1918, Catholics numbered at least four in any one year. Moreover, Samuel Gompers, the Jewish president of the AFL, had a similar ideological perspective as his good friend and advisor Father Peter Dietz. Dietz organized the Militia for Christ as a pro-union but adamantly anti-radical force in the labor movement.

The AFL in organizing the more conservative, highly skilled workers, in avoiding establishing a labor party or an alliance with the Socialist party, in supporting strikes based purely on practical issues, was clearly acceptable to the Catholic leadership in contrast to the radical Industrial Workers of the World (IWW) which emerged as a formidable AFL rival in the years before World War I.

Although the IWW grew in the first sixteen years of the century, so did the AFL. The federal government aided the nationalistic Federation during World War I while it attacked the IWW as subversive and disloyal. In the 1920s the AFL remained static in numbers and ideas. With the IWW virtually dead, the AFL now received some criticism from Catholic quarters, particularly from one of the country's leading theologians, Father John A. Ryan. Although friendly to the AFL, Ryan attempted to prod the Federation a bit to the left—to take stronger and more active political stands on progressive issues and to organize the great mass of industrial workers.

It was not until the 1930s that a new watershed in labor history would be reached and the unskilled industrial workers of the north would be organized. In the process the labor movement split into two warring camps.

Catholic social activists went in both directions, but for the most part supported the new federation—the Congress of Industrial Organizations (CIO) —which attempted to organize the mass of industrial workers. Even before the conflict between the AFL and the CIO, national Catholic publications such as *Commonweal*, *America*, and the *Catholic Charities Review* scored the elitism of the Federation which, according to a *Commonweal* article in March, 1932, "jealously guarded the privilege of skilled labor." Because the CIO included Communists and accepted the use of the "sit-down strike"— where strikers physically occupied factories to prevent employers from using strikebreakers—some Catholic spokesmen became alarmed. Yet, as a whole, they still supported the CIO. In November, 1938, *Sign*, for example, although critical of the CIO, typically urged Catholics to join the CIO and "direct their movement according to the sound principles of Catholic Sociology." Most Catholic publications took this stance, while vocal members of the hierarchy, such as Archbishop Edward Mooney, Archbishop John T. McNicholas, Archbishop Robert E. Lucey, and Bishop Bernard James Sheil were closely identified with the CIO.

Catholic institutions and individuals helped CIO organizing, and became involved with the labor movement in general. The Social Action Department of the National Catholic Welfare Conference supported labor reforms, such as minimum wages, and condemned management actions in numerous strikes. Monsignor Ryan, its director, emerged as one of the few Catholic spokesmen who defended the sit-down strikes. The Catholic Workers, followers of Dorothy Day, in addition to providing direct aid to the poor and propagandizing for massive social and economic change, walked the picket lines during strikes in support of numerous unions and occasionally provided meals and housing to hard-pressed strikers. The Association of Catholic Trade Unionists, in the late 1930s, provided propaganda for union-organizing drives in industries with a large proportion of Catholic workers, and often refuted claims that Communists controlled the CIO. In addition individual priests, such as Father Charles Owen Rice of Pittsburgh, supported organized labor by picketing, by publishing labor periodicals, and by teaching classes on union techniques. Other clerics, such as Fathers Francis J. Haas and John P. Boland, served on numerous government boards overseeing the labor relations of the country.

In the 1930s the community of interest between organized labor and the Catholic Church continued the close relationship which had traditionally benefited both institutions. In contrast to several European countries, the Church did not have to contend with a hostile, anticlerical labor movement, while organized labor did not have to compete with a rival Roman Catholic labor federation, also existing in some countries. Instead traditional American unionism—the AFL and the CIO—received the support of the religious institution to which millions of American workers remained loyal.

RECOMMENDED READING: Aaron I. Abell, *American Catholicism and Social Action: A Search for Social Justice, 1865–1950* (Garden City, New York: Hanover House, Doubleday & Company, 1960), and *American Catholic Thought on Social Questions*, edited by Aaron I. Abell (Indianapolis: Bobbs-Merrill Company, 1968). Henry J. Browne, *The Catholic Church and the Knights of Labor* (Washington, D.C.: Catholic University of America Press, 1949). Mary Harrita Fox, *Peter E. Dietz, Labor Priest* (Notre Dame, Indiana: University of Notre Dame Press, 1953).

DR. BETTEN is an associate professor of history in Florida State University, Tallahassee.

53

Frederick P. Kenkel,

Social Critic

PHILIP GLEASON

Frederick P. Kenkel died in 1952 but many of the things he cared about are still timely in 1976. He loved history, for one thing. And he wanted the story of his ethnic group—Catholics of German origin—to be more fully appreciated as a part of American history. In this he resembles our more recent spokesmen for the new ethnicity.

First and foremost, Kenkel was a social commentator and critic. For almost a half-century he directed the social reform program of the country's leading German-American Catholic society, the Central Verein (now called the Catholic Central Union). As editor of its journal, *Social Justice Review*, he analyzed social issues from the days of Theodore Roosevelt to the Korean War. He denounced injustice and applied the norms of Catholic social teaching in calling for a better world.

But while he was a reformer, Kenkel was not a liberal. He was proudly and self-consciously a conservative. He drew inspiration from the past and looked to the Middle Ages for the model of his ideal society. If this seems paradoxical, it can perhaps be understood as growing out of his life experience.

Frederick Kenkel was almost forty years old before he found his true vocation in life. He was born in Chicago in 1863. His parents had immigrated as newlyweds in 1848 and were active in the German theater in this country for several years. The family was cultured and well-off financially. "Fritz" Kenkel's education came from tutors and private schools, and as a youngster he traveled to Germany.

At eighteen Kenkel returned to Germany to begin his higher education

FREDERICK P. KENKEL

This photograph was taken in the library of his home in Saint Louis in 1930, when he was sixty-seven years old. (*NC Photos*)

as a mining engineer. But in spite of his boyhood fondness for geology, his real bent was toward the artistic and literary, not the scientific or technical. He soon left the mining school and spent the next two or three years in travel and private studies. But when he fell in love and wished to marry, Kenkel's days of leisured intellectual pursuits were over. In 1885 he returned to Chicago and entered a bookselling business.

The next epoch in Kenkel's life (until about 1900) included domestic tragedy and a kind of spiritual crisis. At age twenty-six he suffered the shattering loss of the death of his young wife after only three years of marriage. After this shock, he found consolation in the Catholic religion. He had been baptized as an infant but his family were not practicing Catholics and Kenkel's return to the Church in 1890 was like a true conversion.

Faith gave new meaning to his life, but it did not solve his search for a vocation. He considered a religious vocation for a time but felt an even stronger call to marriage after he met a young German girl engaged by his sister as a governess.

Kenkel's second marriage (in 1892) was happy, fruitful, and long. But domestic responsibility again sent him back into the world of business, which he had already discovered was not to his taste. This time his activities in real estate, insurance, and as business manager of the diocesan Catholic paper contributed to a severe psychological depression lasting many months.

The melancholia took the form of a profound sense of estrangement from the modern world and a detestation of bourgeois civilization. Slowly Kenkel came out of the worst of it, aided by his family and religious counsels. But his cure would never be complete till he found work more suitable to his temperament and abilities. He needed, and had not yet found, a life task into which he could throw himself with all the intensity of his character.

In 1901 Kenkel found such work in the field of journalism. He became the editor of a Catholic German-language paper in Chicago, then moved to the St. Louis *Amerika,* the outstanding German Catholic daily in the country. Kenkel had a scholar's mind and learning, but he also felt a deep need to bring his intellectual energies to focus on the great social and moral issues of the moment. From the editor's desk, he could act the part of educator. His keen and wide-ranging editorials soon won attention and respect.

By 1908 Kenkel's prominent place on the German Catholic scene made it natural for the leaders of the Central Verein to ask his counsel in their efforts to reformulate the aims of that venerable society (founded in 1855). It had just been successfully reorganized and was seeking a new focus for its energies. Thanks mainly to Kenkel's influence, the Central Verein determined to adopt social reform as its primary activity and goal. Kenkel himself became the director of its newly established Central Bureau and the editor of *Social Justice Review,* the first Catholic magazine in the country to make social reform its principal concern.

Kenkel had now truly found his life work and he dedicated himself to it unswervingly till his death in 1952. However, the years 1908–1917 were really the climax of his career. Kenkel himself was in the prime of life and his combined work at the Central Bureau and *Amerika* (which he continued to edit till 1920) made him the most influential German Catholic layman in the country. His message of social criticism and reform meshed beautifully with the dominant currents of American thinking in the Progressive Period and gave him a position of honor among socially conscious Catholics. Even the organizational base improved as the Central Verein flourished and grew in strength.

Then came World War I. The war changed everything. It brought the Progressive Period to a close and made reform unfashionable. Far worse, it made everything German suspect. It put all German-Americans on the defensive and reduced their influence. It speeded the dissolution of their organizations and press and eroded their cultural identity. After 1917, German-Americans found themselves on an irreversible downward course as a self-conscious cultural force in American life.

The war not only weakned the Central Verein organizationally; it also caused a subtle internal shift in Kenkel's social thinking. America, he felt, had made a ghastly mistake in entering the war against Germany. Her doing so confirmed his belief that the whole political and social system was basically defective. The war thus deepened the alienation from modern life that had caused him such anguish in the 1890s. It gave his social commentary a querulous note. It encouraged him to entertain utopian dreams of a complete restructuring of American society that would make of it a truly Christian corporative order, like that of the Middle Ages.

For more than thirty years after World War I, Kenkel fought for a goal that grew more distant with time. He never wavered in his effort, however, or in his conviction that his was the way to true reform. In doing so, he spoke for many a worthy cause—such as cooperatives, credit unions, and the liturgical movement—and undertook practical programs of great value, such as the resettlement of displaced persons in the late 1940s.

Many of the works that he began still continue. Along with the historical riches he collected at the Central Bureau, these works are the monument to a noble and dedicated man.

RECOMMENDED READING: Philip Gleason, *The Conservative Reformers. German-American Catholics and the Social Order* (Notre Dame, Indiana: University of Notre Dame Press, 1968).

DR. GLEASON is professor of history in the University of Notre Dame.

54

John A. Ryan and Social Justice

FRANCIS L. BRODERICK

At the beginning of the twentieth century, Catholics generally feared that every increase in governmental power threatened religion or moved toward socialism. By the end of World War II, the Church in America was comfortable as an ally of progressives and New Dealers. In the years between, no one did more to effect the change in attitudes than Monsignor John A. Ryan.

Priest, teacher, writer, lecturer, even more a reformer than a theologian, he started from the idea that every man was entitled by nature to a living wage. Gradually eroding the Church's fear of the secular state, he brought American Catholic opinion around to the belief that only the government had the power to confront powerful economic groups such as the large modern corporations with enough force to guarantee decent working conditions to the great majority. America moved in the period to legislation for minimum wages and maximum hours, to social security and unemployment insurance, to child labor laws and safety regulations; it attacked trusts like Standard Oil and it regulated monopolies like railroads and telephone companies. Ryan helped Catholics to contribute to the changes and to support the new ways.

The road was long and frequently discouraging, for the hostility of governments to the Church in the nineteenth century had made Catholic thinkers wary of the state. Traditionally Catholics had looked at state and Church as mutually supportive. But the venom generated by the French Revolution and the threats to both religion and property implicit in the spread of socialist thought opened up a new era, and the Church shied away fearfully from any increase in activity by the state. Many churchmen feared secularism and socialism more than they feared for the degradation

Monsignor John A. Ryan

(*NC Photos*)

of the poor. This tradition persisted well into Monsignor Ryan's active years.

To help reverse the trend, Monsignor Ryan's prime resource was Pope Leo XIII's influential encyclical, *Rerum Novarum* (1891). The Pope endorsed private property as a natural right, denounced socialism, and spoke of the reciprocal obligations of employers and employees. Nothing new there. But he also insisted that every laborer had a natural right to enough of the world's goods to live in "reasonable and frugal comfort," and, in a section that to Monsignor Ryan seemed "almost revolutionary," he acknowledged that the "public authority" must step in when the interest of any class was "threatened with evils which can in no other way be met." The "public authority"—that is, the state, the government.

The principle had echoes in contemporary America. Born in 1869, Ryan had grown up in Minnesota where a strong Populist movement sought governmental controls on railroads and grain elevators. Just as Theodore Roosevelt was broadening the power of both the presidency and the national government, Father Ryan wrote his first book, *A Living Wage* (1906). He applied Pope Leo's standard—"reasonable and frugal comfort"—and Pope Leo's authorized solution—the power of the state if necessary—to argue that every man was entitled to a living wage for himself and his family and that the government must guarantee that minimum when employers failed to supply it voluntarily.

A priest (ordained in 1898) and a professor of moral theology at St. Paul Seminary, Father Ryan continued to work out the theology of wealth while supporting, and sometimes even writing, legislation for minimum wages for women in Minnesota, Wisconsin, Pennsylvania, and Massachusetts. In 1915, when he finished his substantial work on *Distributive Justice* and went off to teach in the Catholic University of America in Washington, he had established himself as the foremost Catholic spokesman for social justice in America. When the American Catholic bishops created the National Catholic Welfare Conference in 1919, Father Ryan was the obvious choice to head its Social Action Department. There he stayed for twenty-five years, through the conservative 1920s, through the election of 1928 and the great depression, through the New Deal and World War II. Among reforming groups, he became familiar as the "Catholic spokesman," a blunt, open, witty controversialist, bald, heavy-set, quick-moving. And, conversely, his stature among Catholics grew as he became a force among groups beyond the Church.

His concerns covered a broad spectrum: peace and disarmament, civil liberties, especially free speech; social security; strong unions; child labor amendments; railroad evaluation; public power; Indian rights and, late in his life, Negro rights; Irish independence. In the New Deal years, he defended almost every step of the Administration's program, even the proposal to enlarge the Supreme Court. He served on the Industrial Appeals Board of the National Recovery Administration. He defended President Franklin D. Roosevelt against the attacks of Father Charles E. Coughlin in 1936, and at two inaugurations, 1937 and 1945, the President reciprocated, inviting Monsignor Ryan to give the benediction. Ryan traveled indefatigably, tried never to refuse an invitation to speak, wrote hundreds of articles that gradually found their way into books.

Yet his position was not without difficulties. His liberal friends felt uneasy as he supported orthodox Catholic positions on contraception and Franco's Spain. His Catholic friends wondered at some of the company he kept, curious folk who supported Mexico's attacks on the Church, who disdained religion if they did not despise it. He worked closely with Protestant leaders long before ecumenism became fashionable. Each group could embarrass him with the others, and at various times each group did. Monsignor Ryan kept his head, spoke moderately, reconciled differences.

And in the end he knew triumph. In 1933 Rome recognized his achievement by conferring on him the title of right reverend monsignor. In 1939 a broad coalition of Church and State—archbishops, cabinet officers, Supreme Court justices, and the President—joined in hailing what Justice Felix Frankfurter called a "life greatly lived."

Best of all, in 1938 Congress and the President passed the Fair Labor Standards Act setting minimum wages at forty cents an hour and maximum hours at forty per week. For Monsignor Ryan, who had made the living wage guaranteed by "public authority" his central goal in achieving social justice, passage of the law was a triumphant laurel for a lifetime of struggle.

RECOMMENDED READING: Francis L. Broderick, *Right Reverend New Dealer, John A. Ryan* (New York: Macmillan Company, 1963).

MR. BRODERICK, past president of the American Catholic Historical Association, is Commonwealth Professor at the University of Massachusetts at Boston.

55

Father Haas and Labor Disputes

THOMAS E. BLANTZ, C.S.C.

Throughout the turbulent decade of the 1930s, with its massive unemployment, sit-down strikes, and industrial violence, Father Francis J. Haas, a professor of economics in Washington and later Bishop of Grand Rapids, Michigan, served as one of the government's most effective labor mediators. Newspapers at the time called him "the ace of federal peace-makers" and "one of the Government's most able trouble-shooters," and Father Haas himself once remarked facetiously: "I've been at it so long that I can sense the trouble in a labor dispute just like an old family doctor who comes into the sick room, sniffs the air, and says 'measles.' "

Father Haas was born in Racine, Wisconsin, in 1889, was ordained for the archdiocese of Milwaukee in 1913, and in 1931 was appointed director of the National Catholic School of Social Service in Washington. From 1933 until his appointment as Bishop of Grand Rapids ten years later, Father Haas probably held more important government positions than any other priest of his time, including membership on the National Recovery Administration's Labor Advisory Board, the National Labor Board, the Labor Policies Board of the W.P.A., and the Wisconsin Labor Relations Board. He was also special commissioner of conciliation for the Department of Labor and in 1943 chairman of the President's Fair Employment Practice Committee.

Father Haas received early national recognition as a labor mediator for his part in the settlement of the Milwaukee Electric strike in 1934. Employees of the Milwaukee Electric Railway and Light Company had voted to strike on June 26, demanding reinstatement of thirteen dismissed workers, union elections, and an increase in wages. After one worker was killed in violence erupting near a power plant, the company announced it would have to close the plant each evening, thus leaving the city without electricity.

FATHER FRANCIS J. HAAS

(*NC Photos*)

Father Haas was assigned to the case on June 28 and arrived in Milwaukee that same evening. He met with union leaders until midnight and with company officials until four o'clock in the morning. Hoping to settle the strike before a night of total darkness, he continued the negotiations throughout the day. Shortly before six o'clock, both sides accepted the compromise Father Haas had offered and, weary but smiling, he confided to the assembled newsmen: "It's all over." He characteristically declined major credit for the settlement: "It just happened that I came in twenty-four hours before the truce was signed. A good many of my friends were inclined to give me entire credit for working out the agreement. Of course I did nothing of the kind and for that reason felt I was flying under false colors."

Even more widely acclaimed was Father Haas' intervention in the Minneapolis Truckers' strike later that summer. This dispute over union jurisdiction and minimum wages lasted thirty-six days, cost the city an estimated $50,000,000, and, in the violence that accompanied it, left four persons dead and hundreds injured. The basis for the final settlement was once again a compromise, the so-called "Haas-Dunnigan Plan," named for the two federal mediators and providing for immediate termination of the strike, reinstatement of workers in order of seniority, collective bargaining, and minimum wages of forty and fifty cents an hour for different classes of workers. It was the most violent strike in Minneapolis history and one of the most disruptive anywhere in the country in the 1930s, and Father Haas was justly proud of his part in its settlement.

After four years as director of the National Catholic School of Social Service in Washington, Father Haas was recalled to Milwaukee in 1935 and was named rector of St. Francis Seminary. His work of government mediation, however, did not cease because in April, 1937, Governor Philip LaFollette appointed him a member of the three-man Wisconsin Labor Relations Board to investigate and mediate industrial disputes throughout the state.

During the twenty months of its existence, this Wisconsin Board settled approximately 550 controversies, with Father Haas as the chief negotiator in the very difficult disputes at Nash-Kelvinator and Allis-Chalmers in 1938. At the close of the latter, the governor sent his congratulations: "Your mediation of the Allis-Chalmers dispute was, in my judgment, the outstanding accomplishment of the Board up to this time. I am especially grateful to you for your efforts in that case because you averted what would have been the largest strike in the history of Wisconsin."

As a chief trouble-shooter for the United States Department of Labor, Father Haas's activities were not confined to the Midwest. He arbitrated the Tampa cigar makers' strike in 1935, was chief federal mediator in the lumber industry dispute in upstate New York in 1936, and intervened in the textile strike in eastern Pennsylvania and New Jersey in 1937. On that occasion, Secretary of Labor Frances Perkins reportedly telephoned to ask his assistance: "We have a difficult situation in silk here in the East." Father Haas at the time was being fitted for his new robes as a monsignor and replied with a smile: "We have a difficult situation in silk here in Milwaukee too, but I will come!"

Father Haas always considered his work in labor mediation as an outgrowth of his priestly calling—restoring peace to industry and helping to assure a living wage, reasonable hours, and adequate conditions of employment to workers. The union leader Sidney Hillman remarked: "He has given all his time, his efforts, his ability, to help the cause of the common man and the cause of labor. If we only had more men of his devotion, ability, understanding, and readiness to serve the cause of labor, we would have entirely different conditions in the country today." Six feet tall and over 200 pounds, he was called by newspapers "the big friend of the little guy . . . a man who served his God by serving mankind." As priest and public servant, Father Haas must have considered it the highest compliment.

FATHER BLANTZ is an associate professor of history and university archivist at the University of Notre Dame.

56

Catholics and the New Deal

DAVID J. O'BRIEN

The decade of the 1930s in the United States was a difficult period, marked by the most serious depression in the country's history and by a deepening international crisis which threatened to draw the nation from its cherished isolation. Under the leadership of Franklin D. Roosevelt, the federal government launched a series of programs, some of which were experiments aimed at restoring the nation's economic health, while others were reforms whose goal was to provide greater economic security for all, but particularly for the nation's industrial workers. American Catholics had always been predominantly a working-class people; they felt the suffering of depression acutely and had a particularly intense interest in government programs for relief and reform. Their Church endorsed their demands for social justice, and Catholics and their leaders became deeply involved in the period's burgeoning movements for social change.

When Franklin Roosevelt became President in 1932, he led a Democratic party which had long been the minority party in the nation. Four years earlier Al Smith of New York had been defeated in the presidential campaign, but in losing he had overtaken the Republican lead in the nation's cities. Roosevelt consolidated and advanced these gains, uniting the Democratic party's traditional Southern support with the big city blocs of ethnic, Catholic, and minority voters. While the main reasons for his success were his policies, Roosevelt well knew the need to touch all the bases. He spoke frequently at Catholic events, welcomed honorary degrees from Catholic universities, cultivated well publicized friendships with prominent ecclesiastics, and appointed many Catholics to high positions. While some Catholic spokesmen feared the growth of the power of the federal government, many more saw in Roosevelt's New Deal an implementation of the traditional

PRESIDENT AND MRS. FRANKLIN D. ROOSEVELT ARRIVING AT THE
CATHOLIC UNIVERSITY OF AMERICA

The President is shown as he was greeted by the rector, Monsignor James
H. Ryan, before the commencement exercises at which he received an
honorary degree on June 14, 1933. Occurring only three months after his
inauguration, this was the first public manifestation of Roosevelt's close relations with American Catholics. The main speaker on this occasion, Cardinal
Patrick Hayes, Archbishop of New York, praised the President's "courage
and intelligence" in combating the economic depression and advancing the
common good. (*Department of Archives and Manuscripts of the Catholic
University of America*)

Catholic teaching that the state bears a general responsibility for the maintenance of justice in economic life.

In his 1931 encyclical *Quadragesimo Anno,* Pope Pius XI restated this principle and also endorsed the worker's right to a living wage and to some control over the conditions of his employment. Inspired by papal teaching and the critical problem of unemployment, the bishops, acting individually or through the National Catholic Welfare Conference, endorsed the principles behind such federal legislation as unemployment relief, old age pensions, support for agricultural prices, and legal protection of the right of labor to organize and bargain collectively. While maintaining a stance of strict nonpartisanship, the major figures in the American Church provided moral support for many New Deal policies, and gave indirect encouragement to Catholics to support candidates and officials who sponsored such legislation.

Yet a significant minority of Catholics resisted Roosevelt's appeal, and their numbers grew as the decade progressed. Most Catholics were critical of Roosevelt's foreign policy, which included diplomatic recognition of the Soviet Union and friendship with the anticlerical government of Mexico. Foreign policy issues became more prominent with the rise of Nazi Germany. While several American bishops were outspoken foes of Fascism, others feared that the danger of communism would be lost from view in the rising tide of anti-Fascist feeling. Criticism of Roosevelt's domestic policies grew sharper, too, particularly after he attempted to "pack" the Supreme Court in 1937. In the midst of the depression many felt a responsibility to support emergency programs; the easing of the crisis allowed policy differences to re-emerge.

One result of the political prominence of Catholics during these years was that their internal differences became more apparent to outside observers. In 1936 the famous radio priest, Father Charles E. Coughlin, organized and campaigned for a third party and its candidate for President, while Father John A. Ryan of the National Catholic Welfare Conference went on the radio to defend Roosevelt against Coughlin's attack. Later, advocates of isolationism and advocates of American support for the Allies against Germany both courted Catholic support and found active Catholic leaders to speak for their cause. In both domestic and foreign policy, the bishops generally provided guidance with general statements of principles, while abstaining from direct endorsement of particular policies, programs, or candidates.

Many priests, sisters, and active lay people felt that the real place for Christian action on social problems was apart from the government. Catholic charities continued to meet a wide range of human needs while parish priests always spent large portions of their time and energy helping with the social and economic hardships of their people. The Catholic Worker movement, founded in 1933, soon had houses in major cities to which young Catholics came to offer themselves in service to the poor while exploring new approaches to social justice. Most importantly, the decade witnessed massive strikes and labor unrest. Priests around the country entered into these struggles, some as active union supporters, others as mediators of disputes. Labor schools spread rapidly and the labor priest became a common figure at union meetings. Catholics, like others, differed over the relative merits of the American Federation of Labor and the Congress of Industrial Organizations, but they agreed almost without exception on the right of workers to organize in unions of their choice.

Many Catholics benefited directly from New Deal programs; many others benefited from the new union strength which New Deal policy made possible. In later years they would recall the 1930s as a time when unemployment and hardship threatened all that they had built in America; whatever their reservations about Roosevelt's foreign policies, they were grateful for what he had done to make life a little easier and more secure. They were equally grateful for the recognition which he had given to their Church and to their ethnic communities. They emerged from the decade as solid supporters of social justice legislation and labor unionism. Like other Americans, they would become more politically independent in later years, but until our own day Catholic working people remain among the strongest supporters of public policies aimed at equalizing opportunity, increasing social and economic security, and extending the benefits of economic progress to America's dispossessed citizens.

RECOMMENDED READING: David J. O'Brien, *American Catholics and Social Reform. The New Deal Years* (New York: Oxford University Press, 1968). George Q. Flynn, *American Catholics & the Roosevelt Presidency, 1932–1936* (Lexington: University of Kentucky Press, 1968). Charles J. Tull, *Father Coughlin and the New Deal* (Syracuse: Syracuse University Press, 1965). Sheldon Marcus, *Father Coughlin. The Tumultuous Life of the Priest of the Little Flower* (Boston: Little, Brown and Company, 1973).

DR. O'BRIEN is a professor of history in the College of the Holy Cross, Worcester, Massachusetts.

57

American Catholics and

The Spanish-American War

THOMAS E. WANGLER

The Havana harbor was moonlit on the evening of February 15, 1898, making clearly visible a rocking United States warship, the *Maine*. Suddenly, at about 9:40 p.m., an explosion ripped the ship apart and sent it to the bottom of the bay. By 12:30 a.m. cables began reaching the White House informing President William McKinley of the incident and indicating a preliminary death toll of about 260 Americans. This event, which greatly contributed to a growing fever in the United States to intervene militarily in Cuba against the Spanish government that ruled there, created, when coupled with a widespread national distrust of Catholics, a serious threat to Catholic interests.

As events moved toward war with Spain during March and April, 1898, American Catholics were faced with a dilemma. Spain was a Catholic country and American Catholics had ties of faith with the Spanish people, and yet, who in this country, given its own revolution against a European power and the highly inflated accounts of Spanish atrocities appearing in the press, could not sympathize with the oppressed Cubans? Complicating the Catholic conscience, some of the Protestant periodicals defined the issue in religious terms, demanding that a primarily Protestant America assume its God-given destiny of eliminating, by military means if necessary, the vestiges of "ecclesiastical dominion" in Cuba. Others hinted that if war broke out the nation could not count on Catholic loyalty. It is difficult for American Catholics today to grasp the extent to which our forefathers were subjected to anti-Catholic prejudice.

The general national suspicion of Catholics took clear focus in early

ARCHBISHOP JOHN IRELAND OF SAINT PAUL

After Spain was blamed in the United States for the sinking of the U.S.S. *Maine* in the harbor of Havana on February 15, 1898, Pope Leo XIII asked Archbishop Ireland, who was known as an influential supporter of the Republican Administration, to go to Washington and to confer with President McKinley and congressional leaders in order to prevent the American Government from declaring war on Spain.

April when the dynamic archbishop of St. Paul, Archbishop John Ireland, unexpectedly arrived in Washington. This great patriarch of American Catholicism had received on March 27 a cable asking him, in the name of Pope Leo XIII, to proceed to Washington and attempt to prevent war. Archbishop Ireland was approached because he was a close friend of McKinley. He was at first reluctant to accept the papal request as he had, over the years, carefully fostered a pro-American image for himself before the American public. The proposed mission would make him the instrument of papal intervention in American affairs, and it was bound to arouse anti-Catholic sentiment. But a genuine desire for peace made him "risk everything," as he wrote a friend, and he boarded the train for Washington.

Archbishop Ireland saw the President on April 1 and urged caution. The reaction from some was predictable: "We want no overtures from our government . . . based upon propositions emanating from Rome," announced one Protestant minister. Archbishop Ireland ceased dealing directly with McKinley, for the most part, and instead worked through an intermediary, Senator Stephen Elkins. The archbishop wrote a friend that he experienced as never before "the anti-Catholic prejudice of a large fraction of America."

The Elkins diary from this period portrays Archbishop Ireland working day and night to prevent war. While dealing with the President through Elkins, he met with the Spanish representative to Washington, the Senate leadership, and the major European ambassadors. The results of these contacts were cabled to Rome and in effect called on the Vatican to secure from Spain a declaration of the suspension of hostilities against the Cuban people. After several delays, Spain finally indicated its willingness to proclaim an armistice, and the Vatican so cabled Archbishop Ireland. McKinley was "delighted" with the news, but then, when he learned that this concession did not include a Spanish willingness to grant independence to Cuba, an essential American condition, he felt that he had no alternative but to send his war message to Congress, which he did on Easter Monday, April 11, 1898.

As the United States and Spain prepared for hostilities, the anti-Catholic press continued its attack. Some claimed that they had "reliable information" that the Pope, who allegedly favored Catholic Spain, had ordered Catholics in the United States not to fight. Other reports claimed that 700,000 armed Catholics in the United States were poised for an uprising, and that the explosion of a powdermill in California was caused by Jesuits living in a nearby monastery.

In the end Catholics reacted, as they almost always have in a time of national crisis, by supporting the American cause. Archbishop Ireland, while indicating in his private correspondence a sympathy for Spain, called upon American Catholics to accept "the mandate of the supreme power of the nation." The Vatican issued a statement of neutrality and the Catholic archbishops of the country proclaimed Catholic loyalty to "our country and our flag." These statements, the active involvement of Catholics in the war effort, and the quickness of American victory, quieted the suspicions of the nation.

If Protestant Americans were concerned about Catholic loyalties before hostilities began, the war and its aftermath gave rise to serious Catholic concerns about the behavior of their government and non-Catholic fellow citizens. What started in April as a humanitarian venture to liberate an oppressed Cuban people, turned, with the coming of May, into a bold United States land-grab. On May 1 a small American fleet destroyed a larger Spanish one in Manila bay, in the Philippine Islands. Then Guam was taken. By July not only had American troops occupied Cuba and Puerto Rico, but this country had annexed Hawaii. This burst of American imperialism shocked many and created new problems for American Catholics, since most of the people in the occupied territories were Catholics. To have the island governments, intimately allied with the Catholic clergy, suddenly removed from office and replaced with an American-administered authority involving a "separation" of Church and State would present a serious threat to the Catholic faith in the islands. Symbolic of the new difficulties was the announcement in July that Spanish-language editions of the Protestant Bible were ready for mass distribution in the territories. Unfortunately, some Protestants interpreted the new expansionism of the nation as a providentially arranged opportunity to spread a purified, reformed religion to savage peoples kept ignorant by Catholic governments and priests. And then there were news reports of American military mistreatment of Catholic clergy, nuns, and churches. One photo from the Philippines showed three soldiers at a telegraph station set up on the altar of a Catholic Church, with wires attached to the tabernacle, apparently using the standing crucifix as an antenna. American Catholics, generally allied with the Democratic party, demanded from McKinley and his Republican Administration some concern for Catholic interests. The term "McKinleyism" came to mean in Catholic circles the presumed anti-Catholic behavior of authorities in the territories.

Here again the ever-vigilant Archbishop of St. Paul, fearful of a significant parting of the ways between Catholic and American interests, rushed into the public arena. Having joined the Republican party precisely to prevent the identification of the Church with a single political group, he was able to secure from his Republican friends in the Administration a sensitivity to Catholic interests. Archbishop Ireland had to fight a double battle, one with the Administration and a second with Catholics who distrusted Republican policy, assuming it to be anti-Catholic. The archbishop urged McKinley to name a Catholic to the Peace Commission, and one was invited; he explained that the new civil marriage law in Cuba was unacceptable, and it was rescinded; he provided the government with a list of people to name to public office in the islands and another list of teachers for the new public school system in the Philippines, and they were appointed. Archbishop Ireland even went to New York to twist the arms of Protestant journalists to support Administration policy, especially the sending of William Taft to the Vatican for negotiations over unsettled religious issues in the islands. On the other hand, Archbishop Ireland publicly reprimanded his fellow Catholics, and at one point even a fellow bishop, for their tirades against what they believed was a basically anti-Catholic Administration.

It took some three years to settle all of the religious questions which resulted from the Spanish-American War. But in the end the Vatican could look back on several years of successful negotiations with the United States, a country with which it had had little to do until then. Archbishop John Ireland, who defined the priesthood in terms of mediating between Church and society, rather than between God and man, retired to a less public arena. He had been his own ideal priest and had launched the Catholic community into the twentieth century and toward the status of trusted citizenship, which is, or appears to be, for good or evil, their present, though not traditional, lot.

RECOMMENDED READING: Frank T. Reuter, *Catholic Influence on American Colonial Policies, 1898–1904* (Austin: University of Texas Press, 1967). James A. Moynihan, *The Life of Archbishop John Ireland* (New York: Harper & Brothers, 1953).

DR. WANGLER is an associate professor in Boston College.

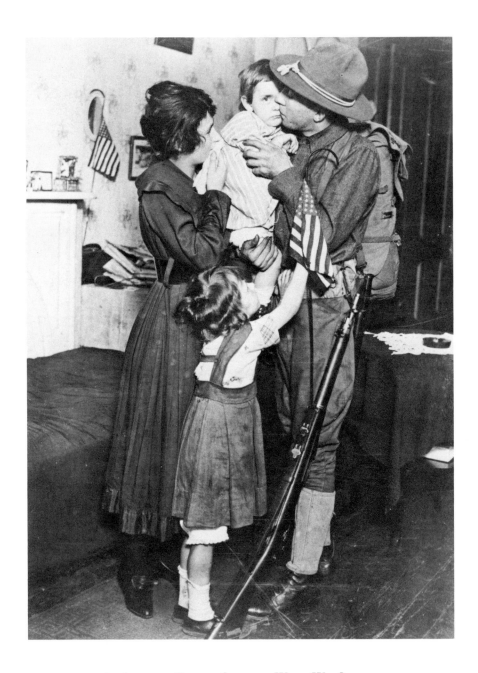

AN AMERICAN CATHOLIC SOLDIER IN WORLD WAR I

Private T. P. Laughlin, an Irish-American of the Fighting 69th, bids fare-well to his family before going off to war. (*NC Photos courtesy of the National Archives*)

58

Catholics and Neutrality in the

Great War, 1914-1917

DEAN R. ESSLINGER

I didn't raise my boy to be a soldier,
I brought him up to be my pride and joy,
To live to place a musket on his shoulder,
To shoot some other mother's darling boy . . .
There'd be no war today
If mothers all would say
I didn't raise my boy to be a soldier.

The rumble of guns that shattered Europe's delicate peace in the summer of 1914 echoed loud enough across the Atlantic to make many a mother thankful that her boy would not have to be a soldier. President Woodrow Wilson proclaimed America's neutrality and urged citizens to be impartial in thought as well as in action. For the next three years Americans clung to the hope that the war in Europe would end before they would be drawn into it. But the position of neutrality was gradually eroded by the British interference with American business, the confiscation of private mail and goods on the high seas, and by the German U-boats that prowled the dark depths of the Atlantic. In the end it was the deadly submarine attacks that persuaded President Wilson to ask Congress for a declaration of war against the Central Powers in April, 1917.

Though most of the nation's 16,000,000 Catholics, like other Americans, swore their loyalty to the new national cause, a significant number found the loss of neutrality a bitter disappointment. The reasons for resisting the drift toward war, however, may not sound familiar to recent critics of warfare. The Catholics who were reluctant to give up American neutrality sixty years ago said little about the inhumanity and injustice of warfare, and there were few references to Christian teachings against war. Instead most of the Catholic opposition to America's entry into war was inspired by political and ethnic motives.

The loudest and most persistent voice among Catholics in favor of neutrality between 1914 and 1917 came from the German- and Irish-Americans who were afraid American involvement would be on the side of Great Britain. At its annual convention the German Catholic Central Verein, the largest German-American organization, applauded Wilson's announcement of neutrality and expressed sympathy for Germany. As Wilson's policies became more pro-British, the Central Verein informally joined with the German-American Alliance to exert greater national influence. Throughout the Midwest, the stronghold of the German-American population, the German-language press and even many priests urged a neutral course that would bring no harm to Germany. Some like Joseph Matt, editor of *Der Wanderer*, and Bishop Vincent Wehrle of Bismarck, North Dakota, were frightened by the German unity movements and warned German Catholics not to separate themselves from other Americans. When war came in 1917, the German-Americans pledged their allegiance to the United States but not without disappointment.

Irish-American Catholics had a similar view of neutrality but for different reasons. For the Irish a victory by the Central Powers over England might mean the achievement of a national dream—the independence of Ireland from British rule. When Wilson refused to intervene on behalf of the captured Irish insurgents after the unsuccessful Easter Rebellion in 1916, the Irish-Americans turned their votes to the Republican candidate in the fall presidential election. Anglophobia rather than a genuine support for Germany put many Irish Catholics in opposition to the Allied cause.

Other groups of Catholics were also influenced by their ethnic origins and political attitudes. A study of the Italian-language press in Chicago at the time shows that the nationalist faction of the ethnic community campaigned against the Central Powers after Austria invaded Italy, while the socialist faction continued to firmly advocate American noninvolvement. The Polish-American Catholics were also divided among the Polish National Alliance and Roman Catholic Union, which followed Paderewski in demanding a new Polish nation after the war, and the Polish-Americans who remained loyal to the concept of strict neutrality for the United States.

If the Catholic press was an accurate reflection of the readers' opinions, then Catholics, more than other Americans, tended to favor Germany and Austria-Hungary in the war. *America*, a Jesuit magazine edited by Father Richard Henry Tierney, an Irish-American, slanted its news and comments in favor of Germany. Some, like *Ave Maria*, published at Notre Dame, Indiana, and the *Sacred Heart Review* tried to tread a strictly neutral path, but many Catholic newspapers in the Midwest, such as the *Western Catholic* of Illinois or the *Indiana Catholic*, were consistently anti-British in viewpoint. Outside the Midwest papers such as the *Tablet* of Brooklyn or *The Catholic News* of New York tended to be more impartial.

On the whole the Catholic press suggests that before the United States entered the war, editors and readers chose sides for several reasons. Most powerful were the ethnic and national ties that drew German-American sympathy for the fatherland and Irish-American hatred for England. But Catholics were also influenced by the treatment of the Church by the governments at war. Austria's traditional role as a defender of the Church was often cited in Catholic newspapers, and the anticlerical attitude of the French government was indignantly denounced.

Among those bishops and other Church leaders who spoke publicly about the war before 1917 there was general support of American neutrality. Cardinal James Gibbons, Archbishop of Baltimore, praised Wilson for choosing peace and refusing "to draw the sword." When war finally did come, the bishops were unanimous in announcing Catholic loyalty to the nation. Those Irish- and German-Americans who had opposed any aid to Britain and its allies now put aside their dual loyalties and pledged full support to the American effort.

What is surprising about this brief glimpse of Catholic reactions to the war in Europe is that the response was more often based on ethnic and national allegiances than on Christian values. Too seldom did those who commented on the war in Catholic organizations and in the Catholic press mention the issues of justice, of humanity, or of the necessity for Christian love and peace.

Dr. Esslinger is a professor of history in Towson State University, Baltimore, Maryland.

ALFRED E. SMITH

*(Department of Archives and Manuscripts of the
Catholic University of America)*

59

Alfred E. Smith and American Catholicism

GEORGE Q. FLYNN

Al acted almost instinctively, as he had been taught at home. As dozens of reporters looked on, the Governor of New York dropped to his knee and kissed the ring of the papal legate. The year was 1926; the setting, New York City Hall. One can only guess at the reaction such a scene produced when readers in Oklahoma City saw photographs of it. These same readers suspected that this man on his knees would soon run for the highest office in the land. The thought of a future President paying homage to a foreigner and a representative of the Pope enraged Protestant America. But Alfred Emanuel Smith was never one to deny his heritage. This heritage was both his great strength and, ultimately, the source of his tragedy.

Born on the lower East Side of New York City on December 30, 1873, and later identified with the emergence to political consciousness of immigrant children, Al himself was a second-generation American. He came from Irish, Italian, and German stock, but never thought of himself as anything but an American. To live on Oliver Street in New York was to live within something like a small village inside a large city. There was the church, St. James, with its parochial school, where Al had attended and served as an altar boy. A young boy had identity in such a setting; he felt at home and knew who he was.

But Al Smith had talent and ambition. In nineteenth-century New York to Irishmen with talent the only attractive avenue for advancement was politics, which meant Tammany Hall. Smith began his political career at the age of twelve by folding ballots in Tom Foley's saloon in the Fourth Ward. In 1918 he became the first Irish Catholic to be elected governor. He lost in 1920, but won again in 1922, 1924, and 1926. In 1928 he was the front runner for the Democratic presidential nomination.

Smith's rise from the Fourth Ward to the presidential nomination rested on his record as one of the most progressive and innovative politicians of his age. While in the New York Assembly and as governor, he pushed through such measures as minimum wage, shorter work hours, workmen's compensation, public housing, and rent controls. Above all, Smith worked to streamline state government. Like most progressives Al Smith believed in efficiency of government. In seeking the aid of experts he broke new ground. He promoted the recruitment of the Jewish intelligentsia into New York politics, turning for advice and leadership to such men as Joseph Proskauer, Herbert Lehman, Robert Moses, and Samuel Rosenman. Even more unorthodox, Smith made use of women advisors and social workers. Belle Moskowitz became his most trusted counselor and Frances Perkins served throughout Smith's term as a labor advisor. An unusual, and to some unholy, alliance developed. Smith, the master of the political machine, bridged the gap between the urban politician and the urban reformer.

Now, in June, 1928, at Houston, Texas, the assembled delegates to the Democratic convention cheered as Franklin Roosevelt called for the nomination of the man "who not only deserves success but commands it. Victory is his habit—the happy warrior." Al Smith won the nomination on the first ballot. But while 18,000 applauded Smith at the convention, a Baptist congregation nearby prayed that God would intervene to save the nation from a papist President. Moreover, in Herbert Hoover the Republicans had picked a strong candidate. The country had enjoyed unparalleled affluence under two preceding Republican administrations. The very things that made Smith a hero to the city alienated many non-urban voters. On prohibition he made plain his commitment to revision. Smith knew something of the suspicion with which he was viewed by rural, Protestant America. Yet the candidate took as his theme song "The Sidewalks of New York." He campaigned with brown derby tilted on his head and cigar clenched between his teeth.

Another politician might have trimmed sails and modified his image. Smith could not. His steadfastness reflected both integrity and naiveté. He expected criticism on the issue of prohibition, but he was unprepared for the religious bigotry he encountered. Ironically, he was unprepared because he was not a reflectively religious man. Like most Americans, Smith accepted his religion as part of his heritage, acting on the basis of habits and rituals which he had acquired from his environment.

Some Americans were more reflective, especially about Catholicism. One of them, the attorney Charles C. Marshall, in a 1927 article in the *Atlantic Monthly*, questioned whether a practicing Roman Catholic could reconcile his loyalty to his Church, including the various encyclicals of the popes, with loyalty to his nation. Such issues of political philosophy and canon law held no interest for Smith. But Belle Moskowitz and Franklin Roosevelt both urged Smith to reply. There followed the bizarre arrangement, revealing the pluralism of Smith's support, by which two Jews, Proskauer and Lehman, drafted a statement on Church-State relations for an Irish Catholic, whose father was probably Italian. The man soon to be branded as the Pope's candidate had trouble even pronouncing the word "encyclical."

In the reply, however, Smith articulated a compartmentalized approach to religion which most Americans probably shared and which would later be restated by John F. Kennedy. Smith favored the total separation of Church and State; the clergy could advise only in matters of faith and morals. In any conflict between his duty and his faith, he would let his conscience be his guide. "I believe," he wrote, "in absolute freedom of conscience and the equality of all churches, all sects, all beliefs before the law. . . ." His statement reflected his faith in the American dream, that a man was judged by what he was and not by the church he attended. He mistook the rhetoric of religion in America for the reality.

Reality appeared when his campaign train steamed into Oklahoma City in September, 1928, and flaming crosses glowed from the countryside. After this greeting by the Ku Klux Klan, the candidate felt compelled to speak out again on the religious issue. He attacked those who would made second-class citizens out of all Catholics. The crowd reacted with little enthusiasm. The next night in the same auditorium, 30,000 citizens applauded as Dr. John R. Straton spoke on "Al Smith and the Forces of Hell."

Students of the 1928 election still argue over the significance of the religious factor. Most agree that Hoover won because of prosperity. He captured 21,392,190 popular votes to 15,016,443 for Smith, and carried the electoral vote by 444 to 87. Some argue that Smith launched a revolution in 1928 despite his loss. While losing five Southern states, he won the twelve largest cities for the Democrats and helped forge the coalition of urban-ethnic votes which would elect Franklin Roosevelt. Such ideas have been challenged as evidence exists that, in Western states, the shift of urban votes to the Democrats took place even before Smith. Whatever the importance of the election for American political history, it had tragic consequences for Al Smith himself.

He was a bitter man, convinced that he had lost because of his religion. His faith in the American dream was shattered. He announced that he would not stand again for public office. By 1932 Franklin Roosevelt had inherited most of Smith's support, won the nomination, and was elected President—for life, as it turned out.

During the 1930s Al Smith seemed a different man. He moved from the Fourth Ward to Fifth Avenue, associated with rich supporters, and attacked the New Deal as communistic. He also opposed Roosevelt's re-election in 1936 and 1940. Later the two men had something of a reconciliation when Smith endorsed Roosevelt's foreign policy. The President sent Frances Perkins to represent him when Smith died on October 4, 1944.

Why had Smith's last years been such a contradiction of his earlier career, when he used government to promote social legislation? Envy, bitterness, and new rich associates, some claimed. No doubt there was some truth to these charges. But many old progressives came to share the same disillusionment over the New Deal. Why should Smith have been different? He believed in efficiency of government and in humanitarian legislation. But he had not conceived of government in the gargantuan terms of the New Deal. Rather than government as a broker of special interests, Smith saw it working to harmonize and reconcile class tensions.

Smith's life had the characteristics of an American melodrama. The first act was filled with struggle and courage; the second with success, recognition, and glory. But then the hero reached out for the prize beyond his fate and failed. Smith lingered on in the twilight of power while a new hero emerged. Franklin Roosevelt became the hero of the cities and of the common man. But Al Smith had his glory. His career before 1928 helped transform New York into a modern state. His monuments still surround the visitor. And, as the contemporary ballad has it, Smith did it his own way. Unlike later Irish politicians, Smith advanced in America by bringing his heritage with him. He could never deny his roots. Indeed, even at the most critical moment of his career, he gloried in that heritage.

RECOMMENDED READING: Oscar Handlin, *Al Smith and His America* (Boston: Little, Brown, 1958). Matthew and Hannah Josephson, *Al Smith: Hero of the Cities* (Boston: Houghton Mifflin, 1969).

DR. FLYNN is a professor of history in Texas Tech University, Lubbock.

60

Catholic Pacifism in America

PATRICIA McNEAL

In the fall of 1969 a peace rally was held in Baltimore to support the Catonsville Nine who were on trial for destroying Selective Service records. During the rally an elderly woman with white hair approached the microphone to address the gathering. Although she had not been introduced, the crowd was giving her a standing ovation. A puzzled young man turned to his friend and asked, "Who's the old lady?" The friend replied, "I don't know, but she sure means a heck-of-a-lot to all the Catholics here." The woman at the microphone was Dorothy Day, and to Catholic pacifists she did indeed mean a lot. Since 1933 when she founded the Catholic Worker movement, Dorothy Day has been the one Catholic in the United States most identified with the cause of pacifism.

Dorothy Day and Peter Maurin, a French-born Catholic layman, founded the Catholic Worker, not as a peace group, but as a movement that would witness to a radical Catholic vision of society. The main belief of the Catholic Worker was that the Church was the heart of the hoped-for new society. Their work centered on applying the corporal works of mercy and finding additional ways to aid the poor and oppressed.

When the peace was shattered in the 1930s, first in the Spanish Civil War and then in World War II, the Catholic Worker ideal prompted Dorothy Day to proclaim pacifism. It was never clear in the early years exactly what this meant, but it was sufficient as an ethic for the Catholic Worker to oppose war even after the government of the United States declared war in December, 1941. There have been other Catholic peace groups, but the Catholic Worker was the only one to take this position before the Vietnam War.

Though Dorothy Day never developed a detailed rationale of her pacifist position, it was clear to her that it was based on love. She believed that

PACIFIST CARTOONS FROM THE CATHOLIC WORKER

The upper cartoon, published in the issue for October, 1940, was an illustra-
tion for an article on "St. Telemachus—Martyr," one of the patron saints of
the Catholic pacifists, whom the author, Right Reverend Barry O'Toole of
the Catholic University of America, called a "martyr of Christian peace."
The lower cartoon, printed in October, 1941, and again in June, 1943, was
a contemporary representation of the siege of Jericho; the first time it was
used, the caption recommended reading Joshua 6 and Judges 6 and 7 "for a
Philosophy of War," and the second time the caption stated that the biblical
story demonstrates that it is God who brings the victory. (*Drawn by Ade
Bethune*)

during a time of war, the coercive power of the state reached its zenith. Since war was the most extreme form of opposition to love, the only alternative to the violence of the state was the nonviolence of the Gospels.

The cost of such witness to Dorothy Day and the Catholic Worker movement during World War II was great. Her refusal to relinquish the pacifist position caused a drop in the circulation of the movement's newspaper, *The Catholic Worker*, from 190,000 copies in November, 1939, to 50,500 in November, 1944. Great dissension among members of the movement also arose. Many members, such as John Cogley, were not pacifists and broke with the movement and entered the armed services. Despite such setbacks over the war, the Catholic Worker movement continued to uphold the ideal of pacifism.

One of the principal works of the movement during the war was to support Catholic conscientious objectors. In World War II 135 Catholics registered their dissent within the law and were granted conscientious objector status. They performed their alternative service at Civilian Public Service camps maintained by the Catholic Worker, first at Stoddard and later at Warner, New Hampshire. Only one percent of the conscientious objector population in the camps was Catholic, but this was a marked increase from the four known Catholic conscientious objectors in World War I. The significance of these 135 men was that eighty-four percent of them contended that their Catholic faith had a bearing on their decision.

Though conscientious objection was the main way that an individual opposed war, a broader tactic, nonviolent resistance, was developed after World War II. Ammon Hennacy, a radical from the Midwest and convert to Catholicism, introduced this tactic to the Catholic Worker during the 1950s. It marked a new form of peace witness that Catholics would offer.

Pacifism narrowly defined meant opposition to war, and its main form of expression during a time of war was conscientious objection. Nonviolent resistance when applied to the issues of war and peace differed from pacifism insofar as its aim was to posit a direct action for peace. It also included an element of coercion. Many different actions could be labelled nonviolent resistance, but its main tactic was civil disobedience. In this case a law would be broken because it was in conflict with a higher law.

Hennacy spearheaded the Catholic Worker's nonviolent resistance to New York City's annual air raid drills, which according to the Civil Defense Act, required that all take shelter for at least ten minutes during a practice air raid. In 1954 Ammon Hennacy, Dorothy Day, and a few others refused to take shelter during a drill. The event occurred in City Hall Park in New York. Each year, more and more members of various peace organizations joined them in their act of civil disobedience. On May 3, 1960, approximately 2,000 students and adults throughout New York City resisted the yearly drill. Ten minutes before the sirens were scheduled to blow, about 500 persons assembled in the park, with many more arriving all the time. Among those present were writers Nat Hentoff, Dwight MacDonald, Norman Mailer, and Kay Boyle. It was the largest direct-action demonstration against nuclear warfare. Radio, television, and the press gave it wide publicity. It marked a new direction in the strategy that the American peace movement would use in the 1960s and evidenced a new spirit of cooperation among Catholics with other peace groups in the United States.

The Catholic Worker was also important for its role in fostering the development of two new Catholic peace organizations in the 1960s: PAX and the Catholic Peace Fellowship. It was the founding of these two organizations and the Second Vatican Council's support of conscientious objection, as well as its affirmation of religious freedom and nonviolence, which gave much hope to individual Catholics involved in the peace movement during the 1960s. It was nonviolence and not pacifism that characterized the American Catholic peace movement in this decade. Thus, it is to Dorothy Day and the Catholic Worker movement that contemporary Catholic peacemakers look to locate the beginning of their history in America. Since the 1930s Dorothy Day has stood firm in her pacifism, and when asked by a reporter what has motivated her over all these years, her answer was so strikingly direct and simple that it was embarrassing. "The Gospel Beatitude," she replied, "Blessed are the peacemakers for they shall be called the sons of God."

DR. MCNEAL is an associate member of the Department of History in Indiana University at South Bend and has published several articles on peace and on the American Catholic peace movement in learned journals.

Index